LONDON RECORD SOCIETY PUBLICATIONS

VOLUME IV
FOR THE YEAR 1968

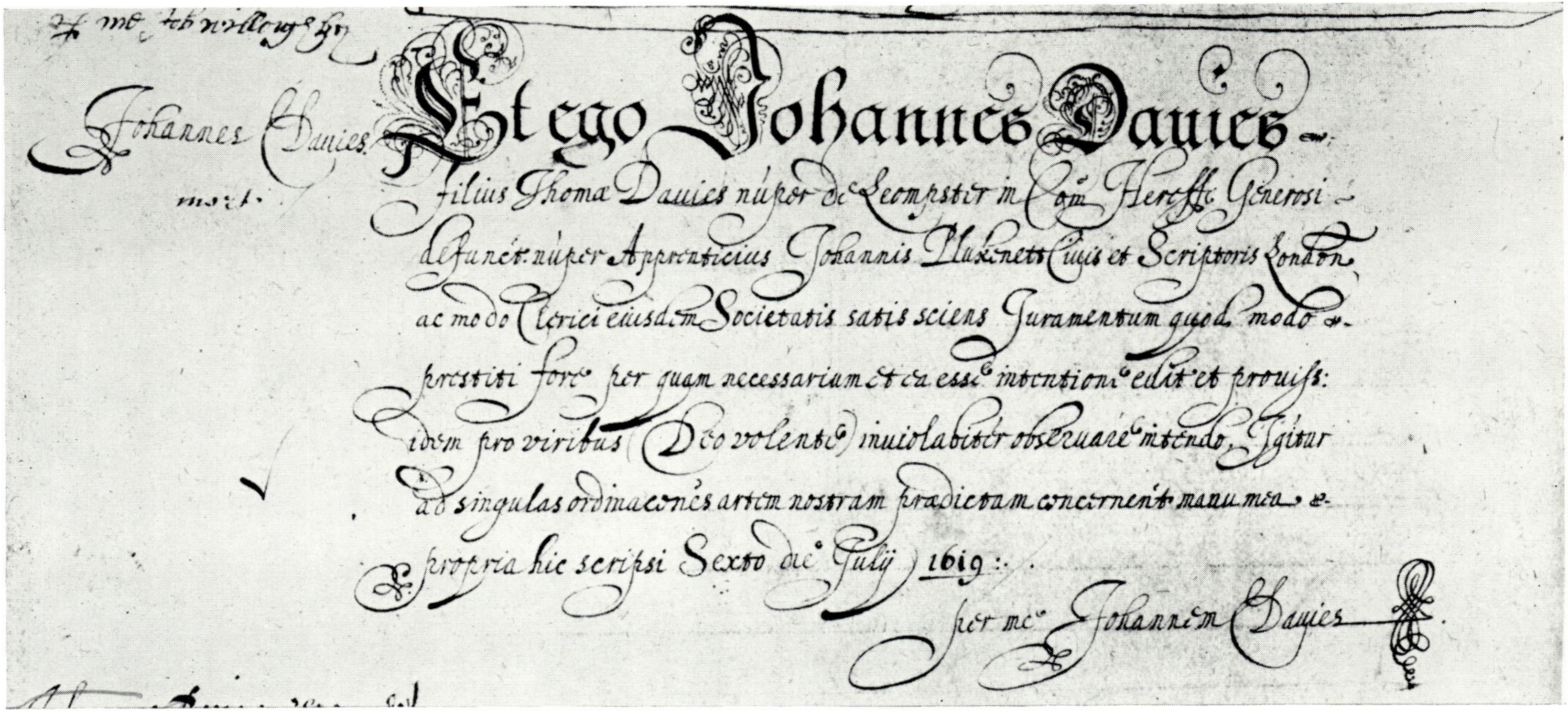

Johannes Davies.

Et ego Johannes Davies
Filius Thoma Davies nuper de Leompster in Com Hereff Generosi
defunct nuper Apprenticius Johannis Pluknett Civis et Scriptoris London
ac modo Clerici eiusdem Societatis satis sciens Juramentum quod modo
prestiti fore per quam necessariam et ea esse intentione edit et provis:
idem pro viribus (Deo volente) inviolabiter observare intendo, Igitur
ad singulas ordinaciones artem nostram predictam concernent manu mea
propria hic scripsi Sexto die Julij 1619:
per me Johannem Davies

I. Declaration of John Davies (son of Thomas Davies, late of Leominster, Herefordshire), 6 July 1619 (see p. 206 of the Common Paper).

SCRIVENERS' COMPANY COMMON PAPER 1357—1628

With a Continuation to 1678

EDITED BY
FRANCIS W. STEER

LONDON RECORD SOCIETY
1968

The Society is indebted to the Worshipful Company of Scriveners for a generous grant towards the cost of printing this volume

Printed in Great Britain by

W & J MACKAY & CO LTD, CHATHAM, KENT

CONTENTS

PLATES

INTRODUCTION

The Company of Scriveners

The Master, Wardens and Assistants of the Company of Scriveners of the City of London were incorporated under that title by letters patent dated 28 January 1616/17.[1] Of the eighty-four Livery Companies of the City of London, the Scriveners have the forty-fourth place in order of civic precedence. The Company, when incorporated, became the successor of those freemen hitherto called the Writers of the Court Letter of the City of London who, as a society or fraternity, had practised the science, art or mystery of professional scribes and, among other things, performed those functions now associated with notaries public; in fact, by 1477 the term 'scrivener' was synonymous with notary.[2] In their capacities as agents acting as conveyancers, scriveners occupied a very responsible position in society; scriveners acting as witnesses to the signing and sealing of many deeds of title and other legal instruments which they had prepared, gave such attestation a greater authority than that of witnesses not enjoying such high professional status. From what must have been humble beginnings as mere 'writers' of letters and documents, we find these men banding themselves together as a guild and, like those of any other trade or profession in medieval England, taking steps to ensure that they had the monopoly of their calling. The existence of professional writers or notaries in places other than London is recognized, but consideration of them is outside the scope of this brief introduction.[3]

Although the exact date when the 'Writers of Court and Text Letter' formed some sort of guild is not known, they are mentioned, with the limners and barbers, as an accepted professional class as early as 1357.[4] Seven years later, in 1364, the Writers doubtless considered that the general direction for the good government of all the crafts in the City of London applied to them because a copy of the enrolment of that article is the second entry in their records.[5] Decisive action to establish the monopoly of their profession was taken by the Writers of the Court Letter on 26 September

[1] For a translation of this document, see pp. 80–91.

[2] *Oxford English Dictionary*. In the sense of a professional penman, the earliest reference in *O.E.D.* is to Reinaldus le scriueyner, *c.* 1375; the form *escrivener* occurs in 1415. As money brokers, *O.E.D.* quotes from Dekker and Webster, *Northward Hoe!* (1607): 'Here was a scriuener but euen now, to put my father in minde of a bond, that wilbe forfit this night.'

[3] See H. C. Gutteridge, 'The Origin and Historical Development of the Profession of Notaries Public in England', in *Cambridge Legal Essays written in honour of and presented to Doctor Bond, Professor Buckland and Professor Kenny* (1926), pp. 123–37; J. S. Purvis, 'The Notary Public in England', in *Archivum*, vol. 12 (1962), pp. 121–6, and the Bibliography on pp. xxv, xxvi below.

[4] See Common Paper, p. 1.

[5] *Ibid.*

1373 when they delivered a petition to the Mayor and Aldermen of the City which resulted in the promulgation of simple ordinances for the control and administration of this particular craft and the appointment of two Wardens.[1] Thus 1373 must be regarded as the year when the Writers became a corporate body whose members were governed and protected. As we shall see, rules were modified as occasion required, but in the course of almost 250 years—from 1373 to 1616—dissension and disobedience, infringement of ordinances, financial embarrassment and other problems inevitably arose which could only be resolved by obtaining letters patent from the Crown and an approved set of ordinances whereby the actions of members of the craft could be better regulated. The old fraternity of the Writers was automatically dissolved and reconstituted as a Company, with a new name, under the direction of a Master, two Wardens and twenty-four Assistants who had the services of a Clerk and a Beadle. That form of government, *mutatis mutandis*, is exercised over the members of the Livery at the present time. After the charter of incorporation was obtained in 1616/17, the form 'Citizen and Writer of the Court Letter' was gradually abandoned and the simple form 'Citizen and Scrivener' (*Cives et Scriptor*) used instead; that latter had become generally accepted by the end of 1618.[2]

As Margaret James has shown, the movement of crafts and professions towards incorporation reached a climax during the reigns of the first two Stuarts. For example, trades such as the Turners obtained their charter in 1604, the Shipwrights in 1605, the Fruiterers in 1605/6, the Curriers in 1606, the Plumbers in 1611, the Founders in 1614, the Bowyers in 1621 and the Horners in 1637/8, while ancient callings, which amounted to professions, such as the Musicians, the Scriveners and the Apothecaries became incorporated in 1604, 1616/17 and 1617 respectively. Added to these were 'new' occupations like the Makers of Playing Cards (1628), the Spectacle Makers (1629) and the Gunmakers (1637/8), who secured grants of privilege. 'The Statute of Monopolies in 1624 had no effect on the progress of incorporation; indeed, its effect was rather in the opposite direction, for while the way of individual monopolists was made distinctly harder, the privileges granted to corporate bodies were expressly excluded from its provisions.'[3] The Court of Common Council frequently considered how to strengthen a particular Company by compelling all freemen of other Companies who practised that trade to be translated to it. A joint petition to the City was presented by the Bricklayers, Carpenters, Feltmakers, Hatband Makers, Joiners, Plasterers and Weavers 'demanding that an Act should be passed to enjoin all persons using their respective trades to bind their apprentices at the Companies' halls, and to be obedient to their regulations. Similar petitions were presented in 1659 by the Founders, the Scriveners, the Upholders, the Freemasons, the Clockmakers, the Carpenters, and the Gunmakers'.[4]

[1] For a translation of this document, see pp. 2–4.

[2] See Common Paper, p. 205.

[3] M. James in *The City of London. A book reprinted from the special number* [8, 9 November 1927] *of The Times*, p. 32.

[4] *Ibid.*, p. 33. The chapter from which this and the previous quotation are taken is a valuable and concise account of the incorporation movement and the control over trades.

The majority of the members of the Scriveners' Company belong either to the legal profession or to professions which, in some way or other, may be regarded as closely allied to it. Therefore, like the Goldsmiths and the Gunmakers among the older Livery Companies, the Scriveners may be said to be continuing their original guild, whereas the members of so many other Livery Companies are in no way associated with the craft of the Company to which they have the distinction of belonging. It may be mentioned here that, as in other Companies, women were admitted; instances of this practice occur in 1665, 1666, 1675 and 1677; in 1666 two honorary freemen were elected.

After 1373, when the Writers of the Court Letter became self-governing, the Writers of the Text Letter broke away and joined up with the Limners and together they founded a guild in 1403 which was the ancestor of the present Worshipful Company of Stationers that received its royal charter in 1557; there is a close similarity between the armorial bearings of the Stationers and the Scriveners which were granted in 1557 and 1634 respectively.[1]

The editor of a text is probably always tempted to exceed his terms of reference when writing an introduction, thereby spoiling the pleasure of those who persevere in looking through a book to make their own discoveries. Few members either of the original fraternity or the later Company were distinguished, but none the less John Milton—the father of the poet—is found in this record, as, indeed, is the celebrated Sir Robert Clayton (1629–1707).[2]

It is a matter for regret that so few records of this ancient corporation have survived[3] and one can but express the hope that the publication of this present volume will result in the discovery of documents, long hidden away in some forgotten box, which will enable the six centuries of the history of the scriveners of the City of London to be made more complete.

Some aspects of the Company's development and administration

Memoranda in the Common Paper show that from the earliest times some measure of control was exercised over those who practised as scriveners. In 1364, for example, imprisonment and a fine were the penalties for anyone who was a hindrance to the craft, and such penalties increased in severity for each offence.[4] Nine years later, in 1373, the ordinances enrolled in Guildhall[5] indicate the work of a scrivener—the making of wills and the writing of charters and other deeds to which the writer was to append his name as a sign of good faith. Here, too, is an attempt to keep 'foreigners' and unqualified persons out of the craft: only those who were free of the City and of the craft were permitted to 'keep shop'. Thomas Pantier, who set up in business although not qualified, was sent to the

[1] See J. Bromley and H. Child, *The Armorial Bearings of the Guilds of London* (1960), pp. 217, 232.

[2] They are probably the only two scriveners in the *Dictionary of National Biography*. In *The Coat of Arms*, vol. 7, p. 274, attention is drawn to Robert Graves's book, *Wife to Mr. Milton*, where the arms of the Company of Scriveners are wrongly described.

[3] See list on pp. xxvi–xxviii.

[4] See Common Paper, p. 1.

[5] See Common Paper, pp. 2–4.

pillory in the mayoralty of Adam Bamme (1390–1);[1] the rebellious conduct of Robert Huntyngdon[2] is noted on p. 282 of the Common Paper; the submission of John Valentyn, who was guilty of divers offences as well in language as in other things to the Wardens in 1446, is transcribed on p. 62.

The mandate issued by Robert Braybrooke, Bishop of London, in 1391[3] is of considerable importance: it demonstrates the religious feelings of the time and the severity of his rebuke: Sundays and festivals were not being observed by some scriveners who opened their premises for business on such days, and by so doing not only set a wicked example to other crafts in the City but were holding the Church in contempt. This admonition led to the issue of new ordinances[4] which included a set form of oath, penalties for doing business on Sundays or double feasts, the provision of a livery to be worn principally on the day of Pentecost 'in honour of God who has given all knowledge'. The fraternity was to meet on the first Sunday following the feasts of Christmas, Easter, St. John the Baptist's day and Michaelmas day to deal with any mischiefs or administrative problems; each member was to pay four silver pennies at each of the four terms and be fined for absence without reasonable excuse. Penalties were incurred by those who refused the office of Warden or who employed persons either not free of the craft or not bound apprentices. The conditions governing apprentices were very strict and to contravene them could result in a fine of £10 to the City chamberlain and £6 13*s.* 4*d.* to the common use of the craft.

The petition to the Mayor and Aldermen in January 1439/40[5] is further evidence of the desire for good government. In 1450[6] we have details of the livery to be worn (it was of one colour, but the colour is not specified), and of the annual attendance on the Sunday next after St. John the Baptist's day at a sung mass of the Holy Ghost at St. Paul's or some other convenient place. On that occasion, 12*d.* was levied from each man; 7*d.* of that sum was regarded as ordinary quarteridge, 4*d.* went towards the expenses of the mass and the dinner which followed, and although it is not stated what happened to the odd penny, it would seem that that was the offering which every man was to make at the mass.

There was an important meeting of 'the hoole Company of the Felasship' or Mistere of Scryvaners' at the mansion or dwelling-place of Henry Wodecok, one of the Wardens, on 12 January 1497/8, when the ordinances of the fraternity were read, considered and revised.[7] The decisions made at that meeting are of much interest, as they are reflected, to some extent, in the seventeenth-century ordinances.

The first resolution concerned the election of Wardens: it was agreed that the two Wardens elected on the Sunday following St. John the Baptist's day should serve for two years, that one such Warden should be of the older men who had held office before and the other should be a younger man

[1] See p. 3.
[2] His subscription (undated) is on p. 54 of the Common Paper.
[3] See Common Paper, pp. 5, 281.
[4] See Common Paper, pp. 6–8.
[5] See Common Paper, pp. 9, 10.
[6] See Common Paper, p. 15.
[7] See Common Paper, pp. 189–91.

who had not served previously. During each term of two years there were to be in all three suppers and a dinner: in the first year a supper on the Sunday next after the Feast of the Epiphany and another on the Sunday following St. John the Baptist's day. In the second year a supper after Epiphany (as before) and a dinner on the Sunday following St. John the Baptist's day, when the new Wardens were elected. The dinner was to be preceded by a mass of the Holy Ghost at which every freeman was to offer a penny. Within an unspecified number of days the retiring Wardens were to render accounts to their successors in the presence of four members of the fraternity, of whom two were to have already served as Wardens.

Each freeman had to pay 12*d.* for his supper and 2*s.* for his dinner, but if he brought his wife to the dinner, the charge for her was 4*d.* These payments were in lieu of the old quarterly charges of 7*d.* and 1*s.* for the dinner. The number of suppers was reduced because, under the old system, it was found that the money collected did not cover the expenses and each pair of Wardens found themselves five or six marks short at the end of their term of office; neither was the common fund of the society able to bear such losses.

Attention was directed to the question of apprentices, some of whom had what is called an imperfect 'congruyte of gramer', a fault bringing reproach to the fellowship. Every master, therefore, was to bring his apprentice before the Wardens; the apprentice's name was to be entered in the book of the fellowship; the apprentice was to be examined by the Wardens or their assignees and if it was found that his education was below the required standard, the master was to be admonished and charged to send the apprentice to a grammar school until he should have 'posytif gramer' or at least 'be competently erudite and lerned in the bookes of p[er]nula Gendres Declynysons p[re]t[er]ites and supynes Equivox & Sinonimes'.[1] If a master failed to observe this rule within the first year of the apprentice's term, he was fined 100*s.*, of which half was equally divided between the Chamber of Guildhall and the fellowship, and the other half went to the apprentice if he or his friends had acted as informers. Furthermore, when a master took an apprentice, he was to deliver to the Wardens a silver spoon worth 3*s.* 4*d.* or give the same amount in money; a marginal note of 1558 says, however, that the sum was then only 2*s.* 6*d.*

It is likely that the memorandum of January 1497/8 was not copied into the Common Paper until 16 March 1557/8, when the rules regarding apprentices were further clarified.[2] The then Wardens, Thomas Went and William Pierson, with nine other members, met at Waxchandlers' Hall and resolved that every apprentice be brought to the Wardens by his master within six weeks of being bound; his name was to be entered in the common book; he was to be examined as to his proficiency in the Latin tongue; the penalties for default were to be imposed as mentioned above. It was also ordered that no master was to permit an apprentice to certify or witness the sealing or delivery of any deed, evidence, bond, writing or conveyance whatsoever unless he had been bound for at least a year. The penalty for breaking this rule was 10*s.* for the first offence, 20*s.* for the second and

[1] See Common Paper, p. 190.
[2] See Common Paper, p. 191.

40*s*. for the third, the fine to be applied to the same uses as that for failure to present apprentices.

At a dinner at Waxchandlers' Hall on 16 July 1553[1] it was shown that the method whereby the senior Warden had to be a man who had served in office before was impracticable 'as by the obs[er]vac[i]on of this ordre and by reason of deathe thelder sorte of the seide company are worne awey so faste that at this present there are but three of them lyvyng besydes the wardeyns[2] nowe standyng'. It was thought unfair to burden the few eligible members with continual or frequent office and so it was resolved to choose both Wardens from men who had not served before, but the upper Warden was to be selected by those who had held, and were holding, office, and the junior Warden by general election. This rule was to remain in force until there were eight persons living who had been Wardens, plus the two in office; when that number was reached, the old order was to be brought back into use.

An order dated 6 October 1601 is on pp. 194, 195 of the Common Paper:[3] it is very long, recites the order, 16 July 1553, and another, 9 July 1583, which latter stated that a Master should be chosen to serve with the Wardens for two years and to be elected only by those who had held the office of upper Warden. On 26 July 1597, however, it had been decided that the election of Master and Wardens should be an annual event, but as the number of 'Anncientes of the said Company' had grown to nineteen by 1601, which was a sufficient number, and it was realized that the yearly charge of the election dinner would put too heavy a strain on the Company's finances (its stock being little or nothing), it was decreed that the Master and Wardens should serve, as stated above, for two years from the time of their election.

The Master was to be elected by past Masters; the upper Warden by past Masters and Wardens; the puisne (or accountant) Warden by the generality of the Company to whom should be submitted the names of three members of the Court of Assistants who had not previously held office; the generality was to choose one of the three 'whome they shall like of'. At this October meeting in 1601 it was stated that as the Court of Assistants, whether of the 'ancient' or 'younger' sort, was fifty-six, no more should be admitted during the coming seven years unless the number fell to twenty, or twenty-four at the most. In future, any received into the Court would be by the consent of the Master, Wardens and Assistants or the greater part of them.

Such were the efforts to govern the Company: it was not until the charter of incorporation was granted in 1616/17 that still greater powers were given to those who were to direct its affairs. It must be emphasized that scriveners carried a heavy responsibility: they had to prepare deeds of conveyance which, if faulty, could involve a purchaser in litigation and great financial loss. They had to ensure against forgery and they had to testify either as writers of the deeds or as witnesses to signing and sealing; they had to be prepared to defend the truth of that which they had written or to which

[1] See Common Paper, p. 192 (printed pp. 52, 53). The entry is dated 16 July, 1 Mary, which would have been in 1553 if the reign of Lady Jane Grey is ignored.

[2] John Melsham and John Hulson elected in 1553, see p. 28, note 1.

[3] Printed pp. 53, 54.

they had subscribed. The precautions against forgery probably account for the complicated paraphs invented by scriveners; such men had to guard against the unscrupulous actions of their servants and, perhaps more than anything else, the damage that might be done by those practitioners who were not free of the craft. In brief, the integrity expected of a solicitor today is the same as was expected of a scrivener, and in the period with which we are concerned it was the Master, Wardens and Court of Assistants of the Company who exercised or tried to exercise, a control similar to that of the Law Society today.

The Scriveners' Hall

No reference occurs in the records discussed in this book to the Company's hall. Meetings were held in houses, inns, a church or at Waxchandlers' Hall, but in 1631 the Company acquired land in Noble Street on which four houses were built adjoining either side of the great gateway or entry leading from the street to their own hall. Precisely when this hall was acquired is not known, but its site had been the property of Sir Nicholas Bacon (1509–79), lord-keeper of the great seal to Queen Elizabeth I. The hall was held by the scriveners until 1703, when, with property in Oat Lane, it was sold to the Company of Coachmakers and Coach Harness-makers for £1,600. It was described by William Maitland in his *History and Survey of London* (1756), p. 762, as 'a handsome Building'; its west entrance was from Noble Street and its southern end abutted on Oat Lane. The old hall was demolished in 1867 and its replacement, built in 1870, perished in the Second World War. The Hudson's Bay Company leased the Scriveners' Hall from 1682 to 1696, but it was then usually referred to as Hudson's Bay House; there were vines and fig trees in the garden.[1]

The Common Paper

At the end of the fourteenth or the beginning of the fifteenth century the Writers of the Court Letter procured a book in which to record ordinances and memoranda and to serve as a register of members. That volume, known as the 'Common Paper'[2] is the principal subject of this present book; it consists of 296 pages of paper,[3] $15\frac{1}{2} \times 11\frac{1}{2}$ inches, now bound in leather with simple blind tooling and secured by a buckle and strap laced on to the cover. The buckle and strap are replacements and are part of the extensive repairs, following the original style, carried out to the book by skilled craftsmen at the Public Record Office in 1924 and 1925. That the book has had a succession of covers is shown by the later insertion of extra sheets between the original first gathering (pp. 1–8 and 53–66 as now numbered).[4] Two parchment guards, both with slight rubrication and

[1] Thanks are due to Miss A. M. Johnson, archivist to the Hudson's Bay Company, for this information.
[2] It is now deposited in the Guildhall Library (hereafter abbreviated to GL) where it is indexed as MS. 5370.
[3] Those which are blank are noted in the text.
[4] The book was repaired under the direction of the late Sir Hilary Jenkinson, who has inserted in it one of his valuable memoranda describing its composition and appearance.

probably cut from devotional books, a former parchment cover bearing the date 27 March 1607 and the names of John Butler and John May,[1] paper from the inside of a cover (one piece having on it the name Frankelyn[2] and some paraphs), and another pair of parchment covers on which the name Thomas Misson[3] (among others) appears, have all been bound in for their better preservation.

Although the original text of the Common Paper is in generally good condition, it is often untidy, which indicates that the book came to be used for memoranda instead of for the more formal purposes of record and subscription. Most of the earlier records are in barbarous French, which has presented problems of translation;[4] the declarations are mostly in Latin[5] which also leaves much to be desired,[6] and there are instances (e.g. Common Paper, pp. 106–9[7], 128–30, 172–4 of the original) where it is seen that there were delays between the time of admission and subscription which automatically confuses the chronological arrangement. There is a distinct air of casualness about many of the later entries in the Common Paper which contrast sharply with the earlier ones;[8] throughout this vital record of the Company's affairs it is noticeable that many of those admitted can hardly be classed as brilliant exponents of the skills they were supposed to have acquired—calligraphy and the disciplines of grammar and spelling. As there is no evidence to the contrary, it must be assumed that the declarations were written by the persons making them.

Reference to the list of contents on pp. v, vi will show that the Common Paper is a haphazard combination of subscriptions and evidences; the latter, in the form now presented, are self-explanatory and the basis for the detailed history of the development and administration of the Company which are beyond the scope of these introductory comments. But the Common Paper has value in other directions: from 1580 until 1628 the fathers of scriveners are given together with place of residence and occupation. Such information will be of interest to genealogists, besides illustrating that men came long distances in order to qualify for membership of a profession offering a special and essential service to the population at large.[9]

[1] Butler's name does not occur elsewhere in the Common Paper; for John May(e), 1597, see pp. 41, 57, 64.

[2] For Stephen Frankeleyn, early fifteenth century, see p. 21; for Martin Fran(c)klyn, 1557, see pp. 14, 28.

[3] This name does not occur elsewhere in the Common Paper.

[4] See below, pp. xxii, xxiii under editorial method.

[5] An illiterate example in English occurs on p. 47.

[6] See below, pp. xviii, xix, under oaths. When the form of oath became shorter and more standardized after the early years of the sixteenth century, we see that because of their limited knowledge of Latin scriveners often copied—not always accurately—the declaration that preceded their own.

[7] On these pages there is a wide range of dates, from 1539 to 1553; this may account, at any rate in part, for the variations between dates given in the Common Paper and in MS. Rawlinson D51, which is discussed later on.

[8] For the care lavished on these early declarations, see the reproductions in H. Jenkinson, *The Later Court Hands in England* (1927).

[9] The bibliography on pp. xxv, xxvi indicates some of the sources which will explain the place of scriveners in society and their close links with other branches of the legal profession.

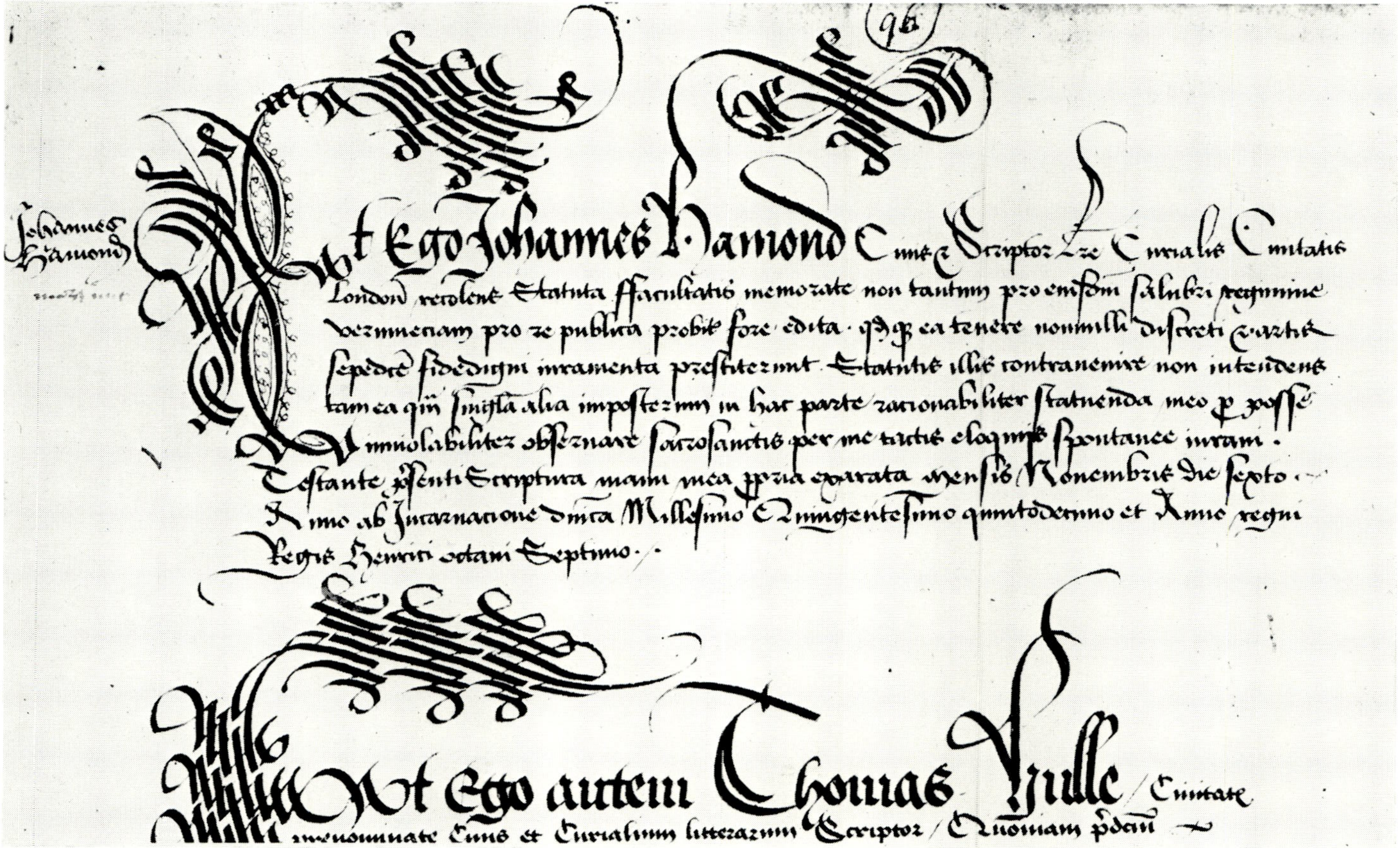

Johannes Hamond

Et Ego Johannes Hamond Civis et Scriptor Lre Curialis Civitatis London recolens Statuta ffacultatis memorate non tantum pro eiusdem salubri regimine verum etiam pro re publica probit fore edita. quo ea tenere nonnulli discreti et artis sepedicte fidedigni iuramenta prestiterunt. Statutis illis contravenire non intendens tamen ea quam similia alia imposterum in hac parte rationabiliter statuenda meo pro posse Inviolabiliter observare sacrosanctis per me tactis eloquiis spontanee iuravi. Testante presenti Scriptura manu mea propria exarata mensis Novembris Die sexto. Anno ab Incarnatione dominica Millesimo Quingentesimo quintodecimo et Anno regni Regis Henrici octavi Septimo.

Et Ego autem Thomas Wulle Civitate prenominate Civis et Curialium litterarum Scriptor Quoniam predict

II. Declaration of John Hamond, 6 November 1515 (see p. 96 of the Common Paper).

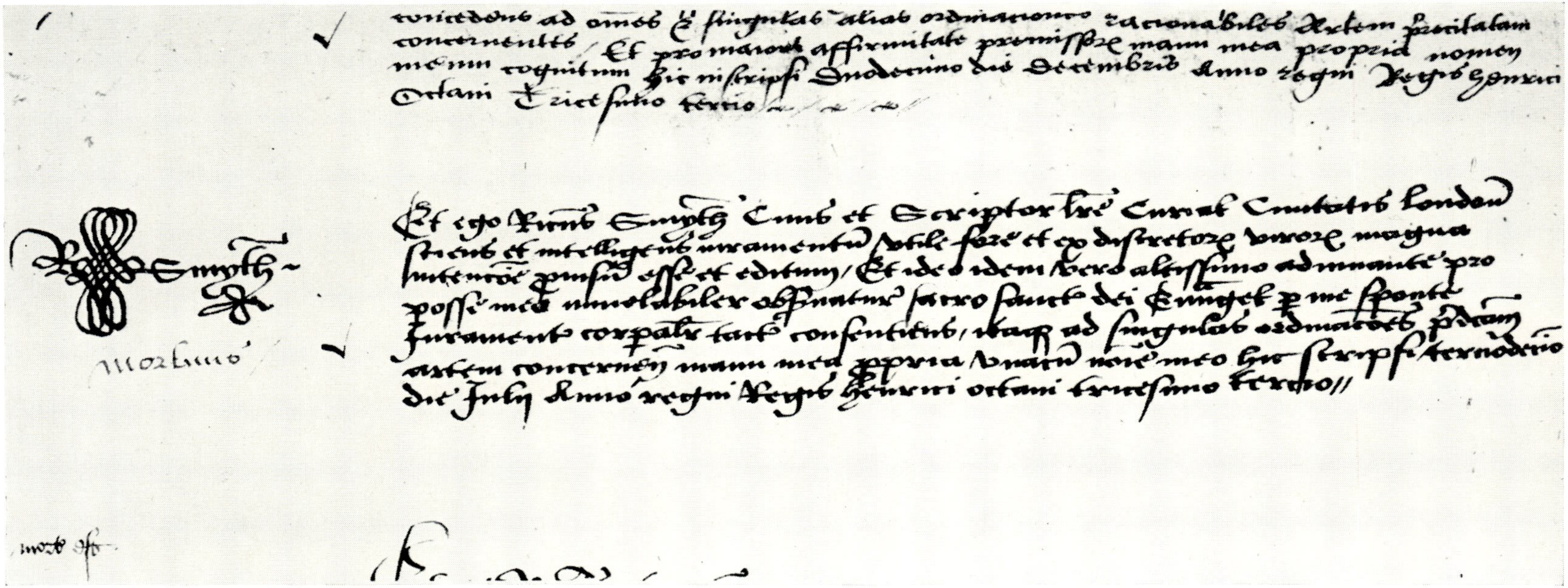

III. Declaration of Richard Smyth 13 July 1541 (see p. 106 of the Common Paper).

An analysis of those entries where territorial and occupational details are available provides the interesting information that the northern and midland counties provided 103 men (group A); the east and south-east counties, 44 (group B); other counties fairly near London, 43 (group C); the western counties, 24 (group D); London (exclusive of men whose fathers were described as citizens and members of Companies), 14 (group E); Wales, 10 (group F); and uncertain, 2 (group G). The groupings are as follows:

GROUP A

Cheshire	10
Cumberland	3
Derbyshire	6
Durham	3
Herefordshire	12
Lancashire	10
Leicestershire	10
Lincolnshire	4
Northamptonshire	9
Rutland	1
Shropshire	6
Staffordshire	9
Warwickshire	2
Worcestershire	3
Yorkshire	15
	103

GROUP B

Cambridgeshire	4
Essex	7
Hertfordshire	6
Huntingdonshire	1
Kent	12
Norfolk	5
Suffolk	9
	44

GROUP C

Bedfordshire	2
Berkshire	6
Buckinghamshire	7
Hampshire	5
Middlesex	7
Oxfordshire	5
Surrey	6
Sussex	5
	43

GROUP D

Cornwall	1
Devonshire	3
Dorset	3
Gloucestershire	13
Somerset	3
Wiltshire	1
	24

GROUP E

London	14

GROUP F

Denbighshire	2
Flintshire	5
Monmouthshire	1
Montgomeryshire	1
Radnorshire	1
	10

GROUP G

Uncertain	2

To the above, totalling 240, there are another 80 men whose fathers are described as citizens of London and members of the following Companies:

Barbers and Surgeons	3	Minstrels	1
Blacksmiths	1	Painter Stainers	1
Clothworkers	4	Pewterers	1
Drapers	7	Saddlers	1
Goldsmiths	2	Salters	1
Grocers	2	Skinners	3
Haberdashers	3	Tallowchandlers	1
Innholders	2	Vintners	2
Ironmongers	2	Waxchandlers	1
Leathersellers	2	Writers of the Court Letter	30
Merchant Taylors	10		

To gain some idea of the social status of the fathers of men who became scriveners, the following is an analysis of occupations excluding those in the preceding table:

Badger	1	Lawyer	1
Baker	1	Linen Draper	1
Blacksmith	2	Mariner or Sailor	2
Bricklayer	1	Mercer	3
Capper	1	Merchant	2
Carpenter	3	Merchant of the Staple	1
Chapman	1	Pewterer	2
Clerk in Holy Orders	13	Saddler	1
Clothier	4	Shoemaker or Cordwainer	6
Clothworker	1	Singingman	1
Cooper	1	Slater	1
Dyer	1	Tailor	3
Esquire	3	Tanner	1
Fellmonger	1	Weaver	1
Founder	1	Woollen Draper	2
Fuller	1	Writer	2
Gentleman	53	Yeoman	98
Husbandman	11		
Innholder	1		229

Also, from 1583 to the end of the record are the names of the masters to whom the newly admitted scriveners had been apprenticed; this information is also provided for the earlier period from MS. Rawlinson D51.

MS. Rawlinson D51

This manuscript, now in the Bodleian Library, Oxford, was compiled between 1664 and *c.*1680[1] and is of great importance because it draws on material now not to be found elsewhere, but which must have been in

[1] The manuscript is hereafter abbreviated to Rawl. D51; I am indebted to the Curators of the Bodleian Library for permission to use it. The manuscript is no. 12869 in F. Madan, *A Summary Catalogue of Western Manuscripts in the Bodleian Library at Oxford*, vol. 3 (1895); a photostat copy of it in GL is indexed as MS. 8721A.

existence towards the end of the seventeenth century. The manuscript is all reproduced (either as additions to the Common Paper or as Appendix I on pp. 76–127 below) except for the lists of contents, abstracts of ordinances, and the index. The original charter incorporating the Scriveners' Company, 28 January 1616/17, the ordinances as approved 29 January 1618/19, and the amendments to the ordinances as approved 28 May 1635,[1] here printed from Rawl. D51,[2] are now in Guildhall Library, where they are indexed as MSS. 8716–18.[3]

MS. Rawl. D51 is a copy of British Museum Harleian MS. 2295, which is a foolscap book, bound in calf, but with a new spine. On the front cover is an ink inscription (perhaps a name) now obliterated; below it is an elaborate paraph formed of interlacing scrolls or flourishes. Harl. MS. 2295 was written *c.*1636–40 on paper; the pages were originally numbered 1–58 (now foliated 1–29), followed by fourteen unnumbered blank leaves, pp. 59–64 (now foliated 30–32), and a blank unnumbered leaf. The manuscript does not contain an English translation of the letters patent, 28 January 1616/17, or any chronological list or alphabetical index of members of the Company. Humfrey Wanley described the volume as 'A Book in folio, formerly (as I suppose) belonging to some Master of the Company of Scrivenors [*sic*] of London; wherein I find divers matters relating to the said Company'.[4]

The compiler of Rawl. D51 was indifferent as to dates: for example, he regarded the calendar year 1450 as the twenty-eighth year of the reign of Henry VI, whereas that regnal year covered the period 1 September 1449 to 31 August 1450. This means that some of the Rawl. D51 entries are actually under the wrong calendar year; we can only be certain of the precise year if the month is stated. Despite this blemish, the manuscript is of value as an extension by fifty years of the Common Paper and particularly as it covers the period of the Commonwealth. It is also of value as the second oldest transcript[5] of the basic documents of the Scriveners' Company

[1] These three documents are printed on pp. 80–113 below.

[2] A detailed comparison between the originals and Rawl. D51 has not been undertaken. The clumsy phrasing and laborious repetition of the ordinances make them tedious to read; I hope to reduce them to a briefer statement for inclusion in a short history of the Worshipful Company of Scriveners.

[3] See pp. xxvi, xxvii for a list of documents in GL belonging to the Scriveners' Company.

[4] See *A Catalogue of the Harleian Manuscripts, in the British Museum*, vol. 2 (1808), p. 643. As the manuscript is excluded from the numerical table in C. E. and R. C. Wright (eds.), *The Diary of Humfrey Wanley, 1715–1726* (1966), we have no clue as to its provenance.

[5] The manuscript is described in W. D. Macray, *Catalogi Codicum Manuscriptorum Bibliothecae Bodleianae, partis quintae, fasciculus tertius, viri munificentissimi Richardi Rawlinson I.C.D.* (1893), p. 27:

> Chartaceus. In folio majori, sæc. xvii. ff. 41. 'Liber Petri Le Neve, Rouge Croix prosecutoris armorum, 1695;' in catal. MSS. ejus, 254.

This is followed by a list of contents of the manuscript in English. For Peter Le Neve (1661–1729), who became Norroy King of Arms in 1704, see *Dictionary of National Biography* and W. H. Godfrey (and others), *The College of Arms* (16th monograph of the London Survey Committee, 1963), pp. 114, 115. Le Neve was Rouge Croix Pursuivant from 1690 to 1704. For Richard Rawlinson (1689/90–1755), see *Dictionary of National Biography* and W. D. Macray, *Annals of the Bodleian Library* (2nd ed., 1890), pp. 231–51.

and for showing the processes in obtaining the charter of incorporation and approval to the ordinances. Sub-headings thoughtfully supplied for convenience of reference by the compilers of Harl. MS. 2295 and Rawl. D51 are reproduced; a modest amount of punctuation and/or capital letters have been inserted to mark sentences or clauses which may otherwise have been obscure.

The make-up of Rawl. D51 is confusing and some explanation is necessary. It is a volume of paper, 16 × 9¾ inches, of which leaves i–iii are unnumbered and, between each of the leaves numbered 2–8 are additional leaves (2a, r. and v., 3a, r. and v., 4a, r. and v., 5a, r. and v., 6a, r. and v., 7a, r. and v.) which are not numbered. The number 16 has been repeated on two leaves; pp. 19–22v., 34–35v. and 44v. are blank, but otherwise leaves numbered 1–41r. bear writing on both sides. To avoid reference problems, the numeration of the leaves of Rawl. D51 given in this present book conforms with that employed for the photostat copy in Guildhall Library, viz. pp. i–iii[1] = 1–6, pp 1–18v. (including the 'a' pages) = 7–54, pp. 19–22v. being blank are ignored, pp. 23–33v. = 55–76, pp. 34–35v. are blank and ignored, pp. 36–41r. = 77–87, and p. 41v. is ignored as a blank.

The forms of oath

As so much of the Common Paper is occupied with the declarations of men admitted to the fraternity, the forms of oath must be treated in some detail. What may be regarded as standard forms will be found on pp. 49, 66, 67, 74, 75 and 105–7 below. The earlier forms which individual scriveners compiled and wrote are more interesting than the later ones because of the variety in expressing basic sentiments and because of their solemn nature; a small selection of them, in translation, is given below.[2]

Fundamentally, an oath is composed of the following elements:

(i) A statement of the person's name and position, e.g. John Tanner, *civis et scriptor litere curialis civitatis predicte*; the formula seldom varies, but *predicte* can be replaced by *London*, and *litere curialis* is sometimes omitted.

(ii) A statement of realization of reason for, or intention of, the oath. This begins with such word as *senciens*, *videns* or *cognoscens*, often with a synonym and/or adverb, and explains that the oath results from necessity (*ex necesse*), hard work (*ex magna industria*) or great faith (*ex magna fidelitate*), for the common advantage (*pro communi utilitate*) of the people (*populi*) or the craft (*artis*). There are many variants of these reasons and any number may be found in one oath in any combination. In more ambitious oaths (e.g. Thomas Guy, p. xxi below) this theme is developed, usually with much circumlocution, and often introducing the idea of stamping out or preventing scandals and deceits.

[1] These numbers are what would be properly accorded to the pages if they had been numbered throughout.

[2] Attention has already been directed (p. xiv) to the indifferent grammar used by scriveners, so these translations, of necessity, are rather broader than would have been the case had the originals been composed in faultless Latin. It would not have been practicable to have included these forms of oath in the calendar. I gratefully acknowledge the enormous amount of help that Mr. J. M. L. Booker has given me in connexion with the oaths.

(iii) The '*tenere et observare*' clause, usually governed by the main verb of swearing (see (v) below), by which the writer swears to 'hold and observe' the oath, but other verbs such as *custodire* or *affirmare* are also found.

(iv) A statement of free will. Either *mea propria* (or *spontanea* or *bona*) *voluntate*, or *sponte* [*mea*], or *non coactus*, and many other variants or combinations. The phrase is generally to be taken with the verb of swearing although it could conceivably belong to the '*tenere et observare*' clause.

(v) The swearing, which contains the first (and occasionally the only) main verb of the passage. It is the crux of the oath. The verb is either *iuravi* or *prestiti* (nothing else) with *iuramentum* (occasionally *sacramentum*) or just an *illud* or *ipsum* referring back to an earlier mention of *iuramentum*. Associated with this verb is the '*tactis sacrosanctis*' clause, occasionally lengthened with an explanation of the sacred objects, e.g. *evangeliis*. The corporal part of the oath is either an adverb (*corporaliter*) with *tactis* or an adjective (*corporale*) with *iuramentum*, and meaning 'having corporally touched the sacred objects' or 'I have sworn the corporal oath'.[1]

(vi) The '*consenciens*' clause, assuring compliance with the ordinances. There is often what seems to be a paradox when *ordinaciones* is qualified by both *novas* and *antescriptas*, but probably only *novas* is strictly temporal in meaning. Sometimes future ordinances are included.

(vii) A statement of subscription of name. *Nomen* is usually omitted in favour of *me*. The expression *scripsi una cum nomine meo* (with no object) must imply that the oath was also written by the swearer.

(viii) The 'credence' phrase which merely explains why the writer has subscribed his name. The usual form is *in fidem et testimonium premissorum*, but more obscure expressions such as *in robur* or *in evidenciam clariorem premissorum* are found; sometimes the whole phrase is omitted.

In the following translations it will be seen that synonyms were so popular that any two scriveners could say almost the same thing with different words. Variants of 'aforesaid' are particularly noticeable; the same English phrases must usually apply to different words in the Latin.[2]

1. I, indeed, John Cossier,[3] citizen and writer of the court letter of London, desiring sincerely to avoid and annul, with all my cunning, whatever deceits, failings and scandals are to be conjectured or exposed in the craft which I use, or will be able to be conjectured or exposed in some way in the future, have sworn the corporal oath (having touched the sacred gospels of God) with my sure knowledge and unprompted free will to observe and inviolately fulfil whatever ordinances are contained in the prescribed oath, drawn up by the masters and worthy men of this craft, as much in the implementation of justice as for the common good, consenting moreover to all other new ordinances previously proclaimed[4] and drawn up by the same masters and worthy men [and] subscribing my [name] here with my own hand in credence and testimony of the aforesaid.

[1] As in the oaths of Andrew Joye and Thomas Froddesham. In the oath of William Slade the corporal word is omitted.

[2] This illustrates the difficulty, if not impossibility, of precise translation.

[3] See p. 20 and note 2 thereon.

[4] See paragraph vi above. Perhaps the true intention here is the subscription to the original ordinances and to any new ones (either additional or amended) drawn up between the date of the original set and the date of signing.

2. And I, Martin Seman,[1] citizen and writer of the court letter of London, knowing full well and understanding that the said oath recently proclaimed and made up by the masters and worthy men of our said craft, and established, as has been said before, by the said master, John Cossier, is profitable and reasonable, and was ordained, for several reasons, for the common advantage and in the implementation of justice, and desiring sincerely and effectually to avoid and annul, with all my power, whatever deceptions or falsehoods, failings and scandals are to be conjectured or exposed in the craft which I use, or will be able to be conjectured or exposed in some way in the future, have sworn this oath (having physically touched the gospels of God) with my sure knowledge and true free will, consenting equally to all other said new ordinances proclaimed and ordained by the same masters and worthy men, and subscribing my [name] with my own hand in credence and testimony of the aforesaid.

3. And I, Robert Huntyngton,[2] citizen and writer of the court letter of the said City, knowing that the said oath has been ordained with great fidelity and for common advantage, have sworn this corporal oath (having touched the sacred objects) of my unprompted free will to observe and fulfil it in every way, and consenting to all the other new ordinances, I have subscribed my [name] here with my own hand in credence and testimony of the aforesaid.

4. And I, Adam Pynkhurst,[3] citizen and writer of the court letter of the oft-mentioned City, although, alas, found to be unworthy and insignificant in mental resources, skill or knowledge of this kind, realizing however that the prescribed oath, made as a result of a great need and with the loyalty and labour of the wise and circumspect men of my said craft, has been equally provided and ordained for the complete avoidance as well as removal (as far as possible) of disinheritances especially and all other scandals, deceptions, disgraces and falsehoods of every kind, and as much for the increase of honour and the good and praiseworthy reputation of the said craft as for preserving the status of the whole nation, in as far as it affects me in my work or will be able to affect me in the future, I have sworn the said corporal oath (having touched the sacred [gospels] of God) spontaneously and not compelled in any way in the above matters and, furthermore, consenting from my own pure and free inclination to other ordinances and whatever wise regulations are firmly provided and now newly ordained for the honour and benefit of my said craft, and desiring to observe these steadfastly and inviolately—as far as I can according to my ability—I have voluntarily made this document, which is clear to view, to be written by my own hand in testimony of the greater deed[4] and in credence of the aforesaid and all and singular that has gone, promising by the good faith with which I am bound to God to be drawn by no other [loyalty] so as to prevent any one or other of the aforesaid [ordinances] being done,[5] without the consent of the greater and more worthy part, of all the men or people of my said craft either now or in the future.

[1] See p. 20 and notes 2 and 3 thereon.
[2] See p. 20 and note 4 thereon. [3] See p. 20.
[4] He probably meant by this his actual observance of the oath in his daily life.
[5] Perhaps this should be understood to mean 'being done away with' or altered.

5. And I, Nicholas Grantham,[1] citizen and writer of the court letter of the oft-mentioned City, although I make unseemly haste in excusing my ignorance in the knowledge of my said craft (seeing that it is rightly said to be more of a divine than a human attribute to know everything and to err in nothing—if men were able to remember all and singular by heart, which is absurd, then it would clearly follow that to write is nothing else than to anticipate labour with labours—writing, therefore, often calls to mind [matters] which lapse and waver[2] through the instability of human nature) wishing nevertheless to conform utterly with the injunctions of my masters and friends, their statutes already written and those to be drawn up in future, and realizing and striving after what is useful and necessary, so that the prescribed oath and the new ordinances prescribed for the common advantage of the people of the kingdom should be steadfastly observed since they are agreed upon by right and reason (because it is lawfully said that the common benefit should come before private), I have of my pure and unprompted will sworn the corporal oath to observe inviolately, according to my strength and ability, the said oath and the new prescribed ordinances and those to be ordained in the future by the masters and friends of my craft, subscribing my [name] here with my own hand so that credence can be applied more fruitfully to the aforesaid.

6. And I, William Acastre,[3] citizen and writer of the court letter of the said City, realizing full well that the prescribed oath has been provided for common advantage and also by much hard work of wise men of the said [craft], have sworn the corporal oath (having touched the sacred scriptures) of my own volition, to hold to it and to observe it as is fitting, consenting moreover to all other articles legally constituted both now and in the future I have written this with my own hand and have set my name to it in credence and as a surer confirmation[4] of the aforesaid.

7. And I, Thomas Guy,[5] citizen and writer of the court letter of the oft-mentioned City, wishing to perform and carry out those things which were and are ordained by my masters and the trustworthy men of my said craft, and especially well realizing that the said oath was drawn up, from necessity, out of the greatest faith, as much for utter avoidance of scandals and wicked deceptions and falsehoods in the said craft as for the profit and honour of the said craft and the principal benefit of all the people, having touched the sacred objects of God, have sworn the said corporal oath of my own unprompted free will, not compelled by force nor by fear, and furthermore consenting and promising to observe justly and faithfully all other ordinances newly drawn up, I have written my [name] here with my own hand to add more weight to the credence of the aforesaid.

8. And I, John Tanner,[6] citizen and writer of the court letter of the said City, although unworthy of [this] knowledge and insignificant in its craft, wishing however to make use of the proposed liberties and transactions in all and singular the points which are drawn up for the profit of my said craft, or will be legally constituted in the future, have corporally sworn the said oath (which I realize was drawn up for common advantage and as a result of the hard work of distinguished men of the said craft), having

[1] See p. 20. [2] Literally 'sink and stagger'. [3] See p. 20.
[4] Literally 'certainty'. [5] See p. 20. [6] See p. 20.

touched the sacred scriptures, induced by my own free will, and I have now written in my surname, to make surer certainty of the aforesaid, with my own hand, warmly entreating the patience of him who reads my writing so that the ignorance of one who is willing to learn may be pardoned among so many and such great scholars.

9. I, Stephen Playne,[1] citizen, writer of the court letter of the renowned City of London, fully examining and clearly observing the oath sworn to by me some time ago, drawn up and carried through, to be in the future interests of the highest expediency of the state and of great loyalty [thereto], will therefore by my own unyielding free will, with the help of God and through my full power, act in accordance with the said oath and all other injunctions of this genuine craft as is mentioned beforehand to those who are newly initiated, and so that greater trust may be summoned I have placed my name, written in my own hand, on this present writing.

10. I, Richard Mulcaster,[2] late apprentice of Francis Mosse, having been admitted to the craft of the scriveners [and] being in some small way skilful, promise to observe, to the best of my ability, all the ordinances of this craft.

11. I, Mark Bradley,[3] having been admitted by the right of redemption, knowing well that the oath which I have now sworn is quite necessary and has been proclaimed and provided with this [i.e. that] intention, intend to observe it inviolately (God be willing) as best I can. Therefore I have subscribed [my name] here, with my own hand, to each ordinance concerning the craft of we scriveners, 25 day of October 1627.

Editorial method

A photographic reproduction of each page with a transcription and/or translation opposite would be the only completely satisfactory method of offering a text so complicated as the Common Paper. The limitations of print and of space have necessitated reducing the text to essentials: this has been achieved by the translation or transcription of those sections of the record which would have lost value by any form of abbreviation, and the submission of the remainder of the volume as a calendar with footnotes to direct the reader to reproductions of some of the entries in other works.[4] Problems of translation[5] have already been mentioned and, in certain instances, footnotes have been provided where some explanation or comment seemed desirable. In the later transcripts,[6] names have been extended in the lists of those assessed, but in headings, preambles and such other places where the character of the document would have been lost or made obscure, those passages are transcribed to correspond as nearly as possible with the original text; footnotes to these difficult sections give further details regarding editorial methods.

So far as the calendared portions of the text are concerned, Christian names have been extended and rendered according to modern usage,[7] but

[1] See p. 29.
[2] See p. 61.
[3] See p. 62.
[4] E.g., H. Jenkinson, *The Later Court Hands in England* (1927).
[5] E.g., pp. 5–8 and 222 of the Common Paper, and many of the declarations.
[6] Pp. 279–95 of the Common Paper.
[7] In cases where there was any doubt, the original spelling has been retained.

surnames are given as written in the original; in those instances where a surname ends with a flourish of which the meaning is not clear, an apostrophe has been introduced,[1] but if it is known that a terminal flourish is mere ornament, it has been omitted. There have been difficulties in deciding whether a letter in some surnames is a 'n' or a 'u': typical examples are Bronn or Broun and Mannsell or Maunsell. With a few exceptions which are noted in the calendar, the place-names in the Common Paper are obvious and as the minor variations in their spelling do not materially add to our knowledge of that subject, such names and the counties are given according to their modern forms. Except in exact transcripts, figures have been converted from Roman to Arabic characters. Discretion has been exercised with regard to contractions when the sense demanded an extension. Thorn has been transcribed as th. Editorial notes or additions to the text are enclosed in square brackets.

In the lists of subscribers to the oath it will be seen that certain information is printed in italic type within square brackets. Such details have been taken from Rawl. D51, which is described above; for example, the entry[2]

William Dodd, 15 July 1577 [. . . *of William Dormer . . . 1564*]

means that the declaration in the Common Paper has been reduced to a bare statement of Dodd's subscription on 15 July 1577, but that Rawl. D51 gives us the additional information that he was apprenticed to[3] William Dormer, who himself subscribed in 1565/6 as William Dermer.[4] Even the minor variations in the spelling of surnames in Rawl. D51 may be important, because we do not know from what sources, other than the Common Paper, that record was compiled; it would appear, however, that the author of Rawl. D51 made some effort to simplify the spelling of surnames. As in the Common Paper, Christian names in Rawl. D51 are given in their modern forms.

Where the phrase 'edited transcript' is used in the printed text of Rawl. D51 it means that contracted words have been extended; that there has been a reduction in, and a standardization of, capital letters; that the 'con' ending of words like 'Corporacon' has been modernized, but spellings such as 'Cittie' and 'scrivenor' have been retained. Superscript letters have been brought down to the level of the line except in those places where it seemed preferable to reproduce the text as precisely as possible.[5]

Acknowledgements

I offer my sincere thanks to the Master, Wardens and Court of Assistants of the Worshipful Company of Scriveners for granting me the privilege of editing the most important of their archives. Likewise I thank the Clerk to the Company (Mr. H. S. S. Trotter, D.F.C.) for his courteous replies to my

[1] E.g., a name written 'Turno' with a terminal flourish may well be Turnor or Turnour.
[2] See p. 32.
[3] In the calendar of the Common Paper I have used the words 'apprentice to' in preference to the 'apprentice of' used in Rawl. D51.
[4] See p. 29 and the last paragraph on p. xvii.
[5] Clarity has been the objective rather than an exact reproduction of a multitude of unimportant scribal mannerisms, but perhaps it would have been wrong to have completely destroyed the character of a document even if it is of late date.

inquiries and for help in other directions. Like all who draw on the resources of the Guildhall Library, I am much indebted to my friends, Dr. Albert Hollaender and his colleagues, for the benefit of their knowledge and for their readiness to assist in every possible way; it is always a pleasure for me to find an excuse to work in the Guildhall Library which I have been privileged to use for forty years. I am particularly grateful to Mr. J. M. L. Booker, who has been untiring in wrestling with knotty problems in Latin and French in the Common Paper; without his generous and willing assistance the translations would have been far less perfect. So many other friends have contributed to this book in one way or another; if they are not named it does not indicate that my gratitude is any the less sincere.

I can hardly expect that this book is flawless; if it contains any errors, then the blame must fall on my shoulders alone.

F.W.S.

ABBREVIATIONS AND SELECT BIBLIOGRAPHY

J. A. R. Abbott, 'Robert Abbott, City Money Scrivener, and his account book, 1646–1652', in *Guildhall Miscellany*, no. 7 (August 1956), pp. 30–39.

adm. — admitted.

app. — apprentice.

A. B. Beaven, *The Aldermen of the City of London* (1908, 1913).

M. Birks, *Gentlemen of the Law* (1960).

J. Bromley and H. Child, *The Armorial Bearings of the Guilds of London* (1960).

City of London Livery Companies' Commission. *Report and Appendix*, vol. 3 (1884), pp. 732–64.

D. C. Coleman, 'London Scriveners and the Estate Market in the Later Seventeenth Century', in *Economic History Review*, Second series, vol. IV, no. 2 (1951), pp. 221–30.

co. — county.

dec'd — deceased.

P. H. Ditchfield, *The City Companies of London and their good works* (1904), pp. 310–13.

Freshfield — E. Freshfield, 'Some Notarial Marks in the "Common Paper" of the Scriveners' Company', in *Archaeologia*, vol. 54 (1895), pp. 239–54.

gent. — gentleman.

GL — Guildhall Library.

H. C. Gutteridge, 'The Origin and Historical Development of the Profession of Notaries Public in England', in *Cambridge Legal Essays written in honour of and presented to Doctor Bond, Professor Buckland and Professor Kenny* (1926), pp. 123–37.

Jenkinson — H. Jenkinson, *The Later Court Hands in England, from the Fifteenth to the Seventeenth Century* (1927).

jun. — junior.

pat. — patrimony.

T. Phillips, *Londonderry and the London Companies, 1609–1629, being a survey and other documents submitted to King Charles I* (1928).

	J. S. Purvis, *Notarial Signs from the York Archiepiscopal Records* (1957).
	J. S. Purvis, 'The Notary Public in England', in *Archivum*, vol. 12 (1962), pp. 121–6.
Rawl. D51	MS. Rawlinson D51, in the Bodleian Library, Oxford.
	T. F. Reddaway, 'The Livery Companies of Tudor London', in *History*, vol. 51 (1966), pp. 287–99.
redemp.	redemption.
Riley, *Memorials*	H. T. Riley (ed.), *Memorials of London and London life, in the XIIIth, XIVth, and XVth centuries* (1868).
s.	son.
s/app.	son and/or apprentice.
Sharpe, *Letter-Book*	R. R. Sharpe (ed.), *Calendar of Letter-Books* [A-L] *preserved among the Archives of the Corporation of the City of London at the Guildhall.* 11 vols. (1899–1912).
subs.	subscribes.
	J. C. Thornley and G. W. Hastings (eds.), *The Guilds of the City of London and their Liverymen* (n.d.), pp. 220–2.
	G. Unwin, *The Gilds and Companies of London* (4th ed., 1963).
	W. Warrell, *Scribes ancient and modern.* (*Otherwise Law Writers or Scriveners*) (1889).

Nearly all the titles mentioned above give references to other sources; see also W. F. Kahl, *The Development of London Livery Companies: an historical essay and a select bibliography* (Boston, Mass., 1960). There are numerous incidental references to the Worshipful Company of Scriveners in general works on the Guilds and in many of the histories of other Livery Companies.

List of manuscripts of the Scriveners' Company in the Guildhall Library

MS.	
366(16)	Case of the Company as to the legality of an assessment on its members towards the rebuilding of their Hall burnt in the Great Fire. With opinion of Sir Thomas Raymond, 14 May 1674.
5370	The 'Common Paper'—the subject of this present book.[1]
6199	Extracts from Court minutes (now untraceable), 1696–1820, chiefly relating to the purchase of the Company's Hall by the Coachmakers' Company and to other premises belonging to the Scriveners' Company, compiled *c.*1830.

[1] For details, see Introduction, pp. xiii, xiv.

8716	Original charter of incorporation granted to the Company by King James I, 28 January 1616/17.
8717	Original ordinances, ratified 29 January 1618/19.
8718	Original ordinances, ratified 28 May 1635.
8719	Copy of grant of arms and supporters, originally granted 11 November 1634, made at the Company's request by Stephen Peters, arms painter, 1738.
8720	Wardens' account book, 1732–1894.
8721	Members' rolls, recording admission to freedom and livery, and offices served, 1732–1892. (There are eighty-four rolls, but the record is incomplete.)
8721A	Photostat copy of MS. Rawlinson D51 in the Bodleian Library, Oxford—this record is also included in this present book.[1]
8722	Bond in £1,000 by the Coachmakers' Company to the Scriveners' Company, 13 May 1703.
8723	Copy bargain and sale by Sir Arthur Savage and Dame Sarah his wife (late wife of George Smithies, Alderman of London, dec'd) and others, to Charles Bostock, Citizen and Scrivener, of— Great messuage with garden known as Bacon House in Oat Lane, St. Mary Staining, City of London 10 June 1628; with copy fine appertaining, 8 July 1628.
9837	Deed of arrangement between (*a*) the Brewers' Company, the Scriveners' Company, the Corporation of London, the Pewterers' Company, the Barbersurgeons' Company and the Carpenters' Company, and (*b*) the Ironmongers' Company, in relation to matters arising out of the Londonderry Estates, 20 November 1884.

List of manuscripts in the Bodleian Library, Oxford, relating to the Scriveners' Company

Rawlinson MS. D51 (*S.C.* 12869), being records of the Company of Scriveners transcribed in the time of Charles II.[2]

Rawlinson MS. D734 (*S.C.* 13504). Miscellaneous papers relating to the City of London and including:

(i) Petition to King Charles II on the issue of a *Quo Warranto* against the Company, expressing their submission, but praying for continuance of such privileges as he shall think fit (f. 79).

[1] For details, see Introduction, pp. xvi–xviii.
[2] For details, see Introduction, p. xvii.

(ii) Two copies of a petition to the Lord Mayor and Aldermen respecting the binding of apprentices, with statement of reasons, and letter, 1672 (ff. 80–87).

(iii) Counsel's opinion, by Sir Thomas Raymond, 14 May 1674, in favour of the power of the Company to levy contributions upon the members for the rebuilding of the Hall, burned down in the Fire of London (f. 88).

Rawlinson MS. D911 (*S.C.* 13677). Fragmentary English papers, historical and legal, but including (f. 196) 'The explanac'on of the clause concerninge scriveners, etc. conteyned in the Act against usury made in the xxi yeare of Kinge James'.

THE COMMON PAPER

[p. 1 translation][1] *The authorities, articles and ordinances for the Company of the Writers of the Court Letter of London, enrolled in Guildhall, London, book G, folio 61*[2]

20 May, 31 Edward III [1357], it was ordered and agreed by Henry Pycard, Mayor, and the Aldermen, that the writers of court and text letter, the limners and barbers [*illuminatores et barbitonsores*] dwelling in the City of London, should not in future be summoned on inquisitions in the sheriffs' courts between any parties pleading in the same. And if any amercement should be taken from them by the sheriffs' officers, the same should be restored without any gainsaying. Saving, however, that if they should be summoned to come to Guildhall on any arduous business touching the City, then they are to come under penalty.[3]

The general articles for all the Mysteries of London, enrolled in the Chamber of the Guildhall, London, book G, folio 135, in the time of Adam de Buri, Mayor, 38 Edward III [1364][4]

Item, it is ordained that all the crafts of the City of London should be loyally ruled and governed, each according to its nature in the proper manner, so that no falsehood nor wrong work nor deceit should be found in any kind of the said crafts, for the honour of the good men of the said crafts; and that, for the common advantage of the people, four or six [men] should be chosen and sworn from each craft, either more or fewer according to the needs of the craft, which men so chosen and sworn would have the full power of the Mayor to do and carry out this, well and loyally. And if anyone of the said crafts should rebel against this or be a hindrance so that they are unable to perform their duty in the proper way, and should be convicted of this, he will remain in prison for 10 days and pay 10*s*. to the commonalty for the contempt. And at the second time he will remain in prison for 20 days and pay 20*s*. to the commonalty. And at the third occasion he will remain in prison for 30 days and pay 30*s*. to the commonalty. And at the fourth occasion he will remain in prison for 40 days and pay 40*s*. to the commonalty.

[1] At the top of the page, above and between the words *Iste* and *sunt*, are the initials W:M.

[2] See Sharpe, *Letter-Book G*, p. 88, and Riley, *Memorials*, p. 295.

[3] Throughout the margins of the manuscript are various memoranda and scribblings, e.g. Henrici Maioris; 1357 31E. These have been omitted unless they shed any light on the content of the paragraphs to which they refer.

[4] See Sharpe, *Letter-Book G*, p. 174.

[p. 2 translation] *The ordinances and articles enrolled in Guildhall, book G, folio 307*[1]

26 September, 47 Edward III [1373], came here the reputable men, the Common Writers of the Court Letter of the City, and delivered to the Mayor and Aldermen a certain petition in these words:

To the honourable lords, the Mayor and Aldermen of the City of London, the Writers of the Court Letter of the said City pray that whereas their craft [*mestier*] is much in request in the same City and it is especially requisite that it should be lawfully and wisely ruled and followed and that by persons instructed therein. And seeing that, for want of good rule, many mischiefs and defaults are, and have often been, committed in the said craft by those who resort to the said City from divers countries, as well chaplains and others, who have no knowledge of the customs, franchises and usages of the said City, and who call themselves scriveners [*escryveyns*] and undertake to make wills, charters and all other things touching the said craft; the fact being that they are foreigners and unknown, and also less skilled than the scriveners who are free of the said City and who for a long time have been versed in their craft and have largely given of their means for their instruction and freedom therein, to the great damage and disherison [*desheriteson'*] of many persons, as well of the said City as of many countries of the realm, and to the damage and offence [*desclanndre*] of all the good and lawful men of the said craft. Therefore, the good scriveners pray that it may please your honourable and discreet lordships to grant and establish for the common profit of the said City and of many other countries and for the well-being and amendment of their condition, that they and their successors for all time may be ruled and enjoy their franchise, in their degree, according to the following points—

First, that no one may be suffered to keep shop [*de tenir shope*] of the said craft in the said City, or in the suburb thereof, if he is not free of the City and also made free of the craft by men of it.

Item, that no one shall be admitted to the said freedom if he be not first examined and found able by those of the same craft who shall, for the time being, by you and your successors, be assigned and deputed in this business and be Wardens of the said craft.

Item, that every scrivener of the said City, and of the suburb thereof, shall put his name to the deeds which he makes so that it is known who has made the same.

Item, that everyone who shall act against this ordinance and institution [*establisement*] shall pay to the Chamber 40*d.* the first time, half a mark the second time, and 10*s.* the third time.

[p. 3] Item, that these articles shall be enrolled in the said Chamber as being firm and established for ever. Which petition being read and heard, and advice thereupon had by the Mayor and Aldermen, it was agreed between them and granted that the said articles shall be henceforth observed and that offenders thereof shall be punished in the penalty in the form written above.

[1] See Sharpe, *Letter-Book G*, p. 312 and Riley, *Memorials*, pp. 372, 373.

After which points and articles had been written, the aforesaid Common Scriveners of the Court Letter had Wardens and used to put their names to the deeds which they made and produced, continuously, by estimation, for about the next three years.

Now it happened that at the time when the article that we should put our names to deeds was drawn up, the custom or the usage then was to write on each kind of deed and writing 'Dat' london'' or 'Done a lonndres', except only in charters and writings of lands, tenements and rents granted outside London which, however, were to have the date when the lands, tenements and rents were granted. And a plan [*un poy*] was then worked out by the wise men of the kingdom, and all means have since been used, as far as concerns the making of them [i.e. the deeds], to remove the date of the grants[1] in the majority of all kinds of deeds and writings with the intention of alleging the date of the grant [and] of the making of the deed when it will be more suitable for the party bringing an action. And, in that the writing of our names must be contrary to this kind of allegation—in a case where the allegation [or alleging] will take place outside the region where the scrivener, who wrote the deed, lives—the aforesaid article, that we should put our names on deeds, was not used any more, nor was the penalty on this injunction ever carried out. For which reason, and for other reasonable causes, and because of the many evils which could have happened by the aforesaid writing of our names on deeds (as appear more fully at the end of this paper),[2] if it had been necessary to have used and continued the process for a longer period, the aforesaid scriveners stopped the said writing of their names on deeds. And the said craft of scriveners of the court letter was afterwards without Wardens [and] without rule and control for 15 years and more.

[p. 4] In which time, through lack of Wardens and of good rule and control over the said craft, many foreign men, not initiated in the said craft, held open shop of it, just like men enfranchised in the said craft, so it happened that one Thomas Pantier, a foreigner, who had been a hireling with a scrivener for two years and was never apprenticed, began to hold shop of the said craft and within a quarter of a year [*dr' quart' dan*] from his beginning through lack of knowledge and ignorance of the science of the said craft, he was sent to the pillory in the time of Adam Bamme, Mayor, in the 14th year of [the reign of] King Richard the Second, to the great slander and shame of all the good men enfranchised of the said craft.[3]

Through [*pur*] which lack [of Wardens] and villainy, the worthy [*p'des*] men of the said craft at once requested, by a petition to the said Mayor, Adam Bamme, to have licence to assemble and discuss the control of the said craft, which Mayor allowed them to make assemblies, in the name of God, telling them they had good reasons for entering the Guildhall and asking why they had no Wardens.

[1] Common Paper, p. 222, has a passage very similar (in places identical) to this. See the note referring to it.

[2] The clause in brackets is inserted above the line in the text; the 'many evils', in fact, are not stated.

[3] See Sharpe, *Letter-Book H*, p. 365, under date 22 Apr. 1391, and Riley, *Memorials*, pp. 527–9.

Upon which all the good men enfranchised in the said craft of scriveners of the court letter, as well by virtue of the aforesaid general article concerning all crafts in London as by virtue and authority of their own points and articles, especially written for and granted to them, assembled and chose two Wardens as appears by the annexed written record:

Enrolled in the Chamber of the Guildhall, London, book H, folio 267[1]

On the 17th day of May in the 15th year of the reign of King Richard the Second [1392] there came into the Chamber of the Guildhall of the City of London honest men of the craft of writers of the court letter in the said City and presented to the Mayor and Aldermen of the same City, Martin Seman and John Cossier, writers, elected by them to be masters of their art for the following year, on which day the same Martin and John were sworn to the good and faithful control of their said art [or craft] by sparing no one through love or oppressing no one through hate, and by presenting shortcomings which they found in the said art to the Mayor, Aldermen and Chamber of the said City, &c.

[p. 5] Also remember that in the aforesaid time when the said foreign men were holding open shop through lack of Wardens and of good rule, as has been said before, the majority of the said craft were holding open shop and writing openly, in public view, as well on festivals and Sundays as on holidays to the very great resulting harm of the said craft, so that the Bishop of London,[2] who then was, issued a mandate, in part concerning the said craft, of which the following is a copy.

Robert, by Divine permission Bishop of London, sends greetings, gramercy [*gram'*] and blessings to all his rectors, vicars and curates whosoever, wherever established within our jurisdiction through our City of London. We declare that it has been laid down by the sacred canons that it is proper for all loyal Christians to be held and effectively constrained to keep holy Sundays and the principal festivals of our Christ Jesus and his most glorious mother the chaste virgin, the apostles and sacred martyrs whose vigils are observed as fasts according to the instruction and advice of the church of England, and to abstain from their tasks and duties and to hear mass and the divine offices in their parish churches and to serve God constantly. With information from very many honest men and with reports being brought back, it has recently come to our ears that several of your parishioners in our jurisdiction of this said City, and particularly the barbers and scriveners, have made very little effort and make little effort [now] to observe Sundays and the principal feasts of this kind, as is lawfully sanctioned and to apply themselves to holy duties on festivals and the said days, but they continue to set about their craft and hold open shop with everyone attending on the said days just as on other days which are not holidays, by collecting their fees for their craft and service to the great danger of their own souls, as a wicked example to other crafts of the said City, and in open contempt of the life-giving mother church. We, wishing to prevent these matters as we are bound by the duty of our pastoral office,

[1] See Sharpe, *Letter-Book H*, p. 375. [2] Robert Braybrooke.

therefore instruct and command you, firmly enjoining you, together and individually, in the virtue of obedience, that you should caution and effectively persuade all those barbers and scriveners whosoever, throughout your parishes in our jurisdiction, and all their apprentices, attendants and servants whom we are advising by the meaning of these presents, and we wish those who have been carrying out these practices[1] and have done it under the penalty of a greater excommunication than if they had disobeyed your warnings—in fact they have scorned to obey ours—and are excelling in sloth, guile and guilt, to undergo the canon law with its warning prescribed in this matter and, afterwards, that on Sundays and festivals of this kind they may devoutly listen to mass and the divine offices in their parish churches just as other good Christians of other crafts of this said City have been accustomed to do, and do now, and that they should serve God and completely abstain on the said days from their craft and work (unless in some emergency) and with their shops closed they should completely desist and refrain from financial matters through which they are more readily trapped by the blindness of greed. If you should find any people at all refusing or contradicting or not effectively obeying your warnings in this matter, you should summon them immediately so they may appear before us, or our commissioners for this purpose, in the chapel of our manor of Stebenheth' [Stepney] on a certain convenient day chosen by you or one of yours, by chastising them with a view to the chaste correction of their souls, to make them answer to us dutifully and, further, to do and to accept what will be ordained and in accordance with reason. And [we wish] that you should inform us what you have done in these matters about the time of the next feast of the translation of St. [p. 6] Thomas by means of your letters patent containing a report of these affairs and subscribed with your own seal, or that one of you should inform us who has first considered our instruction to be carried out. Given under our seal in our manor of Stebbenheth' the 28th day of June 1391 and in the 10th year of our consecration.

The new ordinances

For which above-written reasons, the aforesaid Masters, the said Wardens and all the other good men enfranchised of the said craft [*mestier*] of scriveners, in order to do away with the danger and evils which were able to befall [*cheyer*] as above, assented and agreed to the ordinances written below. That is to say:

That every one that shall be duly enfranchised in the said craft of scriveners shall make especially the following oath, charging himself in the presence of the Wardens of the same craft. And whosoever shall refuse and not make the same oath shall be suspected of falsehood and also presented to the Mayor as a rebel, which oath ensueth here in this form:

I, *N.*, of my own proper will, swear upon the holy evangelists to be true in my office and craft, and to be diligent that all the feats that I shall make to be sealed shall be well and lawfully made after my understanding and knowledge. And especially I shall not write, nor suffer to be written by

[1] In the text, this clause is repeated in another way.

none of mine to my power and knowing, any manner of deed or writing to be sealed bearing a date a long time before the making of the same, nor a long time after, nor a blank charter, nor other deed sealed before the writing thereof, nor closed letters of a date far distant, nor of long time where through any falsehood may be perceived in my conscience, nor no copy of a deed but well examined word by word. And neither for haste nor for covetousness I shall take it upon me to make any deed touching inheritance or other deed of great charge whereof I have no cunning [*sachaunt*] without good advice and information of counsel. So help me God and all the saints.

[p. 7] Item, that every one who shall have made the said special oath, shall testify the same by writing it in his own proper hand in the common paper of the said craft in time to come. And when he is a notary shall put his sign if he pleases.

Item, that none of the said craft shall on Sundays or double feasts keep open shop for any business nor for any money covetousness, nor write openly or privately except in a cause of great necessity which may not be delayed, upon pain of paying double the same money and gain to the use of the said craft. And he that shall keep open shop of the said craft to make open show of his said craft to the view of people upon any Sunday or festival aforesaid shall incur the penalty of paying to the Chamber of the Guildhall of London 6*s* 8*d*. for the first offence, 13*s*. 4*d*. for the second, 20*s*. for the third and so forth.

Item, that every one who shall have made the said oath shall be vested in one suit (and) at the feast of Pentecost by the ordinance of their Wardens. And that every one of them for that shall pay a noble at the beginning of Lent before the buying of the cloth and the rest of the money shall be paid as soon as it may well be after the [de]livery of the said cloth. And that the same vesture be principally used on the day of Pentecost, in honour of God who has given all knowledge. And after that it is to be kept and used honestly for two years at least, that is to say, for the first year for festival days and the second year for holy days. And that their feast is to be held on the day of the Holy Trinity in honour of the same feast.

Item, that every one who is free of the said craft shall come in his proper person four times a year at a certain hour and place in the said City to be appointed by the Wardens to move, declare and dispute among themselves all mischiefs, perils and doubts of their said craft for their information and so that their said oath may be kept, and also to make orders for the good rule and government of the said craft. This is to be on the first Sunday after Christmas, the Sunday next after Easter, the Sunday next after the day of the nativity of St. John the Baptist, and the first Sunday after the day of St. Michael the Archangel, each of them paying to their Wardens, to the use of the said craft, four silver pennies [*quatre den'i's dargent*] at each of the four said terms. And if someone should be absent at any of the four said terms without reasonable excuse, and this should be duly proved, he should pay 40*d*. each time to the Chamber of the Guildhall, except always that if any such person be found excusable he should pay, nevertheless, the four pence for the term, and the expenses then incurred should be paid out of the said four pence and [should be paid] to the Wardens for the time being to be allowed in the account.[1]

Item, that when the election of new Wardens is to be made, it is to take place each year on the Sunday next after the day of the nativity of St. John the Baptist and will be of two people from the said craft of scriveners, of which one person will be chosen by the old Wardens and the other by the rest of the said craft. And if any altercation or discord should occur in the said election of one or the other, it is to be put before the majority [*la greyndre p'tie*] of the said craft at once. [p. 8] And that the old Wardens will immediately be barred from re-holding such office for the next three successive years, but will be at hand for the period of a year, and will help and advise the new Wardens concerning the government of the said craft for the whole year immediately following their own departure from the offices of wardenship. And that vesture for the same year is to be ordered and bought as well by the [? expense] of the two old Wardens as by the two new ones.

Item, if there be anyone duly elected, in this way, to be Warden who is able to carry out this office if he pleases, but refuses the office and responsibility [*charge*] of being Warden, he is to be presented to the Mayor or the Chamberlain of the Guildhall as a rebel and he is to pay for that rebellion 40*s*., half to the said Chamber and the other half to the use of the same craft, without any credit [*grace*] or pardon on the payment. And without delay another is to be elected in his place, and the new Wardens are to be presented to the Court of the Mayor to receive their charge, as is the custom, within eight days of the said election.

Item, that the old Wardens will render their accounts on a certain day fixed and assigned by the new Wardens, after which the new Wardens themselves are to receive their charge at the Guildhall and delivery is immediately to be made to them of their common paper and of their common treasure if there be any.

Item, that no one of the said craft of scriveners will admit any foreign man to hold shop of the said craft under him on pain of paying 40*s*. to the Chamber of the Guildhall and 40*s*. to the use of the said craft, and losing the control [*de voyder*] of such shop, and such kind of foreign man, on pain of paying 10 *li*. to the above-mentioned Chamber.

Item, that no one of the said craft shall take any hired [*allowys*] servant into the same craft, unless the hiring itself is to create an apprentice of the said craft in the above-mentioned City, on pain of paying equally 40*s*. to the said Chamber of the Guildhall and 40*s*. to the use of the said craft, and of losing this kind of servant, on pain of paying 10 *li*. to the above-mentioned Chamber: unless it be through the permission [*grace*] and leave [*conge*] of all the said craft.

Item, that no one of the same craft shall take an apprentice of the said craft in order to release him before his term by deceit, on pain of paying equally 40*s*. to the said Chamber and 40*s*. to the use of the said

[1] This, as much other of the text, is obscure, but it is hoped that this translation conveys the meaning that even if a member of the craft had a valid excuse for absence he still had to pay the 4*d*., but any part of that sum remaining after the payment of the Wardens' expenses in this matter was to be credited to the funds of the craft.

craft. And that each apprentice is to be entered in that paper [*entree en y ceste pap'*], after which the apprenticeship indenture is to be enrolled. And that the Wardens keep good watch to find out who is an apprentice and who is hired.

Item,[1] it is ordained and established by the common consent of all that are of the said mystery, that every person whatever his estate or condition and in or by whatever manner, instance, prayer, commandment, favour, reward he should offer, shall not be received as a freeman of the said mystery or be enfranchised within the said mystery in any manner by the Master and Wardens or by any person belonging to the said mystery but only in the lawful manner and way of apprenticeship; and that when the same person has been apprenticed and has well and truly served his master to whom he was apprenticed or his executors or assigns for the term of his apprenticeship; or by way of birth as the custom of the City requires in such a case; and that especially for the common profit of the realm and the honesty of the said mystery and also to avoid and eschew disorder, especially mischiefs done in the past by strangers ignorant and lacking in good behaviour and good fame and not expert in the said mystery, free[men] shall not be made contrary to this article. And if any Master, Wardens or other person whatever he be in the said mystery shall act hereafter in any way, contrary to this article, ordinance and establishment, which can be proved by the honest company of the said mystery that he has at any time or in any way acted contrary to this ordinance, shall pay . . . to the Chamber of the Guildhall 10 *li.*; and to the common use of the said mystery 6 *li.* 13*s.* 4*d.*; and thereupon he shall be found and accounted a rebel for so doing, by the Master and Wardens of the said mystery and the governance of the same and be without pardon or remission by any means in that case at any time to come.

[p. 9 translation] *Entered in the Chamber of Guildhall, London, book K, folio 182*[2]

13 January, 18 Henry VI [1439/40], there came into the Chamber of the Guildhall of the City of London, before Robert Large, Mayor, John Reynwell', John Gedney, John Welles, John Brokle, Henry Frowyk, William Milreth, Ralph Holand, Thomas Catworth, William Gregory, John Olney, John Sutton', William Combes and William Wetenhale, Aldermen of the said City, good men of the craft of writers of the court letter of London, and laid before the said Mayor and Aldermen a certain bill or supplication in the following words:

[Transcript] *To the full' honorables lordes and sov*[*er*]*aignes Mair and Aldermen of the Cite of london'*

Full mekely besechen the goode folk of the Crafte of Skrivens of Courte l[ett]re in the seid Citee That it plese unto yo' fulle wise discrecions

[1] This article is badly faded in the original; the version here printed is largely based upon the translation in the Report from the Committee of Assistants of the Company delivered to the Master, Wardens, and Court of Assistants, 23 June 1748, and reproduced in the City of London Livery Companies' Commission, *Report and Appendix*, vol. 3 (1884), p. 754.

[2] For a summary of this document, see Sharpe, *Letter-Book K*, pp. 234–5; for another, but inaccurate, transcript, see City of London Livery Companies' Commission, *Report and Appendix*, vol. 3 (1884), pp. 754–5.

tenderly to considre the grete p[er]els and myschiefs that oft tyme haue falle and yit dayly fallen by diu[er]s p[er]sones nat connyng ne experte in the seid Craft Whiche taken vpon' theyme for to make diu[er]s feates aswell touchyng inherytannces as other feates of charge soche as belong to the seid' Craft. Where as in dede thei ar neyther expert ne konnyng and so thurgh' theire ignorannce and vnkonnyng hurten' gretely and disceyuen' the Co[mmon]e peple aswel to theire disherityng as in other caas p[er]sonel[es] to grete hurt and disclanndre of the goode true folk of the seid' Craft And th[ere]vpon' g[ra]ciously to grannte in eschewyng of suche p[er]els & myscheves in tyme here after th[a]t the poyntes and Articles here after folowyng may be hadde' & admitted for ferme & Stable and to be entred & enrolled in the chambre of the Guyldehalle so that the gode rule may be obserued & kept in the Seyde Craft for theire p[ar]tie like as it is Wythin oth[er] Craftes of the seid' Citee.

First that no man[er]e [of] man of the seid' Craft of What condicion' so eu[e]r he be take vpon hym to make eny evidences or munimentes that sownen' to me[n]nes enheritannces ne oth[er]e grete charges soche as mygh[t]e falle to grete hurt of the kynges peple of lesse than he be first Duely examined and founden able by the Wardeyns of the seid' Craft for the tyme beyng and by. vj. or iiij p[er]sones enfrannchesied in the seid' Craft or by the Mair and Aldermen' of the seide Cite And also th[a]t no man' other than suche as haiv serued wethin the seyde Craft by way of app[re]nticialte from hens forward hold eny shop [?as] of the saide Craft wyth'in the seide Citee ne in the subarbes th[er]of lesse than he by the Wardeyns of the seid' Craft for the tyme beyng And by suche vj or iiij p[er]sones of the same Craft or els by the mair & Aldermen' of the seid' Citee haue been examined and founden' able and so for able by hem p[re]sented and th[er]vpon be enfrannchised in the Craft of Screvens aboueseid'.

Item that no p[er]sone enfrannchised in the seid' Craft from hens forward w^t^in his shop' ne in noon' oth[er] place occupie sette on werke ne Colour in the seid Craft and occupacion' of Skryvens ony p[er]sone lesse than the same p[er]son' so sette on' Werke be fore th[a]t tyme haue been' app[re]ntice or enfrannchised in the seid' Crafte W^t^oute Consent and speciall' licence of the Wardeyn[?es] of the seid' Craft And suche vj or iiij p[er]sones enfrannchised in the same craft or of the mair and Aldermen' of the seid' Citee for the tyme beyng vpon the payne of C s' to be arrered of eu[er]iche such' p[er]son' so founden' defectif in doyng the Contrarie of this orden[a]nce And that as ofte as he therof shall' be conuycte And the forseid' C s' to be devided in the fourme suyng that is to seie th[a]t on' half th[er]of to remayn' to the vse of the chambre of the Gildehalle And that other half to the vse of the companye of the seid' Crafte.

Item that from hens forward eu[er]y p[er]sone enfrannchised in the seide Craft that holdeth open Shop' w^t^in the seid' Citee ne subarbes therof paye yerely atte iiij pryncipall' termes of the yere to the supportacion' of the charges of the same Craft. xij d'. th[a]t is to seye eu[er]y quarter iij d' to be disposed and demened by the discrecion' of the Wardeyns and goode men' of the same Craft for the tyme beyng.

Item that from hens forth' no p[er]sone enfrannchised of the same Craft w^t^oute licence of the Wardeyns of the seid' Craft for the tyme beyng

And of vj or iiij of the most sufficiannt p[er]sones of the same Craft occupie ne hold' open w^{t}in the seid' Citee ne subarbes therof but onely 00 [*sic, recte* one] shop' for the grete p[er]els and myschefes th[a]t necclygently hau fallen' And here after may falle thurgh ignorannce and vnkonnyng of theire s[er]u[a]ntes or app[re]ntices the seid' Craft so occupying or kepyng any shop' under[1] his maister In whiche the maister atte all' tymes cannot be p[re]sent to the ou[er]syght and examinacion' of alle feates made be his s[er]u[a]nt[1] ne app[re]ntice in a Shop' so discen[c]ed from his maister opon' payn' of C s' to be arrered of eu[er]y p[er]sone doyng the contra[ry] of this Article [*a word gone and two others illegible*] th[a]t eny so be found' defectyf and to be devided in the fourme aforeseid'.

[p. 10] Item that eu[er]y p[er]sone of the seid' Craft holdyng opyn' Shop' in this seide Citee & subarbes from this tyme for Ward' when and as ofte as he there be warned by the Bedell' or s[er]u[a]nt of the seid' Craft in the name of the Wardeyns of the seid' Craft for the tyme beyng beredy and attendannt at houre & plase to hym assigned vpon' payne to paye at eu[er]y tyme that he th[er]of do the contrarie xijd' to be arrered and devided in the man[n]e[r] and fourme afore rehersed.

[Translation] Which said bill being read to the Mayor and Aldermen and fully understood by them, because it seemed to them that all the articles in the bill are reasonable, redounding to the welfare and honour of the public, unanimously consented to the ordering, decreement and sentencing of the said articles, here among others, to be entered of record in the manner and form in which they are prayed, for the future firmly to be observed, reserving to themselves power to add, diminish and correct according to changes in times and conditions as shall seem expedient. [pp. 11–14 blank.]

[p. 15 *transcript*] This is the orden[a]nce advice and appoyntment made in the tyme of John Grove & Rob't Bale Wardeyns of the Craft of Scriven[ers] of Courte l[ett]re by the Will assent & aggreement of the hole felauship' & company of the same Craft assemblid' togidere in the Chirche of seint Thomas of Akres in London' the xviijth Day of the moneth of Aprill the xxviijth yere of the Reigne of oure sou[er]aigne lord' kyng henry the Sixte as foloweth that is to wite.

The lyu[er]ey of hodyng in the saide Crafte fro hens forth tobe of oo [i.e. one] coloure and' tobe used' in the fourme as hit hath' been of tyme passed accordyng to the Act therof made.

Also to the Worship' and pleasire of god' A masse be note of the holy goste yerely to be holden & kept from hens forth' on the Sonday next after Midsom[er]day at Paules if hit may be hadde goodly or elles at a nother place conuenyent Where as the Wardeyns of the Craft for the tyme beyng will lymet & ordeyn' and a dyner' the same day to be hadde for the same felauship' & Company at suche place as shall be aduysed and assigned by the said' Wardeyns. And' the same masse & dynere tobe gynne & be holden the Sonday after Midsom[er]day next nowe comyng. And' so to contynue forth yerely. And that eu[er]y man of the same Craft & Felauship' aswell he that is absent from the said masse or dyne[r] as he that ther[e] at is

[1] Doubtful word; the manuscript is badly worn here.

p[re]sent paie at eu[er]y tyme to the Supportacion therof. xij.d'. that is to Wite. vijd'. tobe applied for the quarterday as hath been used & hadde afore tyme and iiij.d' toward' a part of thexpenses of the costes tobe doon at the said' masse & dyne[r]. And also eu[er]y man of the said' Company to offre atte the masse. j.d' and to be attendannt at place & houre to him therof by the Wardeyns for the tyme or ony other' in theire name assigned. And ther' to abide att the masse & no p[er]sone in ony wise to absent him thens without that he have a resonable excuse be his othe. And the forsaid xij.d' tobe leveed' & hadde atte all tymes by the Wardeyns for the tyme beyng of eu[er]y man of the said' Craft & Company Prouyded alwey that eu[er]y man' of the Craft and Felauship' abouesaid' paie atte eu[er]y of the iij quart[er] Daies folowyng the vij.d' due as hath been vsed & is enacted' afore. And the Wardeyns for the tyme beyng therof to spend' by theire Discrecions to the use of the said' Company as hem best semyth.

Also it is affermed' assentid' and g[ra]nntid' by the said Felauship' and Company that from hens forth theire Act of xij.d'. conteyned in this boke amonge the Articles of the Craft Whiche is cessed' vpon euery p[er]sone of the said' Craft that geueth not his attendannce atte houre & place by the Wardeyns or ony in their name to him assigned' be put in execucion' & leveed accordyng to thentent of the said' Act for thencrece & availle of the Co[mmo]ne Boxe.

And for the more suretee and euydence of the said orden[a]nces appoyntmentes & accord' to be establisshed & contynued' the seid' Company therto subscriben' Whoos names folowen that is to sey.

[*Edited transcript*] I John Grove (and) Robert Bale, William Brampton', Thomas Clerk, Andrew Joye, William Olov' (and) William Styfford g[ra]nnte & p[ro]mytte to obs[er]ue the same to my power subscribed by myn' owne hand the moneth and yere a[foreseid, *torn away*]. I Thomas Froddesham to all that is aboue Writen except the colour of the hodyng' I consent & aggree.
I Robert Shodewell g[ra]nnte and p[ro]mytte to obs[er]ue the same to my power &c.
I Thomas Plumer g[ra]nnte and p[ro]mytte to obs[er]ue the said' rule & orden[a]nces to my power Writen' with myn' owne hande.[1]
I Robert Spayne (and)[2] Richard Pumfrey, John Parker, Peter Bonauntre, John Geton' (and) Edward Noreys grannte and promytte to obs[er]ue the same to my power subscribed by myn' own hande the moneth & yere aforseid.
I Henry Assheborn' to all that is aboue Written' I consent aggree and it I p[ro]mytte to my power to kepe and observe.

[p. 16 *transcript*] I Walter Culpet grannte to obs[er]ue the said rule and orden[a]nce to my powr Wretyn' With my owne hand'.
I Thomas Tanner grannte and promytte to obs[er]ue the seid rule and ordena[u]nnces to my power Writen' w^t myne owen' hande the xij Day of Juyn the yere aboueseid.

[1] Here is a paraph, the only instance of any form of signature on this page.
[2] The subscriptions of the five other men have minor variations.

[p. 17 *calendar*] The names of apprentices and servants allowed in the craft of writers of the court letter

Apprentices or Servants[1]	*Masters*
John Fordam* and Thomas Masse	William Brampton'
Rowland Forster* and John Pycot* John Jacowe, servant	John Grove
William Aston,* Thomas Hardyng, William Rown'* and Richard Nekke*	Robert Bale
Robert Hedyngham* and Richard Ketrich* Richard Wyse,* servant	Thomas Fermory

1478. The names of apprentices in the craft of writers of the court letter, 26 February, 18 Edward IV, in the time of John Morekok and Henry Wodecok, Wardens

Apprentices[1]	*Masters*
[blank]	Robert Spayne
William Baker	Thomas Masse
Thomas Rows*	William Slade
Edward Langford* and Nicholas Aylove	William Camp'
Nicholas Goswell, Robert Colrede* and Robert Hampton'	John Parker
John Wilkynson', Richard Masham, John Forster, John Clyfford* and Richard Clyfford*	Thomas Clyfford
John Fawconer*	William Pake
[p. 18] John Halmer, Thomas Toker* and Thomas Norwiche*	Robert Leget
Hugh Molyneux,* John Logge* and William Gordon*	William Plofeld
William Hubbard* and Robert Norham*	Simon Lorymer

1481 The names of apprentices in the craft of the writers of the court letter, 2 June, 21 Edward IV, in the time of John Parker and Thomas Masse, Wardens

Apprentices[1]	*Masters*
John Mose	William Carkeke
William Hothersall and William Blakeney*	Robert Leget
Thomas Appulton',* William Shawden,* Richard Rondon'* and Richard Staverton	William Plofeld'
Thomas Davy*	John Barkby
John Davson,* Richard Clerk,* Robert Hampton and Edward Hill*	John Parker
William Bray* and Richard Masse*	Thomas Masse
William Hubbard*	Simon Lorymer

[1] Unless noted as servant, the name is that of an apprentice. All the names have ticks or other symbols beside them; those marked with an asterisk have a small 'o' beside them which presumably indicates (except in the case of Richard Wyse) that these men were never admitted to the Company. The apprentices are noted as *irrotulat*' and the servants as *allocat*'.

[p. 19 *calendar*] 1490 The names of apprentices and servants allowed in the craft of writers of the court letter at the feast of the Nativity of St. John Baptist, 5 Henry VII, in the time of Henry Wodecok and Edmund Tasburgh, Wardens

Apprentices or Servants[1]	*Masters*
Morgan Willliams	John Parker
Richard Brewster,* John Ledar, Nicholas Rutland* and Robert Lynton'*	Henry Wodecok
John Turno'	William Karkeke
John Myllet* and John Wregge*	John Gardyner
Nicholas Bolle	John Gerard
Henry Wilkyn'	Robert Leget
Richard Polley*	Edmund Tasburgh
William Bray,* servant	William Derryvale
William Broun', *filius*, and John Style*	Thomas Broun'
Robert Cook*	John Barkeby
John Worsop	John Mane
Richard Smyth* and John Patynson'*	William Plofeld'
Robert Cressy*	George Nicoll

[p. 20 *calendar*] 1559 The names of apprentices and servants allowed in the craft of the writers of the court letter at the feast of the Nativity of St. John Baptist, 1 Elizabeth, in the time of Thomas Went and William Pierson', Wardens

Apprentices or Servants[2]	*Masters*
William Squyer and Henry Trystram*	Thomas Went
Thomas Browne and Robert Willsonn', servants; William Ownslowe, John Turner and Matthew Sheapard	William Pierson'
William Seward	John Hulsonn'
William Poole, servant; John Walker	Bartholomew Brokesbye
Lambert Thomas and Richard Brend*	John Dalton'
Roger Smythe*	John Scampyon'
John Bennett* and Thomas Redforde	Anthony Bonde
Gregory Astemer	Robert Davyson'
William Fawdyn*	John Lee, jun.
William Bradley* and Richard Tynes*	Bernard Garter
Richard Galle	Francis Brighte
Richard Blake	William Browne
Edward Wynnyngton,* Stephen Playne and John Heathe	Thomas Atkynson'
John Phylpott* and Thomas Shorte	Thomas Wytton'
Jarvacius Grenehurst* and George Smythe	Paul Pope
[p. 21] William Tysdall' and William Softley	Humfrey Broke

[1] See footnote 1 on p. 12, but it is only in most cases on p. 19 of the text that the 'o' indicates that the man was never admitted to the Company.
[2] See footnote 1 on p. 12.

Apprentices or Servants	*Masters*
John Hendon and Richard Rookes*	John Stubberde
Martin Francklyn, servant; John Thatcher	Alexander Rotherforthe
Henry Flete*	Nicholas Kyngston'
Thomas Howes* and John Grome*	Mre Mannsell'
Richard Foster, Thomas Warren* and John Vavaso'	Thomas Bradforthe
Richard Reason and William Searche	Thomas Pierson
Edward Clarvys* and William Juxon*	Augustus Darrys
William Laynge, servant; Simon Wrenche and John Coltherst*	Thomas Brende
Wilfrid Lutie, servant; John Pratt,* William Beere* and Henry Alyson	Peter Baker
William Darmer and John Pigbone	Anthony Higgons
Peter Hardcastell* and Thomas Lane	Edward Holme

[p. 22 *calendar*] 1561 The names of apprentices and servants allowed in the craft of writers of the court letter at the feast of the Nativity of St. John Baptist, 3 Elizabeth, in the time of John Norden and Bartholomew Brokesby', Wardens.

Apprentices or Servants[1]	*Masters*
[blank]	John Norden
John Walker	Bartholomew Brokesbye
[blank]	John Hulson
Lambert Thomas and John Baker	John Dalton
Roger Smythe* and John Langham[2]	John Scampyon
John Bennett* and Thomas Redforde	Anthony Bonde
Gregory Astmer	Robert Davison
William Fawdyn*	John Lee, jun.
Richard Gale	Francis Bright
[blank]	William Browne
Stephen Pleyne, John Hethe, Edward Jones,* Michael Coke and Nicholas Clergyn	Thomas Atkynson
Edward Wright* and Richard Holdernes*	Paul Pope
William Dran*[3] and John Pygborne	Anthony Higgyns
John Turn', Matthew Shepperde, Michael Butler* and Thomas Farrand	William Pyreson
[p. 23] John Pratt,* Henry Alison and Lawrence Rotes [?]*	Peter Baker
Simon Wrenche	Thomas Brende
Richard Reason, William Searche and Jasper Stacye	Thomas Pyreson

[1] See footnote 1 on p. 12. The entries on pp. 22 and 23 of the text are badly arranged, but by comparing them with those on pp. 20 and 21 the apprentices and masters have been correctly paired.
[2] Not shown as apprentices here, but are so described on p. 23 of the text.
[3] This name should be 'Darmer'; see entry on p. 21 of the text.

Apprentices or Servants	*Masters*
Henry Evans*[1]	Wilfrid Lutye
Thomas Lane and Edward Clarvys*	Edward Hulme
Thomas Stapulton and Jasper Berde	Thomas Wytton
William Softley and William Broke	Humfrey Brooke
Humfrey Kyrry*[2]	George Kevall'
[blank]	William Tysdall'
John Thatcher* and Thomas Lawton	Alexander Rotherforthe
Henry Flete*	Nicholas Kyngston
Richard Galle	Francis Bright
Roger Smyth'* and John Langham	John Scampyon

[p. 24 blank.]

[p. 25 *calendar*] 1563. The names of apprentices and servants allowed in the craft of writers of the court letter at the feast of the Nativity of St. John Baptist, 5 Elizabeth, in the time of Thomas Pierson and Thomas Atkynson, Wardens

Apprentices or Servants[3]	*Masters*
William Searche, Gaspar Stacye and [blank]	Thomas Pierson
Stephen Playne, servant; Nicholas Clergye, John Forber and George Samuell	Thomas Atkynson
John Walker, servant; Edward Henson'	Bartholomew Brokesbie
Thomas Stapleton and Gaspar Bearde	Thomas Wytton
Matthew Shepperd, Michael Butler,* Thomas Farrande and Thomas Gamall*	William Pierson
John Bettes* not presented	Thomas Wente
Thomas Redford, Christopher Cory and John Munslowe* [the said Munslowe not presented, *deleted*]	Anthony Bonde
Lawrence Sutton* and Matthew Smythe	William Charnocke
Henry Alyson, Thomas Hedd* and William Jackson	Peter Baker
Simon Wrenche, servant; Lambert Osbolton[4] and William Sansburie* neither of these two be presented	Thomas Brende
John Pighbon', Henry Evans, William Sparke and Nathaniel Dillon*	Anthony Higgons
[p. 26] Robert Preston and Richard Hawkyns* [the said Richard is not presented, *deleted*]	Thomas Bradforthe
John Baker and Andrew Turner, the said Turner is not presented	John Dalton
William Shoftlay, William Broke and Eliachim Whall	Humfrey Broke

[1] This man was admitted, 26 Aug. 1567.
[2] No indication as to whether apprentice or servant.
[3] See footnote 1 on p. 12.
[4] In the left-hand margin, opposite this name, is the word 'not'.

Apprentices or Servants	*Masters*
Ralph Garthe* and Thomas Martyn	Nicholas Kyngston
Robert Gunsley* and Thomas Chapman, neither of them be presented	John Lee, jun.
Richard Gall and Judas Alcocke, the said Judas is not presented	Francis Bright
Thomas Brende and Robert Pedley*	William Braynewood
Stansfelde Cooke* and Robert Awgar	Francis Kydd
Peter Holmes, not presented	Paul Pope
Jonas Fringg [not presented, *deleted*] and William Bonar	Thomas Browne
Edward Prycharde,* not presented	Barnard Garter
George Gunby	George Kevall'
Thomas Layne	Edward Holme
George Crakall,* Clemens Robynson* [Richard Lewtye and Edward Brachye the said Richard and Edward be not presented, *deleted*]	Wilfrid Lewtie
Edward Hooper,* not presented	Richard Dunkyn
[George Astment, *deleted*], Erasmus Sansburye*	William Laynge
Ralph Holte and Edward Powell [neither of them presented, *deleted*]	William Onslowe
Robert Richardes,* not presented	Thomas Shorte
Francis Roffe,* not presented	John Langham
[p. 27] William Cutler and William Nicolls, neither of them be presented	Richard Reason
John Anderson*	Thomas Hulson
Samuel Stronge,* not presented	Lambert Thomas
John Cowper and Robert Pedley*	John Hethe
William Flynte*	Richard Thompson

[p. 28 *calendar*] The names of apprentice servants allowed in the craft of writers of the court letter at the feast of the Nativity of St. John Baptist, 7 Elizabeth, 1565, in the time of William Peyrsone and Stephen Alexsanndre Wardens

Apprentices[1]	*Masters*
Thomas Hedd* and John Wyvas*	Peter Baker
George Taillor* and Richard Mee	Thomas Atkynsone
William Nicholles and William Cuttell*	Richard Reassone
Peter Dewes and Clement Robynsone*	Wilfrid Lewty
Bartram Chapman* and Robert Eastfelde	Humfrey Broke
Lambert Osboltun and William Sandesbery*	Thomas Brende
John Cumeforde'* and Richard Wetenhall;* Jerome Amery*	John Heathe

[1] See footnote 1 on p. 12, but it is only in most cases on pp. 28 and 29 of the text that the 'o' indicates that the man was never admitted to the Company. Jerome Amery is the only name not designated an apprentice on p. 28 of the text.

Apprentices or Servants	*Masters*
John Mounsloo*	Anthony Bonde
William Benedic	Paul Pope
Andrew Turner	John Dalltune
Richard Hawkyns*	Thomas Bradforde
William Webbster*	Richard Clarvis
William Bonner	Thomas Broune
Edward Howper*	Richard Dunkyn
Francis Roulphe*	John Langham
Gregory Astemer	William Laynge
Henry Rowse*	William Braynewoode
William Flynt*	Richard Thomsone
[Edward Henson', *deleted*], Henry Beverley	Bartholomew Brokesby
Henry Dwffe*	William Annesloo
[p. 29] John Andersone*	Thomas Hullsone
William Dodd	William Dormer
Philip Bartun*	Barnard Gartune
Henry Leventhorpe*	Thomas Hullsone
Anthony Hyll*	Edward Hollme
Stephen Gysborowe*	George Kevalle
Ralph Rogers*	Lambert Thomas
Samuel Stronge*	Simon Wrenche
John Humfrey*	Thomas Shorte
Roger Bothe*	William Soffeley
Edward Jones*	Stephen Playne
Samuel Stronge*	Lambert Thomas
Richard Goldewell	John Norden
Richard Williamsone*	Stephen Playne
Robert Somerskale	Henry Burre
William Jetter*	Anthony Hyggons
Sallamon Cole*	Thomas Went
Richard Clerke*	Robert Wyllsone
Edward Nicholas* and William Brokebancke	Thomas Persone
Henry Anthony	Wilfrid Lewty
William Tilley*	Thomas Raddford
[Edward Jones, *deleted*]	[Stephen Playne, *deleted*]
William Eden	Matthew Sharpe
Baldwyn Castelltun[1]	Thomas Broune
David Lewes	Simon Wrenche
Thomas Fynard*	Francis Kydd
Humfrey Wylbloud*	William Serche
William Hayes*	John Hendun
William Glover*	Stephen Playne
Thomas Waller*	William Laigne
Robert Marshall*	John Turner
Richard Williams*	Thomas Wytton

[p. 30 blank.]

[1] All the names previous to this on p. 29 of the text are marked as apprentice; this and the rest of the names on this page are not designated.

[p. 31 *calendar*] 1566.[1] The names of apprentices and servants allowed with writers of the court letter at the feast of the Nativity of St. John Baptist, 9 Elizabeth, in the time of Thomas Wytton and Anthony Bonde, Wardens

Apprentices or Servants[2]	*Masters*
Peter Dewes, Henry Anthony* and Edmund Brashey,* the said Brashey not presented	Wilfrid Lewtye
Thomas Chapman and John Layton*	John Lee
William Cutler and William Nicoll	Richard Reason
Ralph Holt, Edward Powell* and Henry Dove*	William Oneslowe
John Ormeshawe*	Richard Dunkyn
Thomas Hedd,* William Jackson, John Vyneashe and John Petoe	Peter Baker
William Bonner, Baldwin Castleton, John Shawe* and Jonas Fryngge	Thomas Browne
Nicholas Hardy,* Paul Hopkins,* Andrew Turno' and George Kinge,* none of them presented	Henry Alyson
Thomas Farrand and William Eden	Matthew Sheppard
Richard Goldwell and Thomas Bacham,* the said Bacham not presented	John Turno'
William Devet*	Thomas Redforde
Richard Clerke*	Robert Wilson
William Sparke, William Jetter* and Nathaniel Dillon*	Anthony Higgens
[p. 32] William Benedick and Golding Fitche	Paul Pope
John Anderson* and Henry Leventhorp*	Thomas Hulson
Edward Henson, Henry Beverley and Thomas Rushbroke*	Bartholomew Brokesbie
Ralph Rogers	Lambert Thomas
William Flynt and John Williams*	Richard Thompson
John Baker, Thomas Rochester,* Christopher Lambert and Thomas Mathew	John Dalton
Philip Barton* and William Fulstowe*	Bernard Garter
Richard Williamson and William Glover*	Stephen Playne
John Cowper, Richard Whetenhall and John Parson	John Heathe
Roger Bouthe and Robert Sandwiche	William Softlaye
Bertram Chapman,* Robert Estfelde and Matthew Otes,* the said Otes not presented	Humfrey Brooke
George Gonbye,* John Thompson and William Randall*	George Kevall

[1] This date is wrong: it should be 1567.

[2] See footnote 1 on p. 12. All the men listed on pp. 31–33 of the text are designated apprentices, but it is only in most cases on pp. 32 and 33 that the 'o' indicates that the man was never admitted to the Company.

Apprentices or Servants	*Masters*
John Humfry* and Raynes Lawe* not presented	Thomas Short
Richard Hawkins* and Thomas Wrightson	Thomas Bradforthe
[p. 33] Ralph Garthe,* Thomas Marten and Robert Preston	Nicholas Kingeston
Nicholas Atkins,* Judas Alcock* and John Craforthe*	Richard Gall
Matthew Smythe and Thomas Fytche	William Charnocke
David Lewes and Jasper Marshall* not presented	Simon Wrentche
Robert Somerscall and William Somerscall*	Henry Burre
Hugh Quernbye	Robert Preston
John Cowlinge, not presented	John Langham
Robert Auger	Francis Kydd
William Dodd	William Dermer
[blank]	Thomas Wytton
Samuel Smythe	Anthony Bonde
George Bellot* and William Atkinson*	Thomas Godfraye
John Hayward	William Searche
Henry Gruicking*	Edward Holme

[p. 34 blank.]

[p. 35 *calendar*] 1573. The names of apprentices and servants allowed in the craft of writers of the court letter of the City of London at the feast of the Nativity of St. John Baptist, 15 Elizabeth, in the time of Thomas Wente and John Dalton', Wardens[1]

Bartholomew Brokesby,* Thomas Godfrey, Thomas Wente, John Norden, Geoffrey Caldwell,* William Bowland,* Anthony Bond,* Peter Baker,* Thomas Brend, sen.,* Anthony Higgyns, John Dalton',* Humfrey Broke,* Nicholas Kyngeston, Francis Kydde, [p. 36] Thomas Turno', Ralph Melsham', Paul Pope, Thomas Browne,[2] Thomas Staverton, George Kevall', Wilfrid Luty, William Onslowe, Hugh Whaplet, Thomas Shorte, Richard Reason, Thomas Hulson, William Squire, Lambert Thomas, John Langham, Richard Foster, [p. 37] Edward Clarvaux,* Richard Ruck, John Turno', John Walker, William Dermer,* Richard Thomson, Ralph Carkeke,* Simon Wrenche, William Softley, Thomas Redford, Robert Preston, Richard Dunkyns,* Henry Burre,* William Serche, Richard Gall', Henry Allyson,* Robert Mannsell', [p. 38] Emanuel Mannsell', John Tailo', Henry Evans, George Wapull', Thomas Brende, jun.,* Thomas Lane, George Cracall',* William Broke,* Jasper Stacy, John Pierson, Thomas Stapleton, George Gunby, Thomas Farrand, John Baker,* William Cutler,* Ralph Holte. [pp. 39–52 blank.]

[1] The names which follow are written on the right-hand sides of pp. 35–38 of the text and are those of scriveners who were already members of the Company. They are in order of seniority, Brokesby having been admitted in 1540 and Holte in 1571. All the names have a tick against them and those marked with an asterisk also have a cross. The left-hand sides of the pages, for the names of apprentices and servants, are blank.
[2] This name has a tick and a dash against it.

[p. 53][1] John Cossier [*Cosier*][2]
Martin Seman[3]
[p. 54] Robert Huntyngton'[4]
Geoffrey de Keteryngham [*Keseringham*]
[p. 55] John Lonne
John Clonne[5]
Thomas Lincoln' [*Lincolne*]
[p. 56] Adam Pynkhurst [*Pinckhurst*]
Thomas Spencer
[p. 57] William Sandsted' [*Stansted*]
[William, *deleted*] Robert Frannceys [*Fraunceys*]
William Wanstall
William Grone
[p. 58] Richard Claidich' [*Olaidich*]
John Ronceby
William Kyngesmylle [*Kingesmyll*]
Edmund Mille
[p. 59] Nicholas Grantham
Matthew Honycod alias Frome [*Honycodd alias Frome*]
John Hakedy [*Hackedy*]
[p. 60] William Acastre
John Spark [*Sparke*]
William Burton [*Burcon*]
William Broun [*Bronn or Broun*]
[p. 61][6] Thomas Guy
John Bydeford'[7]
John Tanner [*Fanner*]
Simon Sandsted' [*Sansted*]
[p. 62] Edward Forster
John Warner
Richard Watkyns [*Watkins*]
Philip Vygerous [*Vigerous*]

[1] Pp. 53–185 and 196–218 of the text are printed as a calendar; for specimen forms of oath, see pp. xviii–xxii. Unless a date is given, it may be assumed that declarations are undated. Names or other information printed in italic type and enclosed in square brackets are variations in spelling, etc., provided by Rawl. D51. See also p. xxiii.
[2] Notarial mark reproduced in Freshfield, p. 241, and Jenkinson, Plate I. Rawl. D51, f. 54, gives John Cosier and Martin Seman as Wardens under the year 1392; then follow thirty-nine names in roughly alphabetical order with a note, 'All these are wthout date but appear to have been of ye Brotherhood between 1392 & 1404 there being next one Jno: Chelsham in 1404.' The names are given on pp. 53–64 (up to Robert Clerk') of the Common Paper, but in a different order; Robert Huntyngton on p. 54 of the Common Paper is omitted, but William Brampton (given in Rawl. as Scrampton) on p. 65 is included.
[3] Notarial mark reproduced in Freshfield, p. 242, and Jenkinson, Plate I.
[4] Occurs in Rawl. D51 as Rob. Huntingdon under the year 1412 with a note: 'Rob. Huntingdon is menc'on^{d} to be in ye time of Hen. 4. whose Last Year was this Year.'
[5] Notarial mark reproduced in Freshfield, p. 243.
[6] See Jenkinson, p. 124 and Plate II.
[7] Notarial mark reproduced in Freshfield, p. 243, and Jenkinson, Plate II.

William Burdon' [*Burden*]
[p. 63] Nicholas Kyngeston' [*Kingston*]
Edmund Rede [*Read*]
Roger Vygrus [*Vigerous*]
Simon Porkele
John Bussch
[p. 64][1] Henry North'folk' [*Norfolk*]
Stephen Frankeleyn
Robert Clerk' [*Clerke*]
John Chesham, 14 June 1417[2]
Richard Lyndesay[3]
[p. 65][4] John Massemyle' [*Massenyley*]
William Brampton
William Kyngeston' [*Kingeston . . . of Nic. Kingston before 1404*]
Thomas Clerk' [*Clerke . . . of Rob. Clerke before 1404*]
Peter Anketill [*Turketill*]
[p. 66] Walter Culpet [*Culpett*], 20 July 1425[5]
John Kendale, 18 Sept. 1425 [altered from 18 Sept. 3 Henry VI]
Robert Wade, 4 Dec. 1425
William Fanside, 14 Mar. 1425/6
John Daunt, 15 Oct. 1440[6]
[p. 67] John Daunt, 23 Mar. 1425/6
John Middelton [*Middleton*], 8 June 1426
Nicholas Stone, 5 Oct. 1430
Thomas de Bosdon' [*Bosden*], 9 Oct. 1432
William Clove [or Clone], 8 Oct. 1432
[p. 68] Robert Clifton', 17 Oct. 1432
John Stodeley, 2 Apr. 1433
Robert Shodewell [*Shoddwell*], 4 June 1434
Peter Bonauntre [*Bonauntre*], 4 June 1434
Thomas Fermory, 17 June 1434
[p. 69] John Grove, 20 June 1436
William Barker alias Derlyngton' [*Darlington*], 14 Nov. 1437
William Hunter alias Hunte, 14 Nov. 1437
[p. 70] John Combe[7]
Andrew Joye, 18 Nov. 1437
Thomas Froddesham, 1 Mar. 1439/40[8]
John Ecton [*Geton*], 29 Feb. 1439/40
William Styfford' [*Stifford*], 20 Apr. 1440
[p. 71] Thomas Plum'er [*John Plummer*], 26 Oct. 1440[9]

[1] See Jenkinson, p. 125 and Plate III.
[2] Notarial mark reproduced in Freshfield, p. 243, and Jenkinson, Plate III. Occurs as John Chelsham under the year 1404 in Rawl. D51.
[3] As Ric. Lindsay under 1425 in Rawl. D51.
[4] None of the declarations on p. 65 are dated, but in Rawl. D51 they are under 1425.
[5] Notarial mark reproduced in Freshfield, p. 244.
[6] The date is correct, but the entry is obviously on the wrong page: it fills up a space at the bottom of p. 66. The notarial mark is reproduced in Freshfield, p. 245.
[7] Under 1438 in Rawl. D51.
[8] Before this name, Rawl. D51 gives John Grove and Robert Bale as Wardens, 1440.
[9] Signature and paraph reproduced in Freshfield, p. 246.

Robert Bale, 12 Nov. 1440
John Parker, 28 June 1442
John Valentyn', 6 Nov. 1442
Richard Claidich' [*Cladich*], 2 July 1445
Richard Hegge, 5 Oct. 1445[1]
[p. 72] Thomas Wynchecombe [*Winchcombe*], 12 Apr. 1443
Robert Spayne [*Spaine*], 17 July 1445
Richard Pumfrey, 1 Mar. 1446/7
John Thorp' [*Thorpe*], 5 Mar. 1446/7[2]
Edward Noreys [*Norreys*], 12 Mar. 1446/7
[p. 73] Henry Asshborn' [*Ashborne*], 17 Aug. 1447
Thomas Bernard', 18 July 1448
John Boner' [*Bonner*], 6 Aug. 1449
Robert Porter, 24 Feb. 1449/50[3]
Robert Spaldyng [*Spalding*], 14 Jan. 1450/1
[p. 74] Thomas Tanner, 12 June 1451
Richard Wyse alias Lynton' [*Andrew Hinton*], 10 Dec. 1452
Thomas High'wode [*Highwood*], 25 Sept. 1453
Richard Pays, 18 Aug. 1457
William Lettres [*Letters*], 27 Apr. 1462
John Jacowe, 27 Apr. 1462 [. . . *of John Grove . . . 1436*]
[p. 75] Robert Leget [*Legett*], 27 Apr. 1462
Thomas Clyfford' [*Clifford*], 29 Apr. 1462
Robert Hydyngham [*Hydingham*], 29 Apr. 1462
John Ponnfret [*Ponufrett*], 27 Sept. 1463
Thomas Masse, 8 May 1464 [. . . *of William Brampton . . . 1425*]
[p. 76] Robert Halle [*Hall*], 8 May 1464
John Morecok [*Morecock*], 8 May 1464
Richard Tikerich', 8 May 1464
William Vernon', 11 July 1464
Richard Domy, 18 July 1464
[p. 77][4] William Slade, 30 July 1465[5]
John Wormelee, 19 Sept. 1467
Thomas Hardyng, 21 Sept. 1467 [*Harding . . . of Robert Bale . . . 1440*]
Richard Grene [*Green*], 22 Sept. 1467
Nicholas Wykyn', 24 Sept. 1467
[p. 78] William Plofeld' [*Plofeild*], 27 Sept. 1467
William Misterton, 6 Oct. 1467
Richard Padworth', 1 Nov. 1467
William Pake, 15 June 1469
[p. 79] John Pays, 6 Aug. 1469 [*supposed of Richard Pays . . . 1457*]
William Wade, 17 Jan. 1470/1

[1] Given as Richard Kegg under 1446 in Rawl. D51, and the name is preceded by those of John Stodley and Thomas Froddesham as Wardens.
[2] Signature and paraph reproduced in Freshfield, p. 246.
[3] Before this name, Rawl. D51 gives John Grove and Robert Bale as Wardens, 1450, and the name of William Glover as a member of the Company.
[4] See Jenkinson, pp. 128, 129 and Plate VI.
[5] Notarial mark reproduced in Freshfield, p. 246, and Jenkinson, Plate VI; signature and paraph reproduced in Freshfield, p. 247.

Thomas Browne, 27 Jan. 1470/1 [*supposed of William Browne before 1404*]
Henry Wodecok [*Woodcocke*], 20 Jan. 1470/1
[p. 80][1] Simon Lorymer, 9 July 1474
Richard Broun', 9 July 1474 [*Browne supposed of William Broune . . . 1404*]
William Camp', 20 Sept. 1475[2]
John Manee, 20 Sept. 1475[3]
Thomas Barker, 20 Sept. 1475
[p. 81] John Sprotley, 20 Sept. 1475
William Carkeke, 27 Aug. 1477[4] [. . . *of Richard Pays . . . 1457*]
Thomas Hardyng [*Harding*], 27 Aug. 1477
Walter Clyfford' [*Clifford*], 27 Aug. 1477
Hugh Standyssh' [*Standish*], 27 Aug. 1477
[p. 82] Thomas Kyffyn', 16 Oct. 1477
George Nicholl', 13 Jan. 1478/9[5]
Michael Towne, 13 Jan. 1478/9
John Gyllyngale [*Gillingale*], 18 Feb. 1478/9
John Marcannt [*Marcaunt*], 3 Oct. 1479
[p. 83] John Barkby, 25 June 1480
Ed[mund] Tasburgh', 13 Mar. 1480/1[6]
John Wilkynson', 26 June 1481 [*Wilkinson . . . of Thomas Clifford . . . 1462*]
Nicholas Goswell', 26 June 1481 [. . . *of John Parker . . . 1494* (*but? 1434*)]
[p. 84] Henry Mayour', 24 Nov. 1481 [*Maynor . . . of Robert Legett . . . 1462*]
John Halmer, 12 Dec. 1481
John Gerard, 14 Mar. 1482/3[7]
John Gardyner, 9 Dec. 1484[8]
Richard Barton', 17 Dec. 1484
[p. 85] John Mose, 9 July 1487 [*Mosse . . . of William Carkeke . . . 1477*]
William Duryvale [*Durivale*], 17 Jan. 1487/8
William Hothersall', 12 Feb. 1487/8 [. . . *of Robert Legett . . . 1462*][9]
Thomas Butside, citizen and goldsmith of London, *Secundarius Computatorii* in Bread Street, London, adm. at a quarterly meeting of the Company of Writers of the Court Letter of London held on the Sunday next after the feast of St. Michael [3 Oct.] 1490 in the tavern called 'le Cardynalles

[1] See Jenkinson, pp. 130, 131 and Plate VII.
[2] Notarial mark reproduced in Freshfield, p. 247, and Jenkinson, Plate VII.
[3] Notarial mark reproduced in Freshfield, p. 248, and Jenkinson, Plate VII.
[4] In margin: Mortuus temp'e Ra' Feltwell & Joh'is Wylford gardianor' A^{o} Dni Mill'mo V^{c} xxiiij^{to}.
[5] In Rawl. D51, before this name, John Morecock and Henry Woodcock are given as Wardens, 1478.
[6] In Rawl. D51, before this name, which is recorded as Edward Tasburgh, John Parker and Thomas Masse are given as Wardens, 1481.
[7] In margin: Obiit in mense [blank] A^{o} D'ni M^{l} V^{c} xxvij.
[8] Omitted from Rawl. D51.
[9] After this name, Rawl. D51 gives the date 1490 and the names of Henry Woodcock and Edward Tasburgh as Wardens.

Hatte' in Lombard Street, when Henry Asshborn', John Parker and others were present, and Henry Wodecok and Edmund Tasburgh were Wardens.[1]

[p. 86] George Venables, 5 Aug. 1491
John Wollaston', 5 Aug. 1491
Richard Massam, 2 Sept. 1491 [. . . *of Thomas Clifford . . . 1462*][2]
John Forster, 2 Sept. 1491 [. . . *of Thomas Clifford . . . 1462*][3]
[p. 87][4] Henry Walter, 3 Sept. 1491
William Broun', 15 May 1492 [*Brown . . . of Thomas Browne . . . 1469*]
Thomas Laurens [*Laurence*], 31 Jan. 1492/3
Richard Smyth', 6 Feb. 1492/3 [*Smith . . . of William Plofeild . . . 1467*]
[p. 88] Nicholas Bolle, 6 Feb. 1492/3 [. . . *of John Gerard . . . 1482*]
John Worsopp', 28 June 1493 [*Worsope . . . of John Mane . . . 1475*]
Henry Wilkyns, 28 June 1493 [*Wilkins . . . of Robert Legett . . . 1462*]
John E'ghes [*Eghe's*], 28 June 1493
Richard Feltwell, 27 Dec. 1493
[p. 89] John Turnour', 28 June 1494 [*Turnor . . . of William Carkeke . . . 1477*]
John Parker, 3 Oct. 1494
John Ledar [*Leadar*], 3 Jan. 1494/5
[p. 90] Robert Cressy [*John Cressey*], 15 Jan. 1495/6
Morgan Williams, notary public, 31 Mar. 1497 [. . . *of John Parker . . . 1494*][5]
Nicholas Rutland', 22 May 1497
Richard Magson', notary public, 8 Oct. 1497
[p. 91] William Baker, 13 Jan. 1498/9 [. . . *of Thomas Masse . . . 1464*]
John Stondon', notary public, 18 July 1501
John Love, 12 July 1499
William Haylles [*Hayles*], 13 July 1499
[p. 92] John Pierson' [*Pyerson*], 17 July 1501[6]
Robert Hampton', 1 May 1503 [. . . *of John Parker . . . 1494*][6]
John Devereux, notary public, 15 Dec. 1504[6]
[p. 93] Richard Staverton', 18 July 1505 [. . . *of William Plofeild . . . 1467*][6]
John Reve, 18 July 1505[6]
Ralph Tilghman' [*Tylghnan*], 18 July 1505[6,7]

[1] The statement (of which this is a summary in translation) is omitted from Rawl. D51, but Butside's name is followed by: *Thomas Mayne . . . of John Mayn*e . . . *1475*.
[2] In margin: morit gardian' A° D'ni M^{l} V^{c} xxij.
[3] Signature and paraph reproduced in Freshfield, p. 246.
[4] See Jenkinson, p. 133 and Plate IX.
[5] Before this name in Rawl. D51 is the date, 1497, 12, 13 H:7, followed by the name of Henry Woodcock and (blank), Wardens, with this note: 12 Jan: Ordeined for the future That the two Wardens chosen com'only on the Sunday next after Midsomer should be for 2 Yeares as had been certaine Years past. Williams's signature and paraph are reproduced in Freshfield, p. 253.
[6] After the date: Hanc meam inscripcoem' perlegentis constanciam probiter deprecand' ut mei distere & reformari volentis ignorancia inter tantos eruditos irriprehensibilit' excusetur. Pyerson, as given in Rawl. D51, so signs in the Common Paper.
[7] In the margin: Obijt ext^{to} Civitate.

John Ruttur [*Rutter*], notary public, 18 July 1505[2]
[p. 94] Everard [*Edward*] Effamatt, 18 July 1505[1]
John Wylford [*Wilford*], notary public, 31 Oct. 1505[2]
Richard Peppes [*Pepps*], 6 Oct. 1507
Richard Baas, notary public, 11 July 1509
John Dugleton [*Duggleton*], 8 Oct. 1510
[p. 95] William Barkby, 7 Oct. 1510
Robert Grenewiche [*Greenwich*], 7 Oct. 1510
William Mathewe [*Mathew*], 8 Oct. 1510
William Swan', 8 Oct. 1510
Thomas Fryser, — July 1511
[p. 96] John Hamond, 6 Nov. 1515 [See Plate II.]
Thomas Hulle [*Hull*], 29 May 1516[3]
William Goldyng [*Golding*], 29 May 1516
John Bullok [*Bullock*], 29 May 1516
[p. 97] Henry Rowce, 29 May 1516
Edward Barboure [*Barbour*], 29 May 1516
Thomas Grey, 1 July 1519
Thomas Snowdon', 19 July 1520[4]
William Yeo, 4 July 1520
[p. 98] Ralph Caldewell [no declaration]
William Garard, 20 Dec. 1518
Richard Moundis, 20 Mar. 1517/18[5]

Carkek and Staverton' [*Wardens*]

John Melsham, 21 Nov. 1519 [altered from 20 Mar. 1519/20]
[p. 99] Thomas Hall', notary public, 21 Nov. 1519
William Carkeke, jun., notary public [undated][6] [. . . *of William Carkeke, sen., . . . 1477*]
Thomas Strother, notary public [undated][6]
John Halmer, 3 Mar. 1513/14
[p. 100] John Wheler, notary public,—July 1522
William Bla'kwell' [*Blackwell*], 4 July 1522[7]
Henry Standyssh [*Standish*], clerk, notary public, 27 June 1525
[p. 101] John Monntague [*Mountague*], 8 July 1526
John Lee, 13 Jan. 1526/7
John Pyne [*Pine*], 13 Jan. 1526/7
Richard Staverton', jun., 13 Jan. 1528/9 [. . . *of Richard Staverton, sen., . . . 1505*]
[p. 102] (blank) Lany, mort' [no declaration]
Nicholas Bristowe [no declaration][8]

[1] See footnote 6 on p. 24.
[2] Signature and paraph reproduced in Freshfield, p. 246.
[3] This and the next four names are under 1518 in Rawl. D51.
[4] This and the next four names are omitted from Rawl. D51.
[5] Signature and 'mark' reproduced in Freshfield, p. 248.
[6] Under 1519–20 in Rawl. D51.
[7] Marginal note: this man was afterwardes Towneclerk of london'.
[8] Marginal note: M^{d} Bristowe abfuit usq' tempus Thome Wytton et tunc Reductus solvens pro omnibus suis arreragiis xls. viz ese [sic] A^{o} 1563.

Alexander Whitehed [*Whitfeild*], 5 Mar. 1528/9
[John Hol'and, deleted] Stephen Allexsanndre, 24 [14 deleted] Apr. 1529[1]
[p. 103] Martin Gowsse [*Gowse*], 4 July 1529
John Muklowe [*Mucklow*], 4 July 1529
Henry Bright, 16 Jan. 1529/30

John Devereux and John Rutter, Wardens

Hugh Ruck, 14 Jan. 1531/2
[p. 104] John Hulson, notary public, 13 July 1532
William Abbott [*Abbot*], notary public, 18 June [Aug. deleted] 1533
John Muschamp' [*Muschampe*], 18 Jan. 1533/4
John Stoberd, 12 Dec. 1539[2]
[p. 105] Richard Mannsell' [*Maunsell*], 10 July 1532
John Wayland, 10 Dec. 1540[3]
Bartholomew Brokesby, 10 Dec. 1540
Thomas Pierson', 10 Dec. 1540
Thomas Carmarden', 14 Oct. 1543[4]
[p. 106] Thomas Atkynson [*Atkinson*], notary public, 12 Dec. 1541
Richard Smyth' [*Smith*], 13 July 1541 (See Plate III).
Richard Caroll', 13 July 1541

John Lee and Edward Barboure, Wardens

Thomas Wytton [*Witton*], 30 Jan. 1541/2[5]
[p. 107] Christopher Dowe, 27 Feb. 1541/2[6] [. . . *of William Baker . . . 1498*]
Thomas Godfray [*Godfrey*], 8 Mar. 1541/2
Thomas Went, 15 Oct. 1543
[p. 108] John Rusburgh', 15 Oct. 1543[7]
William Pyerson', 15 Oct. 1543[7] [*Peirson supposed of John Peirson . . . 1501*]
John Slannyng [*Slanning*], 15 Oct. 1539[8]
Christopher Grigges [*Griggs*][9]
William Sympson' [*Simpson*], 15 Oct. 1543[10]
Brian Barkar [*Barker*], 15 Oct. 1543[10]

[1] With a note that he was admitted in the time of Richard Mannsell and Thomas Peirson, 1 Mary. (See also note 1 on p. 28.)
[2] With John Slanning and Christopher Griggs under 1540 in Rawl. D51. Stoberd's signature and paraph are reproduced in Freshfield, p. 253.
[3] This and the two next admissions were in the time of John Lee and Edward Barber [*Barbour*], Wardens.
[4] Admitted in the time of John Worsop' and John Lee, Wardens.
[5] Following this entry: Admissus tamen & Juratus cu' aliis quintodecimo die Octobr' A° RR H viij xxxv^{to} (i.e. 15 Oct. 1543). Signature and paraph reproduced in Freshfield, p. 249.
[6] Following this entry: Admissus tamen & Jur' cu' aliis subsequen'. Signature and paraph reproduced in Freshfield, p. 249.
[7] Admitted in the time of John Rutter and William Blackwall; under 1544 in Rawl. D51.
[8] Admitted in the time of John Rutter and William Blackwall, but under 1540 in Rawl. D51; the regnal year, 38 Henry 8, has been deleted and 31 written instead.
[9] No declaration, only the words: jur' per me Crestoffor grygges. See note 2 above.
[10] Admitted in the time of John Lee and Edward Barbour added to the declaration.

Edward Wailand, 23 Nov. 1543 [*Wayland supposed of John Wayland . . . 1540*]
[p. 109] John Norde' [*Norden*], 24 Oct. 1553[1]
William Dawson', 24 Oct. 1553
Geoffrey Caldwall [*Geffery Caldwell*], 28 Mar. 1547[2]
William Bowland, 14 Mar. 1546/7[3]
William Browne, 14 Mar. 1546/7[3]
Edward Braynwoode [*Braynwood*], 1 Aug. 1547[4]
[p. 110] Anthony Bonde [*Bond*], 12 Mar. 1546/7
Edmund Bright [no date][5]
William Charnocke [*Charnock*], 12 Mar. 1546/7
[p. 111] Robert Hodgekynson' [*Hodgkinson*], 14 Mar. 1546/7
John Scampion', 14 Mar. 1546/7
Ellis Philips [*Elizius Phillips*], 14 Mar. 1546/7
Peter Baker, 28 Mar. 1547 [*supposed of William Baker . . . 1498*]
Thomas Brend, 12 Oct. 1551
[p. 112] Edward Pettyngar [*Edmund Pettinger*], 12 Oct. 1551
Anthony Higgins [*Higgons*], 12 Oct. 1551
Thomas Bradforth, 12 Oct. 1551
John Dalton', 12 Oct. 1551
Michael Howman, 12 Oct. 1551

[1] Admitted in the time of John Reve and William Swane, Wardens, 27 [Henry VIII], added to the declaration.
[2] Admitted in the time of William Swane and William Carkeke.
[3] Admitted in the time of William Blakwall and John Rutter.
[4] Admitted, 5 Sept. 1544, in the time of William Blakwell and William Garard.
[5] The long declaration by Bright is in such ungrammatical Latin that a perfect translation is impossible. So far as the statement can be rendered in English, it says:

And I, Edmund Bright, citizen and writer of the court letter of the City of London, having been received as one man into the number of esteemed and wise men of the said most illustrious craft or science of this City of London, which craft now and for many generations past in this City has been so deserving of honour for many and various reasons, and very necessary reasons at that, since, because of the manifold uses to be created, which lie hidden and very delicately concealed in this most splendid science, it was always not unjustly considered one of the most illustrious [crafts]—may it be permitted [to me], as one initiated, to follow [it] with my clumsy skill—and was considered so for this reason, chiefly because, being first and foremost [among] its equals, it understood the rudiments and, as it were, the foundations of other crafts and, moreover, the origin of those matters which touch upon human intellect, in its very essence, and reality itself; which gift the great God and Creator of things has caused to be so instilled in human minds that we rightly judge it to be called the most excellent of all other outstanding [crafts] as it spreads abroad and descends from the same Father to his creatures. As far as I can, and inasmuch as I am able to follow it up with my meagre talent imparted to me by this same Creator, I make witness and admit that I am in no way qualified either to represent with the tongue, play on the pipe, or follow up in my thoughts the sacred mystery, lying hidden as if in the most secret places, with the many and varied rites and customs, precepts and institutions included —and very beneficially so—in this science, with which it comes about that one may reach the exalted peak of this same science; nor is it permitted to celebrate such things with deserved eulogies however much one's spontaneous and self-inspired freewill agrees to adorn it, [but] one should hope for the future, at length, and humbly beseech even the great Creator that He will be an aid and a help to this science so that it may flourish for evermore with His assistance and compassion. Let us earnestly implore with one mind that God will grant this through His goodness.

Humfrey Broke, 15 Jan. 1551/2
John Rydgeley [*Ridgley*], 1 Oct. 1552
[p. 113] William Harlowe, 5 Oct. 1552[1]
Ralph Hall [*Sall*], 24 Oct. 1553[2]
Nicholas Kyngston', 24 Oct. 1553 [*Kingston supposed of William Kingston . . . 1425*]
Augustus Darrys [*Darryes*], 25 Oct. 1553
John Lee, jun., 25 Oct. 1553 [*supposed of John Lee, sen., . . . 1526*]
Alexander Rotherforth, 3 Jan. 1553/4
John Cogan', 14 July 1554
[p. 114] Robert Poole, 12 Jan. 1553/4
James [altered from 'Rober'] Saunders, 15 Jan. 1553/4[3]
Valerian [*Valerius*] Lucas, 16 July 1554 [altered from 1 Mary]

Thomas Godfraye and John Stubberde, Wardens, 15 June 1557

Francis Bright, 15 June 1557 [*supposed of Edmund Bright . . . 1546*]
Robert Davison, 15 June 1557
[p. 115] William Braynwoode, 15 June 1557 [*Braynwood supposed of Edward Braynwood . . . 1545*]
Bernard [*Barnard*] Garter, 15 June 1557
William Poole, 15 June 1557 [. . . *of Bartholomew Brokesby . . . 1541*]
Francis Kyd [*Kidd*], 15 June 1557
[p. 116] Martin Franklyn, 15 June 1557 [. . . *of Alexander Rotherforth . . . 1554*]

Thomas Went and William Pyreson, Wardens, 29 June 1559

Thomas Turner, 29 June 1559 [*Turnour . . . of William Peirson . . . 1544*]
Ralph Melsham, 29 June 1559 [*Mesham . . . supposed of John Melsham . . . 1520*]
Paul Pope, 29 June 1559
Thomas Browne, 29 June 1559 [*allocat' William Peirson . . . 1544*]
Robert Willsonn', 29 June 1559 [*Wilson . . . allocat' William Peirson . . . 1544*][4]
Edward Blakwelle, 23 Aug. 1559 [*Blackwell . . . supposed of William Blackwell . . . 1523*]
[p. 117] Francis Seager [*Segar*], 29 June 1559
Thomas Staverton, 29 June 1559 [*supposed of Richard Staverton . . . 1529*]

[1] After this name, in Rawl. D51, John Melsham and John Hulson are entered as Wardens, 1553/4; then follows the name of Stephen Alexander (see p. 102 of the Common Paper).
[2] After this and the next eight entries is a note that they were in the time of Richard Mansell and Thomas Pierson, Wardens, but in Rawl. D51, after Hall [*Sall*], Nicholas Maunsell and Thomas Peirson are named Wardens, to be followed in 1555 by Richard Maunsell and Thomas Pierson.
[3] In Rawl. D51, after the name of James Saunders, the following are noted as 'Taken in Assistants': William Blackwell, John Lee, sen., John Melsham, Anthony Wayte, John Stubbard, Thomas Godfrey, Bartholomew Brokesby, Thomas Atkinson, Thomas Went, William Peirson, Thomas Witton, John Norden.
[4] After this name in Rawl. D51 occurs that of Thomas Witton supposed of Thomas Witton, 1542.

George Kevall', 29 June 1559,[1] sometime app. to Christopher Dowe [*1542*] and then to Edward Pettingar
Richard Mawcam, 29 June 1559
John Appulbie, 29 June 1559

[p. 118] *John Norden' and Bartholomew Brokysbie, Wardens, 1 July 1561*
Edward Holme, 1 July 1561[1]
Wilfrid Lewtie, 1 July 1561[1] [. . . *of Peter Baker* . . . *1546*]
Roland Mucklowe[2] [*Rowland Mucklow*], 1 July 1561
William [*John*] Layng, 1 July 1561 [. . . *of Thomas Brend* . . . *1551*][3]
Francis Cowper, 1 July 1561
William Tisdale, notary public, 1 July 1561 [. . . *of Humfrey Brooke* . . . *1551*]
[p. 119] William Onslowe, 1 July 1561 [*Onslow* . . . *of William Peirson* . . . *1544*]
Hugh Wapplad[4] [*Whaplad*], 1 July 1561
Humfrey Penythorn' [*Penithorne*], 1 July 1561
Thomas Shorte, 12 July 1561[1] [*Short* . . . *of Thomas Witton* . . . *1542*]

Thomas Wytton', sole Warden after the death of John Hulson, 1562[5]
Richard Reason, 1 Apr. 1563[1] [. . . *of Thomas Peirson* . . . *1541*]
Thomas Hulson, 1 Apr. 1563
William Squyer, 1 Apr. 1563 [*Squire* . . . *of Thomas Went* . . . *1544*]
[p. 120] John Pyne, 1 Apr. 1563
Lambert [*Lambart*] Thomas, 1 Apr. 1563 [. . . *of John Dalton* . . . *1551*]
John Langham, app. to Richard [*John*] Scampion' [1546], adm. *non expertus in scientia* [no date][6]

11 Jan. 1564/5. Thomas Pierson' and Thomas Atkinson', Wardens
Richard Foster, 11 Jan. 1564/5[1] [. . . *of Thomas Bradforth* . . . *1551*]
Edward Clervaulx [*Clervaux*], 11 Jan. 1564/5
Richard Ruck, s. of Hugh Ruck, dec'd, citizen and writer of the court letter of London [*scrivener* . . . *1532*], 11 Jan. 1564/5
Thomas Baker [*Paker*], 11 Jan. 1564/5
John Turner [*Turnour*], 11 Jan. 1564/5
George Webbe [*Webb*], 10 Dec. [rest gone][1]
[p. 121] John Walker, 10 Dec.[1] [. . . *of Bartholomew Brokesby* . . . *1541*]
John Hethe, 10 Dec.[1] [. . . *of Thomas Atkinson* . . . *1542*]
William Dermer, 21 Jan. 1565/6 [. . . *of Anthony Higgons* . . . *1551*]
Richard Thomson [*Thompson*], 24 Jan. 1565/6[8]
Stephen Playne [no date][7] [. . . *of Thomas Atkinson* . . . *1542*]

[1] Elaborate paraph.
[2] Signs Muckelo.
[3] Marginal note: Admiss' tamen in tempore Mr. Went and W. Pyreson.
[4] Signs Whaplod.
[5] Under 1562, Rawl. D51 gives John Hulson and Thomas Witton as Wardens, and Jeff. Coldwell and John Dalton as taken in Assistants; then follows 1563 with the names of Thomas Witton and John Hulson as Wardens bracketed with Thomas Peirson and Thomas Atkinson.
[6] Under 1563 in Rawl. D51.
[7] Signature and paraph reproduced in Freshfield, p. 250.

[p. 122] *William Peyrsone and Stephen Alexsanndre, Wardens, 1566*[1]

John Hendon' [*Hendun . . . of John Stubbers*]
Thomas Halmer
Ralph Carkeke
Simon Wrenche [2] [*Wrench . . . of Thomas Brend . . . 1551*]
William Softlay[2] [. . . *of Humfrey Broke . . . 1551*]
Thomas Redford[2] [. . . *of Anthony Bond . . . 1546*][3]
Thomas Blakwell'[4] [*Blackwell supposed of William Blackwell . . . 1523*]
[p. 123] Robert Preston[2] [. . . *of Thomas Bradforth, 1551, or Nicholas Kingston, 1554*]
Richard Gawton', 11 July 1566
Richard Dunkyn[2]
Henry Burr[5]
John Pigbon[6], 10 Dec. 1566[2] [. . . *of Anthony Higgons . . . 1551*]
Richard Blake, 10 Dec. 1566[7] [. . . *of William Browne . . . 1545*]
Matthew Sheperd, 10 Dec. 1566[2] [. . . *of William Pierson . . . 1544*]
William Serche [*Serch*], 10 Dec. 1566, app. to Thomas Pierson [*1541*]
[p. 124][8] Richard Gall', 10 Dec. 1566 [. . . *of Francis Bright . . . 1557*]
Henry Alyson, 10 Dec. 1566 [*Alison . . . of Peter Baker . . . 1546*]
Gregory Astmer, 10 Dec. 1566 [. . . *of Robert Davison . . . 1557*]
Robert Mannsell', 26 Aug. 1567 [*Maunsell . . . supposed of Richard Maunsell . . . 1533*]
Emanuel Mannsell', 26 Aug. 1567[9]
John Tailler, 26 Aug. 1567
Henry Evans, 26 Aug. 1567 [. . . *of Wilfrid Lewty . . . 1561*]
[p. 125 r.] George Wapull' [*Whapull*], 26 Aug. 1567

Thomas Witton and Anthony Bonde [*Wardens*]

Thomas Brende, jun., 23 Jan. 1568/9 [*Brend, jun., . . . of William Brainwood . . . 1555*]
Thomas Lane, 23 Jan. 1568/9 [. . . *of Edward Halme or Hulme . . . 1561*]
Gaspar [*Jasper*] Berde, 23 Jan. 1568/9 [. . . *of Thomas Witton, jun., . . . 1559*]

[1] In Rawl. D51 these names are followed by those of Richard Horne, John Tomes, Richard Ravener, Lawrence Owen, William Butt, Nicholas Johnson, William Laigne, and James Hendon, with no other details. These and all the entries, up to and including Henry Burr, on pp. 122, 123 of the Common Paper are under 1565 in Rawl. D51, where Burr is followed by Matthew Sharpe.
[2] Elaborate paraph.
[3] In Rawl. D51 the names of *William Rudderford . . . of* (blank) and *Philip Playne supposed of Stephen Playne . . . 1564* have been inserted between those of Redford and Blakwell.
[4] Incomplete declaration; no signature.
[5] Incomplete declaration.
[6] In Rawl. D51 this name is preceded by those of William Peirson and Stephen Alexander as Wardens, bracketed with those of Thomas Witton and Anthony Bond, and the date 1566. Pigbon's signature and paraph are reproduced in Freshfield, p. 250.
[7] Signature and paraph reproduced in Freshfield, p. 250.
[8] From here onwards many signatures have paraphs, but they are not noted unless of exceptional interest.
[9] Rawl D51 gives this entry as Laurence Sutton [app. of] Emanuel Maunsell.

Nicholas Clergye, 1 Sept. 1568 [*Clergie . . . of Thomas Atkinson . . . 1542*]
William Broke, 21 Apr. 1569 [. . . *of Humfrey Broke . . . 1551*][1]
[p. 125v.] George Craicall, 12 May 1569 [. . . *of Wilfrid Lewty . . . 1561*]
Jasper Stacy, 12 May 1569 [. . . *of Thomas Peirson . . . 1541*]

Thomas Godfrey and Peter Baker, Wardens

Thomas Farrand, 14 Oct. 1569 [*Ferrand . . . of William Peirson, 1544, or Matthew Shepard, 1566*][2]
Thomas Chapman, 18 July 1571 [. . . *of John Lee, jun., . . . 1554*]
John Baker, 18 July 1571 [. . . *of John Dalton . . . 1571*][3]
Ralph Holte, 18 July 1571 [*Holt . . . of William Onslow . . . 1561*]
[p. 126r.] Thomas Stapleton, 19 July 1571 [. . . *of Thomas Witton, jun., . . . 1559*]
William Cutler, 20 July 1571 [. . . *of Richard Reason . . . 1563*]

Thomas Wente and John Dalton, Wardens

George Gunby, notary public, 17 Apr. 1572, app. to G[*eorge*] Kevall [*1559*] notary public
William Sparke, 17 Apr. 1572 [. . . *of Anthony Higgons . . . 1551*]
William Stackforde [*Stackford*], 17 Apr. 1572
[p. 126v.] Christopher Corey, 17 Apr. 1572 [. . . *of Anthony Bond . . . 1546*]
Peter Dewes, 17 Apr. 1572 [. . . *of Wilfrid Lewty . . . 1561*]
Lambert Osbolston,[4] 17 Apr. 1572 [*Osborne or Osbolston . . . of Thomas Brend, sen., . . . 1551*]
Matthew Smythe, 17 Apr. 1572 [*Smith . . . of William Charnock . . . 1546*]
Edward Powell', 17 Apr. 1572 [. . . *of William Onslow . . . 1561*]
Thomas Marten, 17 Apr. 1572 [. . . *of Thomas Kingston*]
[p. 127] John Crafford, 22 June 1573 [. . . *of Richard Gall . . . 1566*]
William Nicoll, 22 June 1573 [*Nicholl . . . of Richard Reason . . . 1563*][5]
Edward Henson, 1 July 1573 [. . . *of Bartholomew Brokesby . . . 1541*]
John Cooper, notary public, 31 July 1573 [*Coopere . . . of John Hethe . . . 1564*][6]
William Bonner, 9 Mar. 1572/3 [. . . *of Thomas Browne . . . 1559*]
Thomas Wrightson,[7] 9 Mar. 1572/3 [*Wrighton . . . of Thomas Bradforth . . . 1551*]

1 In Rawl. D51 this name is followed by that of Michael Butler [app. of] William Peirson.
2 In Rawl. D51 this name precedes those of the following taken in as Assistants: Edward Blackwell, Nicholas Kingston, Paul Pope, Thomas Browne, Thomas Staverton, Wilfrid Lewtie, William Onslow, Thomas Hulson, William Squire and Ralph Carkeke.
3 In Rawl. D51 this name is followed by that of John Anderson [app. of] Thomas Hulson, 1563.
4 Marginal note that in the time of John Norden and Thomas Brend this man transferred to the Haberdashers, of which Company he became Clerk.
5 In Rawl. D51 this name is followed by that of John Pierson, app. of (blank).
6 In Rawl. D51 this name is followed by that of John Turnor, app. of (blank).
7 Elaborate paraph.

Henry Bev'ley, 9 Mar. 1572/3 [*Beverley . . . of Bartholomew Broksby . . . 1541*][1]
Robert Awgar, 9 Mar. (deleted) [*Augar . . . of Francis Kidd . . . 1557*][2]
[p. 128] John Forber, 9 Mar. 1572/3 [. . . *of Thomas Atkinson . . . 1542*]
John Peyto, 22 June 1573 [. . . *of Peter Baker . . . 1546*]
Henry Anthony, [22 June 1573 deleted and] 15 July 1577 [substituted][3] [. . . *of Wilfrid Lewtie . . . 1561*]
Jonas Fring, 15 July 1577 [*Fringe . . . of Thomas Browne . . . 1559*]
Ralph Rogers, 22 June 1573 [. . . *of Lambert Thomas . . . 1563*][4]

John Norden and Thomas Brende, Wardens

William Benedyck, 24 June 1575 [*Benedick . . . of Paul Pope . . . 1559*]
Andrew Turno', 15 July 1577 [*Turnor . . . of John Dalton . . . 1551*][5]
[p. 129] William Sansbury, 20 Nov. 1574[6] [. . . *of Thomas Brend, jun., . . . 1568*]
Richard Mey,[7] 15 July 1577 [*May . . . of Thomas Atkinson . . . 1542*]
George Samwell, notary public, 15 July 1577,[8] app. to Thomas Atkynson, notary public, dec'd [*Samuell . . . of Thomas Atkinson . . . 1542*]
Robert Eastefeild, 24 June 1575 [*Eastfeild . . . of Humfrey Broke . . . 1551*]
Robert Som[er]scale, 14 May 1578 [*Somerscall . . . of Henry Burr . . . 1565*]
William Brokebank, 24 June 1575 [*Brokesbanck . . . of Thomas Person . . . 1541*]
Golding Fitch, 24 June 1575 [. . . *of Paul Pope . . . 1559*][9]
[p. 130] Samuel Smythe, 24 June 1575 [*Smith . . . of Anthony Bond . . . 1546*]
Roger Bouthe, notary public, 2 Aug. 1575 [. . . *of William Soffley . . . 1565*]
David Lewes [*Hewes*], 24 June 1575
Richard Goldwell, 24 June 1575 [. . . *of John Norden . . . 1554*]

Peter Baker and Anthony Higgons, Wardens

William Dodd, 15 July 1577 [. . . *of William Dormer . . . 1564*]
John Parson, 15 July 1577 [. . . *of John Heath . . . 1564*]

[1] In Rawl. D51 this name is followed by those of Thomas Went and John Dalton as Wardens, bracketed with those of John Norden and Thomas Brend, and the date 1573. Then comes the name of William Jackson, app. of Peter Baker, 1546, which is omitted from the Common Paper.
[2] In Rawl. D51 this name is followed by that of Edward Witton, with no other details.
[3] Under 1577 in Rawl. D51.
[4] In Rawl. D51 this name is followed by that of William Rowland, with no other details; then is the date 1574 and the names of Richard Norden (no other details) and William Sansbury (see footnote 6).
[5] Under 1575 in Rawl. D51.
[6] The regnal year is given as 16 Elizabeth, which would make this date 1573. Perhaps Sansbury, on 20 Nov., had forgotten that the new regnal year had begun on 17 Nov., four days previous to his making his declaration.
[7] Signs as May.
[8] Notarial mark reproduced in Freshfield, p. 251.
[9] In Rawl. D51 this name is followed by that of John Fineash, with no other details.

Thomas Fitche, 15 July 1577 [*Fitch . . . of William Charnock . . . 1546*]
[p. 131] Anthony Gall, 15 July 1577
John Haward, 15 July 1577 [. . . *of William Search . . . 1566*]
John Hatton, 15 July 1577 [. . . *of John Walker . . . 1564*]
Israel Jordayne, 15 July 1577 [*Jordan . . . of Thomas Lane . . . 1568*]
Edward Ledesham, 15 July 1577 [*Edmund Ledsham . . . of Paul Pope . . . 1559*]
John Tompson [*Thompson*], 15 July 1577, app. to G[*eorge*] Kevall, notary public [*1559*][1]
John Welles [*Wells*], 15 July 1577[2]
Baldwin Castelton', 15 July 1577 [*Castleton . . . of Thomas Browne . . . 1559*]

[p. 132] *John Dalton and Humfrey Broke, Wardens*

Thomas Newman, 5 Nov. 1577, app. to G[*eorge*] Kevall [*1559*]
Robert Sandwithe, 13 Oct. 1578 [*Sandwith . . . of William Softlay . . . 1565*]
Christopher Lamb[ar]te, 13 Oct. 1578 [*Lambert . . . of John Dalton . . . 1551*]
John Yarington', 13 Oct. 1578 [*Yarrington . . . of Francis Kidd . . . 1557*]
John Miller, 13 Oct. 1578 [. . . *of George Whapull . . . 1566*]

1580. Thomas Brende, sen., and Francis Kydd, Wardens

John Skyllicorne, 18 Aug. 1580 [*Skyllycorne . . . of Edmund Maunsell . . . 1567*]
Thomas Smythe, 18 Aug. 1580 [*Smith . . . of William Onslowe . . . 1561*]
[p. 133] John Good, s. of John Good of Kingston-upon-Thames, co. Surrey, gent., 18 Aug. 1580 [. . . *of William Cutler . . . 1571*]
Richard Fletcher, s. of Henry Fletcher of Abingdon, co Berks., yeoman, 18 Aug. 1580 [. . . *of Lambert Osbolston . . . 1572*]
John Dixon', 18 Aug. 1580 [. . . *of Paul Pope . . . 1559*]
Walter Meredith, s. of David Thomas ap Meredith of Glasbury, co. Radnor, yeoman, dec'd, 18 Aug. 1580 [. . . *of Lambert Thomas . . . 1563*]
Edward Banckworth[e], s. of Robert Banckworth of Aylesbury, co. Bucks., shoemaker, dec'd, 18 Aug. 1580
Richard Russhall, s. of John Russhall, citizen and draper of London, 18 Aug. 1580 [. . . *of Simon Wrench . . . 1565*]
Matthew Smyth[e], s. of Griffith Smythe of Exeter, co. Devon, pewterer, dec'd, 18 Aug. 1580 [*Smith . . . of Thomas Redford . . . 1565*]
Thomas Lucas, s. of Valery Lucas, citizen and writer of the court letter of London dec'd, 18 Aug. 1580 [. . . *of Valerius Lucas, scr., . . . 1555, or of Thomas Preston*][3]

[1] In Rawl. D51 this name is followed by that of John Wetts, app. of John Dalton, 1559.
[2] In Rawl. D51 this name is followed by that of John Carver, app. of (blank) Went, 1544, and that of Edmund Smithson with no other details.
[3] Below his signature and elaborate paraph, Thomas Lucas has written: 'Post Tenebris Lux'; see reproduction in Freshfield, p. 251. In Rawl. D51 the entry for Lucas is followed by these names of men taken in as assistants: Barnard Garter, Thomas Short, John Turnor, John Walker, William Dermer, Simon Wrench, Thomas Redforth, Robert Preston, Henry Burr, William Serch, Robert Maunsell, Emanuel Maunsell, John Taylor and Thomas Brend, jun.

[p. 134] William Wattes, s. of Robert Wattes, citizen and merchant taylor of London, dec'd, 4 Apr. 1581 [*Watts . . . of Peter Dewes . . . 1572*]

Edward [*Edmund*] Pierson, s. of Thomas Pierson [*1541*], citizen and writer of the court letter of London, dec'd, 4 Apr. 1581

Henry Christofer [*Christopher*], s. of Robert Christofer of Stanway, co. Glos., slater, 10 Apr. 1581[1]

Henry Dowe, s. of Christopher Dowe [*1542*], citizen and writer of the court letter of London, 10 Apr. 1581[2]

John Lawe [*Lane*], s. of Thomas Lawe of Edgware, co. Middx., yeoman, dec'd, 2 June 1581

John Cowling, app. to John Langham [*1563*], adm. *Sed non expertus in Scientia*, 19 July 1581

William Mannsell' [*Maunsell*], s. of Richard Mannsell' [*Maunsell . . . 1533*], citizen and writer of the court letter of London, dec'd, 19 Nov. 1582

[p. 135] *30 May 1583. Anthony Higgons and Paul Pope, Wardens*

George Breese, s. of William Breese, citizen and writer of the court letter of London, app. to Henry Burr [*1565*]

Robert Hill, s. of William Hill of Shelton, co. Staffs., carpenter, app. to Thomas Shorte [*Short . . . 1561*]

Augustine Erell', s. of James Erell' of Winchester, co. Hants., yeoman, app. to Bernard Garter [*1557*][3]

James Carter, s. of Thomas Carter of Ashwell, co. Herts., tailor, app. to Thomas Farrande [*Farrand . . . 1569*][4]

William Chamberleyne [*Chamberleyn*], s. of John Chamberleyne of Sparsholt, co. Berks., gent., app. to Roger Bouthe [*1575*]

William Garter, s. of Bernard Garter, citizen and writer of the court letter of London [*1557*][5]

[p. 136] Robert Taylboys, s. of Robert Tailboys, citizen and goldsmith of London, dec'd, app. to George Kevall' [*1559*]

Walter Filkins, s. of William Filkins of Osbaston, co. Leics., husbandman, dec'd, app. to Peter Baker [*1546*]

Henry Best, s. of Richard Best of Middleton Quernhow, co. Yorks., yeoman, app. to John Walker [*1564*][6]

John Greene [*Green*],[7] s. of Thomas Greene of Norton, co. Heref., yeoman, app. to Simon Wrenche [*Wrench . . . 1565*]

Walter Wood, s. of Richard Wood of 'Naneby', co. Leics., yeoman, app. to Emanuel Mannsell [*Maunsell . . . 1567*][8]

[1] In Rawl. D51 this name is followed by that of Thomas Boys [app.] of Thomas Lane, 1568.

[2] In Rawl. D51 this name is followed by that of Benedict Atkinson, son of Thomas Atkinson, 1542.

[3] In Rawl. D51 this name is followed by that of Val. Penson, with no other details.

[4] In Rawl. D51 this entry is followed by the surname, Thomas; no other details.

[5] In Rawl. D51 this name is followed by that of Richard Hopkins [app.] of Ralph Carkeke, 1565.

[6] In Rawl. D51 this name is followed by: Paul Typotts . . . Straunger.

[7] Marginal note that Greene transferred to the Salters' Company.

[8] In Rawl. D51 this name is followed by that of Abraham Robinson [app.] of William Dermer, 1564; then comes the name of Roger Rowe, with no details.

John Dalton, Master, William Squier and George Kevall, Wardens[1]
13 September 1583

Thomas Spensley [*Spenceley*], s. of Ralph Spensley, citizen and saddler of London, dec'd, app. to Thomas Browne [*1559*]

Hugh Base, s. of John Base of Westhall, co. Suff., gent., dec'd, app. to Anthony Higgons [*1551*].

[p. 137] William Lightwood, s. of Robert Lightwood of Bradley, co. Derby, yeoman, app. to John Norden' [*1554*], 11 Oct. 1583

John Partridge, s. of Martin Partridge, citizen and barber and surgeon of London, dec'd, app. to Robert Eastfeilde [*Eastfield . . . 1575*], 11 Oct. 1583[2]

John Deane, s. of John Deane of Wallingford, co. Berks., yeoman, dec'd, app. to Emanuel Mannsell [*Maunsell . . . 1567*], 18 Dec. 1583

William Pizley, s. of William Pizley of Wittenham, co. Berks., yeoman, dec'd, app. to David Lewes [*1583*], 18 Dec. 1583

William Phillipotte [*Phillipott*], s. of Gregory Phillipotte of Langham, co. Rutland, husbandman, app. to Matthew Smythe [*Smith . . . 1572*], 27 Feb. 1583/4[3]

Francis Lomelyn [*Lumley*], s. of James Lomelyn of London, gent., app. to Thomas Chapman [*1571*], 27 Feb. 1583/4[4]

[p. 138] Maurice Hackett, s. of Simon Hackett, citizen and clothworker of London, app. to John Hawarde [*Haward . . . 1577 or of William Search . . . 1566*][5]

Robert Symond[es] [*Simonds*], s. of Thomas Symond[es] of Stowmarket, co. Suff., cordwainer, dec'd, app. to Christopher Corey [*1572*]

Thomas Buckshawe, s. of William Buckshawe of the City of York, capper, app. to Paul Pope [*1559*][6]

Alexander Wytton [*Witton*], s. of Thomas Wytton [*1559*], citizen and writer of the court letter of London, adm. *sed non expertus in scientia*[7]

Robert Banckworth, s. of Robert Banckworth of Aylesbury, co. Bucks., shoemaker, dec'd, app. to Peter Baker [*1546*]

Francis More [*Moore*], s. of Brian More of London, blacksmith, dec'd, app. to Richard Gawton [*1565*]

Geoffrey [*Geffery*] Place, s. of William Place, citizen and merchant taylor of London, app. to Anthony Higgons [*1551*][8]

[1] In Rawl. D51 this heading is followed by: Richard Blake taken in Assistant.

[2] In Rawl. D51 this entry is followed by the date, 26 Eliz., and then the names of William Eden [app.] of Matthew Shepard, 1566; James Evans [app.] of Godfrey Reynor, 1595; Richard Dawson [app.] of William Dawson, 1554, and William Deerring [app.] of William Sparke, 1572.

[3] In Rawl. D51 this name is followed by that of David Lewis [app.] of Simon Wrench, 1565.

[4] In Rawl. D51 this name is followed by that of John Lawe [app.] of John Heathe, 1564.

[5] This and the following eight undated entries are under 26 Eliz. (1583–4) in Rawl. D51.

[6] In Rawl. D51 this name is followed by that of Cornelius Speering, with no other details.

[7] In Rawl. D51 this name is followed by: James Witterongle—Straunger.

[8] In Rawl. D51 this name is followed by that of William Newman [app.] of Ralph Rogers, 1573.

John Hallywell [*Halliwell*], s. of Nicholas Hallywell, citizen and skinner of London, app. to John Dalton' [*1551*]

[p. 139] James Smythe, 26 May 1585 [incomplete declaration] [*Smith . . . of Henry Allison . . . 1566*]

Paul Pope, Master, William Onslowe and John Langhame, Wardens 1 Aug. 1585

John Wynton [*Winton*], s. of Richard Wynton of Whaddon Chase, co. Bucks., yeoman, dec'd, app. to William Dermer alias Dormer [*1564*]

Thomas Donnyngton [*John Donnington*], s. of William Donnyngton of Stoke Newington, co. Middx., yeoman, dec'd, app. to Samuel Smithe [*Smith . . . 1575*][1]

[p. 140] *William Squyer, Master, Bernard Garter and William Dermer, Wardens 16 December 1588*

Edward Charnock, s. of William Charnock, citizen and writer of the court letter of London [*1546*]

Jeremy Spracklinge [*Sprackling*], app. to John Le'gham [*Langham . . . 1563*], adm. *sed non expertus in scientia*[2]

Richard Spittull, s. of Richard Spittull, dec'd, app. to William Benedyck [*Benedick . . . 1575*]

William Hallmar [*Halmar*], s. of Thomas Hallmar [*1565*], adm. *sed non expertus in scientia*

John Barrett, s. of John Barrett of Knutsford, co. Ches., husbandman, app. to Richard Dunkyn [*1565*][3]

William Peckston, app. to Emanuel Mannsell [*Maunsell . . . 1567*]

Edward Crook [*Crooke*], s. of Henry Crook, dec'd, app. to George Samwell [*Samuell . . . 1577*], notary public

[p. 141] Leonard Browne, s. of Thomas Browne, dec'd, app. to Christopher Corey [*1572*][4]

Robert Androwes [*Andrews*], s. of William Androwes of Merkett [Markyate] co. Herts., yeoman, dec'd, app. to William Dermer alias Dormer [*1564*][5]

John [Robert, deleted] Woodhowse [*Woodhouse*], s. of William Woodhowse, citizen and blacksmith of London, app. to Roger Bouthe [*1575*]

John Coles, s. of Thomas Coles, dec'd, app. to John Crafford [*1573*]

Edward White, s. of Alexander White, citizen and draper of London, dec'd, app. to Henry Evans [*1567*]

[1] In Rawl. D51 this entry is followed by a heading: 1587, 29 Eliz., Paul Pope, Master, William Onslow and John Langham, Wardens, and then the admission of William Mathew, but with no other details.

[2] Just below this entry is written the name, James Fryer, but in Rawl. D51 it precedes that of Spracklinge and gives Fryer as app. of John Thompson . . . 1577.

[3] Just below this entry is written the name, John Johnes; he occurs as Jones in Rawl. D51 as the app. of Robert Preston . . . 1565.

[4] Strapwork notarial mark reproduced, with signature, in Freshfield, p. 252.

[5] 'Robert Andrewes, scr.', with his apprentice, Henry Lawrence, witnessed the mortgage, 10 March 1612/13, of William Shakespeare's house within the precinct of Blackfriars in the City of London. This document is in GL MS. 3738; see also, P. E. Jones and R. Smith, *A Guide to the Records at Guildhall, London* (1951), p. 184.

Thomas Squyer [*Squire*], s. of William Squyer, citizen and writer of the court letter of London [*1563*][1]

[p. 142] *George Kevall, Master, William Searche*[2] *and Simon Wrenche, Wardens. Elected 3 Aug. 1589*

6 Aug. 32 Eliz. [*1590*] *in the time of the said Master and Wardens*[3]

John Stacy, s. of Henry Stacy, citizen and ironmonger of London, app. to Thomas Wrightson [*Wrighton . . . 1572*]

George Ersby, s. of John Ersby of Chelsea, co. Middx., yeoman, dec'd, app. to William Dermer alias Dormer [*1564*]

[p. 143] Anthony Mason, s. of William Mason of Theakston, co. Yorks., yeoman, app. to George Kevall, notary public [*1559*]

John Mayle, s. of Robert Mayle of Forthampton, co. Glos., yeoman, app. to William Nicoll [*Nicholl . . . 1573*]

William Calcott [*Callcott*], s. of Thomas Calcott of Calcott [Caldecott], co. Ches., gent., dec'd, app. to George Gunby [*1572*]

Thomas Radcliff [*Radcliffe*], s. of Humfrey Radcliff of Rugby, co. War., cooper, app. to John Yarington [*Yarrington . . . 1578*][4]

Robert Morgan, s. of Landivic Morgan of Denbigh, co. Denbigh, saddler, app. to Ralph Rogers [*1573*][5]

Peter Blower, s. of William Blower, citizen and goldsmith of London, app. to Thomas Newman [*1577*]

[p. 144] Richard Glover, s. of Richard Glover of Thornby, co, Northants., husbandman, app. to Richard Fletcher [*1580*], adm. *sed non expertus in scientia*

William Sampson', s. of Thomas Sampson, citizen and leatherseller of London, dec'd, app. to Jonas Fring [*Fringe . . . 1577*][6]

Francis Kempe, s. of Francis Kempe, citizen and draper of London, dec'd, app. to Roger Bouthe [*1575*]

Edward Bullock, s. of Roger Bullock, citizen and innholder of London, dec'd, app. to Thomas Chapman [*1571*]

[1] Spaces below this entry are left for William Nicolles, James Hickes and John Lugger; Nicolles occurs in Rawl. D51 in 1589. Hicks is named as app. of Baldwin Castleton, 1577, but there are no details for Lugger, whose name is followed by that of James Latham, app. of John Craford, 1573.

[2] The name has been crossed through and then written in as William Serche after Simon Wrenche, which is also the order in Rawl. D51. This heading was an elaborate one; because of the mistake, a fresh heading was engrossed beneath it with the date, 3 Aug. 1589 in the text, but 1590 written in the loop of the T of *Tempore*.

[3] This is a third heading; there were no admissions recorded between 3 Aug. 1589 and 6 Aug. 1590.

[4] Spaces below this entry have the name John Lugge (see note 1 above), then a few letters deleted, then Edward White, deleted, and Robert Derham. In Rawl. D51, Robert Doreham is given as [app.] of Jonas Fringe . . . 1577.

[5] In Rawl. D51 this name is followed by that of William Petiso, with no other details, and then these entries:

Edward Chambers [app.] of Simon Wrench . . . 1565
Gamaliell Gardiner [app.] of Richard Gall . . . 1566
Nicholas Holcroft [app.] of Simon Wrench . . . 1565
William Nicholls [app.] of John Baker . . . 1571 (see note 1 above)
John Shawe [app.] of Anthony Echell . . . (no date)

[6] This entry is under 1591 in Rawl. D51, but he dates his declaration in the Common Paper, 6 Aug. 1590.

George Wright, s. of Thomas Wright of Astwick, co. Beds., husbandman, app. to Robert Awgar [*Augar . . . 1573*]

Robert Griffith, s. of Peter Griffith of Aston below Harwarden, co. Flint, gent., dec'd, app. to Walter Meredith [*1580*]

William Ledesham [*Ledsham*], s. of Peter Ledesham of Ewloe, co. Flint, yeoman, app. to Edward Ledesham [*Ledsham . . . 1577*]

[p. 145] *20 May 1591. George Kevall, Master, Simon Wrench and William Search, Wardens*

Ambrose Shorter [*Short*], s. of William Shorter, citizen and draper of London, dec'd, app. to William Serche [*Search . . . 1566*]

George Foster, s. of John Foster, late of Wymondham, co. Norf., yeoman, app. to William Onslowe [*1561*], adm. *sed non expertus in scientia*

William Dunce, s. of William Dunce of East Ham, co. Essex, yeoman, dec'd, app. to Francis Kydd [*Kidd . . . 1557*]

Richard Michell', s. of John Michell', citizen and minstrel of London, app. to Edward Henson', dec'd [*1573*]

Robert Kesforthe [*Kesforth*], s. of Thomas Kesforthe, late of Kesforth Hall, co. Yorks., gent., app. to Robert Mannsell [*Maunsell . . . 1567*]

Christopher Holmes, s. of George Holmes of Barnard Castle, co. Durham, yeoman, dec'd, app. to Emanuel Mannsell [*Maunsell . . . 1567*]

William Hix, s. of Adam Hix of Tansor, co. Northants., yeoman, app. to Edward Henson, dec'd [*1573*]

John Bentley, s. of Henry Bentley of Bury St. Edmunds, co. Suff., clothworker, dec'd, app. to Peter Baker [*1546*]

Roger Wager, s. of Roger Wager, citizen and ironmonger of London, dec'd, app. to Thomas Shorte [*Short . . . 1561*][1]

[p. 146] John Ryder [*Rider*], s. of John Ryder of Horsehouse, co. Yorks., yeoman, dec'd, app. to Andrew Turno' [*Turnor . . . 1573*], 1 Apr. 1595[2]

Godfrey Reyner, s. of Robert [all deleted][3]

Zachary Humfrey, app. to George Kevall' [*1559*], 27 Feb. 1603/4[4]

[p. 147] *William Onslowe, Master, Thomas Hulson and Robert Preston, Wardens*

Godfrey Reyner, s. of Robert Reyner of 'Hillome', co. Yorks., yeoman, app. to William Broke [*1569*], 11 Apr. 1595

[1] In Rawl. D51 this name is followed by that of William Sampson (see note 6 on p. 37); then is entered the date 1593, 35º Eliz. and the names of Robert Ward (no other details) and Silvan Williams [app.] of George Kevall . . . 1559.

[2] In Rawl. D51 this name is preceded by that of George Beales [app.] of Henry Burr . . . 1565, and followed by that of John Hard [app]. of John Wells . . . 1577.

[3] See entry on p. 147 of the Common Paper.

[4] The names of Ewen Martyn, William Jolly and George Beales occur in the right-hand margin ready for declarations. Humfrey's admission is entered under 1595 in Rawl. D51 and followed by:

William Brend (no other detail)
Anthony Downes [app.] of John Wells . . . 1577
Walter Holleley (no other detail)
Thomas Watson [app.] of Thomas Buckshawe . . . 1583
Thomas Atkinson (no other detail)
John Purnell [app.] of John Langham . . . 1563.

Thomas Langworth, s. of William Langworth of Marthall, co. Ches., yeoman, app. to Hugh Base [*1583*], 11 Apr. 1595
George Hill, s. of William Hill of Shelton, co. Staffs., yeoman, app. to Robert Hill [*1583*], 1 Apr. 1595
Simon Broome [*Brome*], app. to John Coolinge [*Cowling . . . 1581*], adm. *sed non expertus in scientia*
Robert Marshe, s. of Robert Marshe, citizen and grocer of London, app. to William Benedyck [*Benedick . . . 1575*], 1 Apr. 1595
James Colbron [*Colebron*], s. of William Colbron, late of Freckleton, co. Lancs., gent., app. to Baldwin Castelton [*Castleton . . . 1577*], 1 Apr. 1595
William Woolley [*Wolley*], s. of Thomas Woolley of Abingdon, co. Berks., gent., app. to John Thompson [*1577*], 11 Apr. 1595 [p. 148 blank]

[p. 149] *John Langham, Master, John Taylor and Thomas Lane, Wardens*

Reginald Wray, s. of Roger Wray of Aysgarth, co. Yorks., gent., app. to John Dixon [*1580*] [presumably 11 Apr. 1595]
Henry Adams, s. of Thomas Adams of Wallington, co. Herts., yeoman, app. to Thomas Newman [*1577*], 11 Apr. 1595
Thomas Frith, s. of George Frith of Rainham, co. Essex, yeoman, app. to George Gunby [*1572*], 11 Apr. 1595
Leonard Wallworth [*Walworth*], s. of Ellis Wallworth of Ringley, co. Lancs., yeoman, app. to Maurice Hackett [*1583*], 11 Apr. 1595
Charles Bostocke [*Bostock*], s. of Robert Bostocke, late of Bostock, co. Ches., gent., app. to Roger Bouthe [*1575*], 11 Apr. 1595
Robert Wade, s. of William Wade of Highmeadow below the Forest of Dean, co. Glos., yeoman, dec'd, app. to Andrew Turno' [*Turnour . . . 1575*], 11 Apr. 1595 [p. 150 blank]

[p. 151] *Thursday, 5 Sept. 1594. John Langham, Master, John Taylor and William Brooke, Wardens*

Thomas Mathew, s. of William Mathew of Merstham, co. Surrey, yeoman, dec'd, app. to Henry Best [*1583 or John Dalton, 1551*], 7 Sept. 1594
Edward Draper, s. of John Draper, citizen and merchant taylor of London, dec'd, app. to Bernard Garter [*1555*], 1 Apr. 1595
Thomas Gall, s. of Richard Gall, citizen and writer of the court letter of London [*1566*], 1 Apr. 1595
Peter Holmes, s. of William Holmes,[1] citizen and writer of the court letter of London, 7 Apr. 1595 [p. 152][2]

[p. 153] *Thursday, 7 Oct. 1596. Bernard Garter, Master, Henry Allison and Thomas Chapmann, Wardens*

Richard Nydd, s. of Richard Nydd of Mountsorrel, co. Leics., fellmonger, app. to Henry Anthony [*1577*], 7 Oct. 1596

[1] In Rawl. D51 no date is given for William Holmes, but there is the additional statement 'or Paul Pope . . . 1559', thus expressing the doubt as to whether Peter Holmes was apprenticed to his father or to Pope.
[2] This has the following names in the right-hand margin: William Brende, Anthony Downes, Walter Holleley, Joseph Rawson, Thomas Watson, Thomas Atkinson and John Purnell.

Joseph Rawson, s. of Richard Rawson of the precinct of St. Katherine by the Tower of London, mariner, dec'd, app. to John Dalton' [*1551*], 7 Oct. 1596

Francis Strange, s. of John Orphiu' Strange of the City of London, doctor of laws, dec'd, app. to William Serche [*Serch . . . 1566*], 7 Oct. 1596

Robert Holland, s. of Richard Hollande, citizen and merchant taylor of London, dec'd, app. to John Welles [*Wettes . . . 1577*], 7 Oct. 1596

George Maile [*Mayle* (as he signs)], s. of Robert Mayle of Fortington [Forthampton], co. Glos., yeoman, dec'd, app. to John Mayle [*Maile. . . 1589*], adm. *sed non expertus in scientia*

9 Dec. 1596

Thomas Ruck, s. of Thomas Ruck of Cranbrook, co. Kent, merchant, dec'd, app. to Jeremy Spracklinge [*Sprackling . . . 1588*], adm. *sed non expertus in scientia*

[p. 154] *9 Dec. 1596*

Thomas Nelson, s. of Richard Nelson of Mawdesley, co. Lancs., yeoman, dec'd, app. to Thomas Lane, dec'd [*1568*]

John Savage, s. of Matthew Savage of Northampton, co. Northants., yeoman, dec'd, app. to George Samwell [*Samuell . . . 1577*]

Basil Nicoll [*Basill Nicholl*][1] s. of William Nicoll, citizen and writer of the court letter of London [*1573*]

John Squier [*Squire*], s. of William Squier, citizen and writer of the court letter of London [*1563*], adm. by pat. *sed non expertus in scientia*

John Plukenett [*Plucknett*], s. of David Plukenett of Bridport, co. Dorset, yeomen, dec'd, app. to Thomas Chapman [*1571*]

John Wattes [*Watts*], s. of Richard Wattes, citizen and haberdasher of London, dec'd, app. to Christopher Corey, dec'd [*1572*]

[p. 155] *19 May 1597*

John Woodward, s. of John Woodward of Chaldon, co. Surrey, yeoman, app. to Walter Filkins [*1583*]

Humfrey Pye, s. of William Pye of Haughton, co. Staffs., yeoman, app. to John Yarington [*Yarlington, sen., 1578*][2] [p. 156 blank]

[p. 157] *Thursday, 20 Oct. 1597. John Taylor*[3], *Master, John Cowper and John Crafford, Wardens*

Walter Lewes [*Lewis*], s. of Lewis Jones of Brampton, co. Heref., fuller, dec'd, app. to John Jones [*1589*]

William Childe [*Child*], s. of William Childe, citizen and grocer of London, app. to George Ersby [*1589*]

John Power, s. of Thomas Power of the City of Worcester, clothier, app. to William Sparke [*1572*][4]

[1] Marginal note that he transferred to the Haberdashers' Company.

[2] A space below this entry has the name H. Corey, but in Rawl. D51 is the entry: Henry Corey . . . of Christopher Corey . . . 1572; this is under the date 1596–7 and precedes the entry for Pye.

[3] Thomas Taylor in Rawl. D51.

[4] In Rawl. D51 this name is followed by that of Andrew Palmer, with no other details.

Richard Wotton, s. of William Wotton of Marden, co. Heref., yeoman, dec'd, app. to Walter Meredith [*1580*]

John Maye [*May*], s. of John Maye of Wyverstone, co. Suff., yeoman, dec'd, app. to William Garter [*1583*]

Ralph Hardwicke [*Hardwick*], s. of Anthony Hardwicke of Claverley, co. Salop, yeoman, app. to John Mayle [*1589*][1]

[p. 158] Philip Lugger, s. of Thomas Lugger of Leominster, co. Heref., tanner, app. to John Greene [*1583*], 23 Jan. 1598/9

Henry Burnley [*Burneley*], s. of Robert Burnley of Canterbury, co. Kent, carpenter, app. to Gamaliel Gardner, dec'd [*Gamaliell Gardiner . . . 1589*], 23 Jan. 1598/9

John Fludd, s. of Lewis Fludd of Lydham, co. Salop, gent., app. to David Lewes, dec'd [*Lewis . . . 1583*], 23 Jan. 1598/9

[p. 159] *Thomas Hulson, Master, William Benedicte and George Samwell, Wardens, elected 10 August 1598. Tuesday, 23 January 1598/9*

Hugh Berchley, s. of George Berchley of the City of Chester, gent., dec'd, app. to William Chamberleyne [*1583*], 23 Jan. 1598/9

John Forde [*Ford*], s. of John Forde of Canterbury, co. Kent, bricklayer, dec'd, app. to William Serche [*Search . . . 1566*], 23 Jan. 1598/9[2]

John Waren [*Warren*], s. of William Waren, citizen and tallowchandler of London, dec'd, app. to George Samwell [*Samuell . . . 1577*], 23 Jan. 1598/9

[p. 160] Roland Squyer [*Rowland Squire*], s. of William Squyer, citizen and writer of London, dec'd, app. to William Benedyck [*Benedick . . . 1575*], 23 Jan. 1598/9

Ralph Sumner [*Sum'er*], s. of Peter Sumner of Frodsham, co. Ches., yeoman, dec'd, app. to James Carter [*1583*], 23 Jan. 1598/9

Richard Ley, s. of John Ley of Sutton, co. Lancs., yeoman, dec'd, app. to William Sampson [*1591*], 23 Jan. 1598/9

Richard Lumley, s. of Thomas Lumley of Ainderby Steeple (Aynderbye cu' le Steple), co. Yorks., yeoman, app. to Thomas Lucas [*1580*], 27 Feb. 1599/1600

Richard Chapman, s. of Edward Chapman of Tetbury, co. Glos., weaver, app. to Charles Bostocke [*Bostock . . . 1595*], 27 Feb. 1599/1600

[p. 161] Thomas Reason, s. of Richard Reason, late citizen and writer of the court letter of London, app. to Edward Ledesham' [*Ledsham . . . 1577*], 27 Feb. 1599/1600

John Curtis, s. of Thomas Curtis of Andover, co. Hants., yeoman, app. to John Deane [*1583*], 27 Feb. 1599/1600

John Ellys [*Ellis*], s. of Ellis Demavet of Caerwys[?], co. Flint, yeoman, app. to Godfrey Reyner [*1595*], 27 Feb. 1599/1600

[p. 162] John Milton,[3] s. of Richard Milton of Stanton [St. John], co. Oxon.,

[1] In Rawl. D51 this name is followed by that of Thomas Smith [app.] of (blank) Onslowe . . . 1561.

[2] In Rawl. D51 this name is followed by those of Robert Ayrie [app.] of Paul Pope . . . 1559, and Richard Farrar, the latter with no other details.

[3] The poet's father; see *D.N.B.*

yeoman, app. to James Colbron' [*Colebron . . . 1595*], 27 Feb. 1599/1600
John Robynson [*Robinson*] [no declaration][1]
John Pattenson, *postea*
James Bowler, *postea*
Francis Mosse, *postea*

[p. 163] *Thomas Chapman, Master, William Bonner and Andrew Turnor, Wardens*[2]

Charles Yeoman [*Yeomans*], s. of Thomas Yeoman of Greatford, co. Lincs., yeoman, dec'd, app. to Thomas Chapman [*1571*][3]
John Pattison, s. of John Pattison of Carlisle, co. Cumb., gent., app. to John Dixon [*1580*]
James Boler, s. of John Boler of Brinington in Chesterfield, co. Derby yeoman, app. to Richard Rucke [*Ruck . . . 1564*]
Francis Mosse, s. of Roger Mosse of Ilam, co. Staffs., clerk, app. to Edward Crooke [*1588*][4]
John Jackson, s. of John Jackson of London, founder, dec'd, app. to Baldwin Castelton [*Castleton . . . 1577*]
[p. 164] John Ewen, s. of Thomas Ewen of Great Yarmouth, co. Norf., merchant, dec'd, app., *per assigna'coem*, to Robert Banckworth [*1583*]
Robert Woodford, s. of John Woodford of Leicester, co. Leics., baker, app. to Walter Filkins [*1583*][5]

[1] The spaces for this and the three following declarations have diagonal lines drawn across them.
[2] In Rawl. D51 the year is given as 1599.
[3] Neither this nor the next six entries are dated.
[4] Mosse signs his declaration as a notary public.
[5] In Rawl. D51 this entry is followed by: Roger Price [app.] of John Greene . . . 1583. Next is a main heading: 1600, 43^{0} Eliz. Thomas Chapman, Master, William Bonner and Andrew Turnor, Wardens, and these entries:
Henry Dove [app.] of William Onslowe . . . 1561
Charles Demetrius (no other details)
Bernard Garter, jun. (no other details)
Richard Hartley [app.] of Peter Dewes . . . 1572
John Hiberd (no other details)
Peter Hewes [app.] of Matthew Smith . . . 1580
Nicholas Hacost [app.] of John Petoe . . . 1573
William Jollye [app.] of John Taylor . . . 1566
Hugh Lea (no other details)
Edward Marten (no other details)
Ralph Masters (no other details)
Nicholas Moxey [app.] of Robert Hill . . . 1583
Zoachim Martin (no other details)
William Panck [app.] of Richard Gall . . . 1566
William Roberts [app.] of Jeffrey Caldwell . . . 1546
Charles Raye [app.] of Anthony Gall . . . 1577
John Shewell [app.] of Paul Pope . . . 1559
John Shorter [app.] of Edward Crooke . . . 1587
Robert Tyford [app.] of (blank)
Paul Whitmore [app.] of Ralph Rogers . . . 1573
Then comes the date, 1601, 43^{0} Eliz., followed by an entry: William Swarland [app.] of Simon Brome . . . 1595.

[p. 165] *14 July 1601* Geoffrey [*Jeffery*] Bower, s. of Maurice Bower of Wotton-under-Edge, co. Glos., mercer, app. to John Mayle [*1589*][1]

John Walter, s. of John Walter, citizen and clothworker of London, dec'd, app. to Thomas Brend [*jun., 1568*]

Reginald [*Reynold*] Robotham, s. of John Robotham, citizen and clothworker of London, app. to John Wynton [*Winton . . . 1585*]

Humfrey Browne, s. of Stephen Browne of Stowmarket, co. Suff., yeoman, app. to John Hallywell [*Halliwell . . . 1584*]

Roland [*Rowland*] Beckwith, s. of William Beckwith, late citizen and skinner of London, app. to Robert Andrewes [*Andrews . . . 1588*]

Wilfrid Spicer, s. of William Spicer, citizen and haberdasher of London, dec'd, app. to John Lawe [*1583*]

William Bonner, s. of William Bonner, citizen and writer of the court letter of London [*1572*], adm. by pat., *sed non expertus in scientia*

[p. 166] *John Cowper, Master, Edward Ledesham and Baldwin Castelton, Wardens, 1601*

Thomas Hill, s. of Thomas Hill of 'Gillegate' [Gilligate, par. St. Giles, City of Durham], co. Durham, yeoman, app. to George Kevall [*1559*], 21 Aug. 1601

William Benyon, s. of Simon Benyon of Northampton, co. Northants., yeoman, app. to Francis Strange [*1596*] 7 Oct. 1601

Adam Holland, s. of George Holland of Worsley, co. Lancs., yeoman, app. to John Ryder [*1595*], 7 Oct. 1601

William Hone [. . . *of Henry Allison . . . 1566*] [no declaration] – Oct. 1601

Thomas Brome [. . . *of Simon Brome . . . 1595*] [no declaration], 6 Nov. 1601

Richard Newman [. . . *of Robert Preston . . . 1565*] [no declaration], 23 Dec. 1601

[p. 167] William Knyveton [*Kniveton*], s. of Rowland Knyveton of 'Moginton' [Mugginton], co. Derby, gent., app. to John Crafford [*1573*], 16[or 18] Feb. 1601/2

William Shingler [. . . *of William Dermer . . . 1564*] [no declaration], 18 Feb. 1601/2

Edward Britten, s. of Edward Britten, late of Harpole, co. Northants., dec'd, app. to Henry Best [*1583*]

George Lemme [*Lemm*], s. of John Lemme of Eardington, co. Salop, yeoman, app. to Robert Wade [*1595, or Walter Meredith . . . 1580*], 25 Feb. 1601/2

Philip Gossenhill, s. of Philip Gossenhill of Manchester, co. Lancs., singingman, app. to Thomas Fitch [*1577*], 13 Mar. 1601/2

George Smyth [*Smith*], s. of William Smyth of Maidstone, co. Kent, gent., dec'd, app. to Edward Crooke [*1587*], 27 Apr. 1602[2]

[1] In Rawl. D51 this entry is followed by:
Edward Overy [app.] of William Hicks . . . 1591
Miles Babb [app.] of Jeffrey Place . . . 1583

[2] Under 1601 in Rawl. D51.

[p. 168] Thomas Preene [*Preen*], s. of Thomas Preene of Kenley, co. Salop, 'scisser' [tailor], app' to Thomas Newman [*1577*], dec'd, 20 May 1602

Robert Thwaites, s. of Richard Thwaites of Barnsley, co. Yorks., gent., app. to Zachary Humfrey [*1595*], 4 Oct. 1602

John Smith, s. of John Smith of Baldock, co. Herts., app. to George Wright [*1590*], 14 July 1602

Joseph Jackson, s. of William Jackson, citizen and writer of the court letter of London [*1573*], dec'd, adm. by pat., 14 Jan 1602/3, *sed non expert' in scientia*

[p. 169] Nicholas Slater, s. of Peter Slater of Long Wittenham, co. Berks., yeoman, app. to Maurice Hackett [*1583*], 7 Apr. 1603

John Cutler [no declaration], 7 Apr. 1603

John Symons [. . . *of Richard Gall . . . 1566 or John Ryder . . . 1595*] [no declaration], 6 July 1603

Owen Bett, s. of Edward Bett of Somersham, co Hunts., yeoman, app. to Edward Charnock [*1588*], 3 Nov. 1603

Hugh Osborne, s. of John Osborne of Alton, co. Hants., yeoman, app. to John Dixon [*1580*], 3 Nov. 1603

Robert Yarington [*Yarrington, jun.*], s. of Robert Yarington, citizen and merchant taylor of London, app. to John Partridge [*1583*] 3 Nov. 1603

[p. 170] John Macrow [*Macro*], s. of John Macrow of Lavenham, co. Suff., shoemaker, app. to Henry Adams [*1595*], 8 Dec. 1603

William Benedick, Master, Walter Meredith and Edward Pierson, Wardens, 1603

John Ball, s. of John Ball of Maidstone, co. Kent, dyer, app. to John Cowper [*1573*], adm., *sed non expertus in scientia*, 19 Jan. 1603/4

Francis Archer, s. of Richard Archer, late of Leicester, co. Leics., yeoman, servant to Walter Filkins [*1583*], 22 Mar. 1604/5[1]

William Fellawe, s. of John Fellawe of Little Walsingham, co. Norf., writer, dec'd, app. to John Greene [*1583*], 22 Mar. 1604/5

[p. 171] Edward Gough, s. of Thomas Gough of Cheltenham, co. Glos., yeoman, app. to Thomas Frith [*Frithe . . . 1595*], 22 Mar. 1604/5

John [*William*] Assenden, s. of John Assenden of Henley-on-Thames, co. Oxon., chapman, app. to William Childe [*1597*], 22 Mar. 1604/5

Henry Leverich, s. of Richard Leverich of Ecton, co. Northants., gent., app. to Richard Gall [*1566*], 22 Mar. 1604/5

Luke Boys, s. of Thomas Boys, late of Barfreston, co. Kent, gent., app. to Richard Gall [*1566*], 22 Mar. 1604/5

Ellis [*Elias*] Deane, s. of Thomas Deane, late of Staveley, co. Derby, yeoman, app. to William Woolley [*Wolley . . . 1595*], 22 Mar. 1604/5

Richard Brokebanck, s. of William Brokebanck, late citizen and writer of the court letter of London, app. to Baldwin Castelton [*Chastleton . . . 1577*], dec'd, 26 Mar. 1606

[p. 172] Randal [*Randolph*] Hanmer, s. of Randal Hanmer of Horsmas', co. Flint, gent., dec'd, app. to Walter Filkyns [*Filkins . . . 1583*], 26 March 1606; adm. 2 July 1605

[1] This and the next six names are under 1604 (2 James I) in Rawl. D51. From Fellawe to Deane inclusive the date of the declaration is given as *die et anno p'dict'* or similar.

Arthur Vizer, s. of Ralph Vizer of Hawkesbury, co. Glos., clothier, app. to John Bentley [*1591*], 26 Mar. 1606; adm. 2 July 1605[1]

Richard Bright, s. of William Bright of Walden, co. Yorks., mercer, dec'd, app. to George Wright [*1590*], 27 Mar. 1606

[p. 173] *26 Mar. 1606. George Samwell, Master, John Lawe and Walter Filkins, Wardens*

Thomas [*John*] Farmer, s. of Stephen Farmer of Chetton, co. Salop, yeoman, app. to James Colbron [*1595*], 27 March 1606; adm. (blank) Oct. 1605

Timothy Whithorne, s. of Robert Whithorne of Berkley, co. Soms., gent., dec'd, app. to Basil Nicoll [*Nicholl . . . 1596*], 26 Mar. 1606; adm. 15 Oct. 1605

Henry Farley, s. of John Farley of Keymer, co. Sussex, tailor, dec'd, 27 Mar. 1606

John Langham, s. of John Langham, citizen and writer of London [*1563*], adm. *sed non expertus in scientia* (no date)

John Pile, s. of Robert Pile of Andover, co. Hants., yeoman, app. to Robert Marshe [*1595*], 27 Mar. 1606

[p. 174] Bartholomew Rogers, s. of Ralph Rogers [*1573*], citizen and writer of the court letter of London, subs. 26 Mar. 1606, *sed non expert' in scientia*; adm. by pat., 5 Dec. 1605[2]

Michael Dover, s. of John Dover of Langrigg, co. Cumb., husbandman, dec'd, app. to Edward Bullock [*1590*], dec'd, 26 Mar. 1606; adm. 7 Feb. 1605/6

Thomas Mason, s. of Oliver Mason, citizen and haberdasher of London, app. to George Samwell [*Samuell . . . 1577*], 26 Mar. 1606; adm. 7 Feb. 1605/6

Edward Cooper, s. of William Cooper of Rochford, co. Worcs., yeoman, dec'd, app. to John Cooper [*1573*], adm. 7 Feb. 1605/6, *sed non expertus in scientia*; subs. 26 Mar. 1606

Thomas Maycock, s. of William Maycock of London, clerk [. . . *of John Power . . . 1597*], 27 Mar. 1606

John Wythers [*Withers*], s. of Henry Wythers of Theydon Garnon, co. Essex, S.T.D., app. to John Tayler [*Taylor . . . 1566*], 27 Mar. 1606

[p. 175] John Waterhouse, s. of James Waterhouse, citizen and skinner of London, dec'd, app. to Robert Morgan [*1589*], 27 Mar. 1606[3]

Thomas Randolph, s. of John Randolph of Ticehurst, co. Sussex, gent., app. to John Hibbard [*1600*], 26 Mar. 1607

William Frith [*Frithe, jun.*], s. of William Frith of Bradford, co. Yorks., badger, app. to Thomas Fitch [*1577*], 26 Mar. 1607

John Edwardes [no declaration] [*Edwards . . . of Edward White . . . 1588 or Richard Wotton . . . 1599*]

[1] In Rawl. D51 this entry is followed by Randal Minshall [app.] of John Partridge . . . 1583; a space for his declaration was left in the Common Paper.

[2] In Rawl. D51 this name is followed by: Jeremy Thorneton . . . Redemp. A space for his declaration was left in the Common Paper.

[3] In Rawl. D51 this entry is followed by the date, 1607 5^{0} Jac., and the admission of Thomas Audley [app.] of William Bonner . . . 1601.

Thomas Ayraye, s. of William Ayraye of Houghton-le-Spring, co. Durham, yeoman, app. to Robert Ayraye [*Ayray . . . 1598*], 27 Mar. 1607

Edmund Cobie, s. of John Cobie of Southover near Lewes, Sussex, gent., app. to William Ledesham [*Ledsham . . . 1590*], 26 Mar. 1607

[p. 176][1] Thomas Smythe [*Smith*], s. of William Smythe, sen., of Linton Magna, co. Cambs., innholder, app. to John Mayle [*1589*], 26 Mar. 1607

John Peirse [*Peircey*; signs Pewsey], s. of John Peirse of Milton near Gravesend, co. Kent, gent., app. to Roger Wager [*1591*], 21 Apr. 1607

John Gybson [no declaration] [*John or Thomas Gibson . . . of Thomas Chapman . . . 1571*]

George Gorney [no declaration] [*Gourney . . . of Jeremy Sprackling . . . 1588*]

[p. 177] Bartholomew Gillman [*Gilman*], s. of George Gillman, citizen and merchant taylor of London, app. to George Samwell [*Samuell . . . 1577*] [no date]

Robert Partridge, s. of Robert Partridge of Edmonton, co. Middx., gent., dec'd, app. to William Hickes [*Hicks . . . 1591*], 27 Mar. 1607

Hugh Burrowes, s. of Robert Burrowes of Burton, co. Ches., yeoman, dec'd, app. to Hugh Base [*1583*], 19 Jan. 1607/8

Roger Jones, s. of William Jones, late of Limehouse, co. Middx., sailor, app. to Walter Lewis [*1597*], 19 Jan. 1607/8

Henry Fletchar [*Fletcher*], s. of Richard Fletchar, citizen and writer of the court letter of London, dec'd, [*1580*], adm. by pat., 2 July 1607, *sed non expertus in scientia*,, subs. 19 Jan. 1607/8

[p. 178] *Thomas Fitch, Master, William Dodd and John Partridge, Wardens, 19 Jan. 1607/8*

Michael Hauard [*Havard*], s. of Thomas Havard of Willersley, co. Heref., gent., app. to Edward Crook [*Crooke . . . 1588*], 19 Jan. 1607/8

Nicholas Reeve, s. of John Reeve, citizen and waxchandler of London, dec'd, app. to George Kevull [*Kevall . . . 1559*], late citizen and writer of the court letter of London, and afterwards to Thomas Hill,[2] 19 Jan. 1607/8

Richard Channdler [*Chaundler*], s. of William Channdler of Church Lench, co. Worcs., yeoman, dec'd, app. to Robert Bankworth [*Banckworth . . . 1583*], 19 Jan. 1607/8

Richard Dod [*Dodd*], s. of Peter Dod of 'Shockledg' [Shocklach], co. Ches., gent., app. to William Dod [*Dodd . . . 1577*], 19 Jan. 1607/8[3]

[p. 179] Andrew Lake, s. of Andrew Lake of Brompton Regis, co. Soms., clerk, app. to Thomas Nelson [*1596*], 28 Mar. 1609

Salomon [*Solomon*] Waller, s. of Thomas Waller of Brentwood, co. Essex, linendraper, dec'd, app. to Thomas Lucas [*1580*], 28 Mar. 1609

Richard Alie, s. of Edward Alie of 'Twexburie' [Tewkesbury], co. Glos., gent., app. to Robert Andrewes [*Andrews . . . 1588*], 28 Mar. 1609

[1] At the top of this page is written: Jhe/maria/.

[2] The apprenticeship to Thomas Hill is not mentioned in Rawl. D51.

[3] In Rawl. D51 this entry is followed by a heading: 1609 William Bonner, Master, Thomas Smith and Robert Bankworth, Wardens.

John Cclarcke [*Clarke*], s. of William Clarcke, citizen and innholder of London, app. to George Mayle [*1596*], 28 Mar. 1609 [Declaration in English.]
John Ken [*Kenn*], s. of Matthew Ken, citizen and barber and surgeon of London, dec'd, app. to John Woodward [*1597*], 28 Mar. 1609[1]
[p. 180] Richard Pampion [. . . *of Richard Gall . . . 1566*] [no declaration] *in Rure Comorans*
William Barton [no declaration]
Thomas Sparckes [*Sparke s. of William Sparke . . . 1572*] [no declaration] *Sandwichi com'orans*

William Bonner, Master, Thomas Smyth and Robert Banckworth, Wardens

William Cleyton [*Redemp.*], citizen and writer of the court letter of London, 14 July 1609[2]
Robert Holliland [*Holland*], s. of Richard Holliland, late of London, gent., dec'd, app. to Thomas Chapman [*1571*], 9 Oct. 1610[3]
Joseph Jones, s. of Hugh Jones of Chalfont St. Peter, co. Bucks., clerk, app. to John Mayle [*1589*], 9 Oct. 1610
Robert Pye, s. of William Pye of Haughton, co. Staffs., yeoman, app. to Thomas Preene [*1602*], 20 May 1611
[p. 181] Thomas Newman, s. of Thomas Newman, late citizen and writer of the court letter of London, dec'd [*1577*], adm. by pat.[4]
Thomas Ive, s. of Thomas Ive of London, gent., adm. by redemp.
Richard Stretton [*Streetton*], s. of Robert Stretton, citizen and merchant taylor of London, dec'd, app. to Walter Lewes [*1597 or John Craford . . . 1573*]
Paul Tooley, s. of Nicholas Tooley of Idbury, co. Oxon., app. to William Wolley [*1595*], 13 Mar. 1609/10
James Goodyer, s. of Anthony Goodyer, citizen and vintner of London, dec'd, app. to Andrew Turno'r [*Turnor . . . 1575*], 13 Mar. 1609/10
Robert Egleton, s. of Nicholas Egleton of Ellesborough, co. Bucks., gent., dec'd, app. to Francis Strange [*1596*], 2 Apr. 1610
Laurence Edwardes [*Edwards*], s. of Augustine Edwardes, citizen and barber and surgeon of London, dec'd, app. to Edward White [*1588*], 2 Apr. 1610

[1] In Rawl. D51 this entry is followed by:
Edward Watkinson [app.] of John Squire . . . 1596
Robert Wells (no other details)
John Chester [app.] of John Lawe . . . 1583
Edward Graunt (no other details)
At the foot of this page of the Common Paper, in the left-hand margin, is:
Edward Watkinson/translated to the Goldsmiths/Translated to the Goldsmiths/ John Chester in Rure comorans.
[2] In margin: *quere Pedagogus.*
[3] In Rawl. D51 this entry is followed by (blank) Holliland [app.] of (blank) or George Kevall . . . 1559.
[4] This and the two next entries only have *die et anno supradict'* as a date: it is uncertain whether the date should be 9 Oct. 1610 or 20 May 1611, but in Rawl. D51 the entries are under 1611.

[p. 182] Godfrey Johnson, s. of William Johnson of Hazlewood, co. Derby, gent., app. to William Childe [*1597*], 17 July 1610

Robert Nesfeilde [*Neffeild*], s. of Richard Nesfeilde, late of 'Barwicke' [no county given], gent., dec'd, app. to George Foster [*1591*], adm. *In scientia inexpertus Die et anno præmemoratis*

Anthony Marshe, s. of Paul Marsh of the city of Hereford, yeoman, app. to Robert Morgan [*1589*], adm. *in scientia pred' liber Civit' pred'*, 22 Jan. 1610/11

William Egleston, s. of William Egleston of Rowell [Rothwell], co. Northants., app. to William Hickes [*Hicks . . . 1591*], adm. *in scientia pred' liber Civit' pred'*, 22 Jan. 1610/11[1]

John Hopwood, s. of William Hopwood, citizen and merchant taylor of London [. . . *of Francis Kemp . . . 1590*], adm. *in scientia pred' liber Civitat' pred'*, 22 Jan. 1610/11

John Clerke [*Clerk*], s. of Edward Clerke of Offham, co. Kent, gent., app. to Francis Mosse [*1599*], 22 Jan. 1610/11

Christopher Lawe, s. of John Lawe, citizen and writer of the court letter of London, dec'd [*1583*], adm. by pat., 12 Mar. 1610/11

Henry Rowse, s. of John Rowse, citizen and leatherseller of London, app. to Edward Charnock [*1588*], 5 Apr. 1611

[p. 183] Thomas Tasker, s. of Roland Tasker of Pitchford, co. Salop, dec'd, app. to Robert Bankworth [*Banckworth . . . 1583*], 18 Apr. 1611[2]

Andrew Turnor, Master, Geoffrey Place and John Mayle, Wardens

John Smyther [*Smither*], s. of Robert Smyther of Bramley, co. Surrey, yeoman, dec'd, app. to William Benedick [*Benedicke . . . 1575*], 17 Oct. 1611

Benjamin Bonner, s. of William Bonner, citizen and writer of the court letter of London, dec'd [*1572*], adm. by pat., *sed in Scientia inexpertus*, 3 Dec. 1611

Henry Meye [*May*], s. of John Meye [*May . . . 1597*] of Shouldham Abbey, co. Norf., esq., adm. by redemp., *sed in scientia inexpertus*, 4 Dec. 1611

John Michell, s. of Edmund Michell of Brunthwaite, co. Yorks., yeoman, app. to Hugh Osborne [*1603*], 17 Feb. 1611/12[3]

Martin Swone, s. of Samuel Swone, late of Brasted, co. Kent, gent., app. to George Smythe [*Smith . . . 1601*], 2 Apr. 1612

John Smith, s. of John Smith of London, gent., dec'd, app. to Simon Broome [*Brome . . . 1595*], adm. *sed in scientia inexpertus*, 2 Apr. 1612

[p. 184] Christopher Wilton, s. of Christopher Wilton of Over Woodhall, co. Yorks., gent., dec'd, app. to John Deane [*1583*], 16 July 1612

Thomas Banister, s. of William Banister of Gainsborough, co. Lincs., gent., dec'd, app. to George Hill [*1595*], 16 July 1612

[1] In Rawl. D51 this entry is followed by the admission of Thomas Somerford [app.] of Ralph Hardwick . . . 1597.

[2] In Rawl. D51 this entry is followed by the admission of Richard Fell [app.] of Thomas Short, jun.

[3] In Rawl. D51 this entry is followed by the names of John Hollowey, Thomas Frith, John Woodward, William Childe, Richard Wotton and John Warren, chosen assistants.

William Harsnett, s. of Adam Harsnett of Colchester, co. Essex, yeoman, app. to Edward White [*1588*], 16 July 1612

Thomas Ridgley, s. of Edward Ridgley, citizen and draper of London, app. to Richard Lumley [*1599*], 6 Aug. 1612 [entry deleted]

William Audley [*Audeley*], s. of Thomas Audley of Carleton [East Carlton], co. Northants., yeoman, dec'd, *ac dudum* app. to Francis Strange [*1596*], adm. *attamen in scientia scripto' inexpertus*, 19 Nov. 1612

[p. 185] John Atkyns [*Atkins*], s. of Richard Atkyns of Hartbury in the co. of the city of Gloucester, yeoman, app. to John Mayle [*1589*], 15 Dec. 1612

John Pope, s. of Paul Pope, citizen and writer of the court letter of London, dec'd [*1585*], adm. by pat., *in scientia inexpertus*, 20 Jan. 1612/13

Henry Manly, s. of John Manly, of Halberton, co. Devon, woollen draper (*lanerer*), app. to George Hill [*1595*], 28 Jan. 1612/13

Anthony Hudson, s. of John Hudson of Highgate, co. Middx., yeoman, app. to William Benyon [*1601*], 6 Mar. 1610/11

Henry Welch, s. of William Welch of Belgrave, co. Ches., husbandman, app. to Bartholomew Rogers [*1605*], adm., but in the art unskilful, 13 Apr. 1613 [in English]

[p. 186 translation] *The oath for those who are enfranchised in other crafts and use the craft of the writers of the court letter*

You will swear that you will be loyal in the office and craft of being a writer of the court letter, which you now use, and that the deeds which you will make to be sealed will be well and loyally made. And especially that you will not write, nor allow to be written by any of yours, any kind of deed or writing to be sealed, bearing a date a long time before the making thereof, nor a long time after, nor any blank charter, nor other deed sealed before the writing thereof, nor closed letters of a date a long distance away or a long time away, whereby any falseness can be perceived in your conscience, nor any copy of a deed sealed without careful examination, word by word. And that for no haste or avarice you will take it upon yourself to make any deed concerning inheritance, nor any other deed of great charge of which you are not aware without good advice and information of counsel. So help you God and all the saints. [pp. 187–8 blank]

[p. 189 transcript] *Be it Remembered* that the xijth Day of Janyver The yere of our Lord god[1] M^{l} ccccIxxxxvij And the xiijth yere of the Reigne of Kyng Henry the vijth the hoole Company of the Felasship' or Mistere of Scryvaners of the Courte l're of the Citee of London' in good and honest maner assembled theym' self togider in the Mansion' or Dwellyng place of Henry Wodecok than' one of the Wardeyns of the said Felashep' or Mistere And than' and there by good Delib'acion' herd redde openly amonges theym' the articles Rueles & orden'nces concernyng theym' and their said Mistere beyng Wreten' and conteyned in this Book called their' Co'en papir Of which Articles div's been' regestred and enrolled in the Chamber of the Geldhall of the said Citee And ev'y suche of alle the said Articles as to theym' than' semed to be good and necessary honest and profitable for the

[1] In the right-hand margin at the end of this line: 1497. 13 H.7.

said Felaship' thei than' caused to be marked on the heed w^t [*blank*] Aggreying gen'ally w^t one assent to alle those articles so marked And from hensforth to have theym duely kept and put in execucion' accordyng to the good meanyng and entent of the same And ovir that to the better ordryng comforte and Relief of the said Felaship' than' and there thei ordeyned made and establisshed amonges theym' certeyn' other newe articles here under Wreten'. To the Which new articles thei have hooly condescended and aggired to be kept and put in execucion' as here under is specified that is to sey

First thei have ordeyned and establisshed contynuelly from hensforth to endure that the two Wardeyns for the tyme beyng of the said Felaship' chosen' comenly on the Sonday next after Midsomer Day shall contynue in their' Office of Wardeynship' for two yeres togider as thei have doon' certeyn' yeres past. one[1] Wardeyn' alway to be taken' of the elder men' suche as afore have been' Wardeyns and the other to be taken' of the yonger men' suche as afore that have not been' Wardeyns And to be chosen' alwey after their' use and maner accustumed. And ev'y such' two Wardeyns in their' tyme of Wardeynship' to hold and kepe amonges[2] the Felaship' onely three Sopers and one Dyner that is to sey ev'y of the thire[3] first half yere a Soper And at the last half yere a Dyner therat chosyng the newe Wardeyns So that the first Soper shall alway be kept and holden' the Sonday Sevenyght after the Feest of the Epiphanye of our' Lord. The Second Soper the Sonday next after the Feest of the Natyvyte of Saynt John' the Baptist/The third Soper the Sonday Sevenyght ageyn' after the Feest of the Epiphanye. And the Dyner w^t a masse of the Hooly Goost afore it to be kept and holden' the Sonday next after the Feest of the Nativite of Saynt John' Baptist at thende of two yeres next after the eleccion' of ev'y suche two Wardeyns/At Which' masse ev'y p'sone Freman' of the said Felaship' to offer jd. And at which' Dyner alwey the newe Wardeyns to be chosen and elect as is aforsaid. And upon' ev'y such' eleccion' the old Wardeyns w^{t}in [*blank*] Dayes to make and yeld [p. 190] a Due accomptes unto the new Wardeyns Beyng called alwaye to ev'y such' accomptes iiij others of the Felaship' beside the said old and new Wardeyns that is to say two of the same iiij that have been' Wardeyns And two of theym that have not been' Wardeyns And ev'y p'sone Freman' of the said Felaship' to the mayntenannce of the Co'en charges of the said Sopers and Dyners to pay at ev'y suche said Soper xijd. and at ev'y Dyner ijs. for hym self. And for his Wif if she come to the Dyner iiijd. these paiementes to be in lieue of their' old charges of vijd. a quart' and xijd. the Dyner. the first of the said Sopers now to begyn' the Sonday next after the Feest of the Natyvyte of Saynt John' Baptist next now comyng. And the Dyner that Day twelve moneths And so forth' to contynue alwey in two yeres w^t three Sop's and one Dyner. And the cause why to have so fewe Sopers is for asmoche as afore these tymes hederto Whan' thei had ev'y quarter a Soper their' vijd. a quart' and xijd. a Dyner was not equyvalent unto the payementes and charges used and accustumed to be paide by the Wardeyns for their' Sopers

[1] In the left-hand margin at the beginning of this line: Wardeyns.

[2] In the left-hand margin at the beginning of this line: Three Sopers & one Dyner.

[3] The manuscript is not very clear; this passage should read 'the three first half yeres'.

and Dyner So and in such' Wise that comenly their' payementes and charges exceded their' Receytes ev'y two yeres v. or vj. m'rc Wherthurgh' the Co'en Treso' if eny be of the said Felaship' alway decreseth' and mynyssheth' and so consequently shuld be utterly spent and wasted/

Also[1] forasmoche as div's App'ntices have been' taken' contynued and s'ved their' app'ntishodes w[t]in the said Felaship' that have not had their' p'fact congruyte of gramer Which' is the thyng moost necessaire and expedient to ev'y p'sone ex'cisyng and usyng the science and faculte of the said Mistere. And in default Wherof they can' not have the p'fact knowlege and connyng of the said science. Wherthurgh' often' tymes thei erre/And their' actes and feates been' incongrue and not p'factly doon' to the gret Reproche and sclanndre of the said Felaship'. It is therfore ordeyned and enacted by the Com'en assent abovesaid that ev'y p'sone of the said Felaship' Which' at eny tyme hereaft' shall take any App'ntice to the said science shall bryng and p'sent the same app'ntice to the Wardeyns of the said Felaship' for the tyme beyng the name of the said app'ntice to be Wreten' in the booke of the said Felaship' And than' to be examyned by theym' or their' assignees if the same app'ntice have his congruite or not. And if it be founden' that he have not his said congruite. that than' the maister of the said app'ntice to be monysshed and charged by the said Wardeyns that the same App'ntice be set and founden' to gramer scole unto such' tyme as he have or by resonable capacite may have posytif gramer. or atte lest that he be competently erudite and lerned in the bookes of p'vula[2] Gendres Declynysons p't'ites[3] and supynes Equivox & Sinonimes w[t] the other pety bookes And that w[t]in iiij[4] the first yeres of his t'me upon' payn' that eny' maister of eny' suche app'ntice Which' dooth' or suffer to be doon' the [p. 191] contrary to this acte beyng monysshed as is aforsaid shall forfaite and pay at ev'y tyme[5] that he so doo'th the Contrary. C.s sterlinges to be applyed to thuse herund' writen' that is to sey the one half' therof to be eq'ally devyded bitwene the Chamber of the Guyldhall of London' and the body of the same Felaship'. And the other half' to thuse of the said app'ntice if he or his Frendes woll' therof compleyn' and make Due prouf' of the same. And that also ev'y maister takyng such' app'ntice shall geve and Deliv' to the Wardeyns of the said Felaship' for the[6] tyme beyng to thuse of the Treso' of the said Felaship' A Spone of silver price of iijs. iiijd. or iijs. iiijd. in money for the same spone

And for asmuche as it is not playnely p'scribed at the making of the order last aforespecified W[t]in What tyme eny p'sone of the saide felowshipp' sholde bringe and p'sent the name of his app'ntice or app'ntices to the Wardeyns of the saide Felowshipp' for the tyme beyng not only to cause the name of the saide app'ntice to be Written' in the boke in the saide

[1] In the left-hand margin at the beginning of this line: App'ntices.

[2] The word is *pervula* or *parvula* and refers to a Latin grammar; for printed editions, see *Short Title Catalogue* (1926), nos. 19, 439–42. I owe this identification to the kindness of Mr. A. G. Watson.

[3] The word is preterites.

[4] The sense requires a word or words to follow this figure.

[5] In the left-hand margin at the beginning of this line: pena Cs.

[6] In the left-hand margin at the beginning of this line: A Spone or iijs. iiijd. modo ijs. vjd.

felowshipp' But also to be examyned by them or by some of the saide felowshipp' Whether the same app'ntice have his congruytie in the lattyn' tonge or not To thentent that reformac'on and redresse may be had and taken therin accordingly

It is nowe therfore decreed condiscended and fully agreed by thassentes and consentes of Thomas Went and William Pierson now Wardeyns of the saide company And by the consentes and agreamentes of William Blackwell John lee thelder John Melsham [John, *deleted and*] Richard [*written above*] Mannsell Thomas Pierson' Barthelmew Brokesby Thomas Atkynson' Thomas Wytton and John Norden' at a meating att the Wexchaundelers hall in london the xvjth daie of Marche a^{o} d'ni 1557, That ev'y p'sone and p'sones of the saide Mystery or felowshipp' Whiche fromhensfo'the[1] shall take and have any app'ntice or app'ntices shall W^{t}in Syx Wekes[2] next and imediatly after he or they shall so take and have any suche app'ntice or app'ntices bounde unto hym or them Bring and p'sent the same app'ntice to the Wardeyns of the saide Mystery or felowshipp' for the tyme being to thentent to have his and their names entred in the co'en booke of the saide felowshipp' and to be examyned in forme aforesaide according to the effecte and true meanyng of the saide first recyted order, upon suche paynes and penalties as in the same first order is declared/And further that no p'sone or p'sones of the saide Mystery or felowshipp' shall at any tyme or tymes from hensforthe Willingly suffer any his app'ntice or app'ntices to Certefie or Witnes the Sealling or delyv'y of any dede Evidence bonde Writing or conveyannce Whatsoever, unles he or they have byn bounde app'ntice W^{t}out fraude or covyn W^{t} his M^{r} by the space of one hole yere at the least upon' payne for the First offence contrary to this order xs. and for the second offence xxs. and for the thirde offence xls. to be levied to suche like uses as in the saide first recyted order is lymytted for not p'senting of app'ntices as in the same first order more playnely appereth

[p. 192 transcript] *An order agreed upon the xvjth of Julye A^{o} RR. Marie Primo for the eleccion of the Wardens*[3]

Albeit the anncyent Ordre and custome of the elecc'on of the wardeyns of this Company hath byn' alweyes heretofore at ev'y two yeres ende to no'iate choyse and appoynte two wardeyns (that is to sey) for thupper warden one that had byn' warden before, and thother of the yonger men whiche before that tyme had not byn' wardeyn And Forasmoche as by the obs'vac'on of this ordre and by reason of deathe thelder sorte of the seide company are worne awey so faste that at this present there are but three of them lyvyng besydes the wardeyns nowe standyng in office and that they are lyke so to weare awey more and more, so as w^{t}in shorte space fewe or none of thelder sorte whiche have borne office sholde be lyvyng, (but onely suche as had very shortly before ex'cysed the seid office, whome eft sones to burden therw^{t} it were not meete) yf that olde ordre shulde any longer contynue/It is nowe therfore decreed condescended and fully agreed aswell by thassentes and consentes of John' Melsh'm and John' Hulson nowe

[1] In the left-hand margin at the beginning of this line: vj Wekes.

[2] In the right-hand margin at the end of this line: Wthin vj weekes to p'sent app'ntices.

[3] In a different hand.

wardeyns of the seid company As also by the consentes and agreament of all the seid hoole company gen'ally assembled at a dyn' holden and made at wexchaundelers[1] halle the xvj^{ne} day of July in the Fyrste yere of the Reigne of our Sov'aigne lady Mary by the grace of god Quene of Englande Frannce and Irelande defendo' of the feith and of the Churche of Englande and also of Irelande in erthe the Sup'me hed/ that from that tyme forthwarde at ev'y two yeres ende shalbe elected and chosen two of the yonger sorte of the seid company that have not byn wardeyns before, to be wardeyns of the seid company/And that the same elecc'on shall alwayes be made in fourme folowyng (that is to sey) the elder wardeyn onely by suche of the company as before that tyme have byn' wardeyns and then for the tyme beyng are wardeyns, and thother by a gen'all elecc'on of the seid company accordyng to tholde ordre and custome therin before tyme used And that this p'sent ordre and decree shall contynue and be obs'ved duryng so longe tyme and untill the fulle nombre of eight p'sones that have byn' wardeyns be lyvyng besydes the wardeyns then beyng/And it was further ordred and agreed by the seid hoole company that when assone and as often as the seid nombre of viij anncyentes that have byn' wardeyns of the seid company besydes the olde wardens that shall stande in office at the tyme of ev'y suche newe elecc'on shalbe fully compleete Then and so often this newe ordre of elecc'on shall utterly cease/And then onely tholde ordre heretofore used for the same shalbe obs'ved and folowed (that is to sey) to chose to be the upper wardeyn one that hath byn' wardeyn before and to be the yonger wardeyn one that hath not before byn' wardeyn/[p. 193 blank]

[p. 194 transcript] *An order, for the Contynuance, of the anncient use and custome, for the election of the wardens of the Mistery of the writers of the Court l're of the City of London, and for the establishing of the Choyce and election of the M^{r} of the saide socyetie, and also for the admytting of the Assistantes of the same socyety, 6. Octobr' 1601, a^{o} 43 RR'ne Eliz*:

Whereas the anncient order and Custome for the election of the wardens of the Mistery or Socyety of the Wryters of the Court l're of the City of London, Hath byn tyme oute of mynde at ev'y two yeares end, to nominate Choose and appoynt Two wardeyns, that is to say: For the upper warden, one that had byn Warden before, and the other, of the younge men, being an assistant, wch before tyme had not byn warden/And wherealso, scythence (that is to say) a^{o} primo R Rne Marie upon good considerac'on then had and for that the nomber of the elder sort of the assistantes, were worne oute, and only three then lyving (besides the wardens then lyving) It was ordered that at ev'y two yeares end, two should be Chosen oute of the younger sort wch had not byn Wardens before, to be wardens of the saide Company, and that the elder warden should be no'iated and Chosen by such as had byn Wardens before and such as for the tyme being, were Wardens; and the puisne warden, by a generall election of the saide Company according to the old order and custome, Which saide late order, should contynue no longer then till the nomber of eight anncient men should be lyving, besydes the wardens for the tyme being, and afterwardes to cease:

[1] In the left-hand margin at the beginning of this line: not' the dye the xvj of July.

Scythence wch tyme, that is to saye) the Nyneth day of Julie, a^o D'ni 1583, (upon good considerac'on then had) It was agreed that a M^r should be chosen, to be assocyate wth the other two wardeyns for two yeares, and to be accompted M^r, or governo', of the saide Company, to be taken and chosen oute of such; and by such only, as had byn upper Wardens before, Afterwardes, that is to wytt the xxvj^th day of July 1597 (upon div's considerac'ons) it was then thought mett & ordered That the election of the M^r and Wardens, should be ev'y yeare yearely. As by the sev'all actes & orde' in this behalf made, more plainly app'eth. Nowe forasmuch as by the observac'on of the last menc'oned order; of the yearely choosinge of the M^r and wardens, of the saide socyetie, the nomber of Anncientes of the said Company are at this p'nte growen to be Nynetene yet lyving, wch are a sufficient and a competent nomber, and that in fewe yeares, (if such yearely Choosing should Contynue) the yerely charge of the dynner or banckett at the choosing of the said M^r and wardens would growe so greate (the stock of the Company litle or nothing) as yt would not in any sort support the same—For remedy whereof and for the avoyding of dyvers other inco'venyences wch would thereby growe to the saide Company It is ordered and agreed by the M^r, wardens and assistantes, assembled together at a quarter meetynge the day and yeare abovesaide, That the anncient order & custome, of the nomynating and election of the said M^r and wardens shalbe revyved and put in use (that is to say) That the M^r or Governo' and the two Wardens now being, shall contynue for the space of two yeares from the tyme of their elections And that the M^r and wardens of the saide company from hensforth shalbe elected & chosen once in ev'y two Yeares, as hath byn accustomed, which M^r shalbe first elected & chosen by such of the saide Anncientes and elders, as have byn M^rs before, The second or upper warden by such as have byn before tyme M^r and wardens, and the puisne Warden by the Whole Socyetie or generally of the saide Company To wch generallty the names of Three of the assistantes that have not byn Wardens shall be presented, that oute of them three one (whome they shall like of) may be elected & Chosen puisne Warden or Accomptant Warden for the space of Two Yeares following:

[p. 195] And whereas, the nomber of Assistantes of the saide Company are at this present lvj in all yet lyving accompting both Anncientes and the younger sort altogethers, wch nomber shall be sufficient for dyvers yeares to come Itt ys thought good, ordered, and agreed, that no p'son or p'sons, shall be admytted into the Company of Assistantes, during the space of vij yeares next ensuyng unlesse the nomber of those that be nowe lyvinge, shall be decreased to Twenty or xxiiij^or. at the most. And that afterwardes when any shallbe receyved into the said Company of Assistantes, the same, shall be don by the M^r and wardens, and by the whole Company of assistantes or the greatest p'te of them:

[p. 196 *calendar*][1] Thomas Gregorie, s. of William Gregorie of Branston, co. Leics., husbandman, app. to Thomas Frith [*1595*], 1 June 1613

[1] Pp. 196–218 of the text are printed as a calendar.

Roger Brereton, s. of Edward Brereton of Borras, co. Denbigh, esq., dec'd, app. to John Langham [*1606*], dec'd, adm. *sed in scientia inexpertus*, 1 July 1613

William Lewyn [*Lewin*], s. of William Lewyn of 'Pitston alias Pitchlesthorne' [Pightlesthorne], co. Bucks., yeoman, app. to John Bentley [*1591*], 6 July 1613

Paul Hart, s. of John Hart of Histon, co. Cambs., yeoman, app. to John Maye [*May . . . 1597*], 13 July 1613

Charles Bourne, s. of Edward Bourne, citizen and pewterer of London, dec'd, app. to John Partridge [*1583*], 13 July 1613

Zealdecaies Wood, s. of Leaver Wood late of Boughton,[1] co. Kent, app. to Thomas Ruck [*1596*], adm. 'but in the art of a scrivener unskillfull', 5 Oct. 1613[2]

William Alexander, s. of Michael Alexander, citizen and merchant taylor of London, app. to Thomas Hill [*1601*], 12 Oct. 1613

[p. 197] John Stickley, s. of Richard Stickley of Pillerton, co. War., yeoman, app. to Ralph Hardwick [*Hardwicke . . . 1597*], adm. 'but unskillfull in the trad', 13 Sept. 1613 [in English][3]

Robert [*Richard*] Minchard, s. of Thomas Minchard of Thame, co. Oxon., shoemaker, dec'd, app. to Andrew Turno'r [*Turnor . . . 1575*], 24 Feb. 1615/6

John Wickes [*Wicks*], s. of Robert Wickes of Arrington, co. Cambs., yeoman, app. to Thomas Mason [*1606*], 12 Mar. 1615/6

Caleb Whitfeld, s. of William Whitfeld of Mayfield, co. Sussex, clerk,dec'd, app. to George Smyth[4]

Thomas Powell, s. of Howell ap n'dd' of Llandynam, co. Mont., gent., dec'd, app. to Reginald Wraie [*Wray . . . 1595*] [date left blank]

[p. 198] John Bagshawe [*Bagshaw*], s. of John Bagshawe of Lichfield, co. Staffs., clerk dec'd, app. to Robert Bankworth [*Banckworth . . . 1583*], 6 July 1614

Thomas Smith, s. of Thomas Smith of Kingston-upon-Thames, co. Surrey, yeoman, app. to Francis Kempe [*1590*], 6 July 1614

Edward Duck, s. of Richard Duck of North Mymms, co. Herts., gent. [*. . . of Thomas Chapman . . . 1571*],[5] 15 Sept. 1614

William Fut[t]er [*Futter*], s. of Thomas Futter of 'Tompston' [Thompson], co. Norf., gent., app. to George Smyth [*Smith . . . 1601*], 1 Oct. 1614

[1] This badly written entry in English gives the place-name as 'Blloughton': it is probably Boughton, but there is no indication which of the Kent parishes of that name is intended.

[2] In the left-hand margin is a note between this and the next entry that Edward Ledsham was Master with Henry Best and Robert Hill as Wardens; in Rawl. D51, however, the Wardens at this identical point are given as Francis Kempe and Robert Griffith.

[3] After this entry in Rawl. D51 is the date 1614, followed by the name of Thomas Cleare with no other details, and then by that of John Merick [app.] of Thomas Fitch . . . 1577.

[4] This entry has been partially erased; Whitfeld's admission will be found on p. 205 of the Common Paper.

[5] Duck's apprenticeship to Thomas Chapman is also noted in the margin of the Common Paper.

Henry Lawrence, app. to Robert Andrewes [*Andrews . . . 1588*], 1 Oct. 1614

[p. 199] Richard Alsope, app. to Henry Burnley [*Burneley . . . 1598*], 27 Oct. 1614

William Thomason, s. of George Thomason of 'Gorstelowe' [Gorstella], co. Ches., yeoman, app. to Robert Griffith [*1590*], 20 Jan. 1614/5

Giles Bostocke [*Bostock*], s. of William Bostock of Sevenoaks, co. Kent, carpenter(*lignifaber*) dec'd, app. to Charles Bostock [*1595*], 4 Feb. 1614/5

Edward Chapman, s. of Richard Chapman of Foxton, co. Leics., yeoman, app. to William Bonner [*1572*], dec'd, adm. 'but in the said art of a scryvener unskilfull', 10 Feb. 1614/5 [in English]

Thomas Alkyn [*Alkin*], s. of William Alkyn, late of Melton Mowbray, co. Leics., merchant of the staple of England, app. to John Partridge [*1583*], 28 Mar. 1615

[p. 200] George Beresford, s. of Rowland Beresford late of Rickmansworth, co. Herts., gent., app. to George Samwell [*Samuell . . . 1577*], 24 Apr. 1615

Richard Glover, s. of Henry Glover of Wolverhampton, co. Staffs., app. to Thomas Frith [*Frithe . . . 1595*], 9 May 1615

John Reynolds, s. of John Reynolds of Barton, co. Staffs., yeoman, app. to Henry Fletcher [*1607*], 5 June 1615

John Linton, s. of Anthony Linton of Richmond alias West Sheen, co. Surrey, app. to William Childe [*Child . . . 1597*], 8 July 1615

John Eaton, s. of Humfrey Eaton of Thornbury, co. Heref., clerk, app. to Robert Morgan [*1589*], 8 July 1615

[p. 201] *14 Aug. 1615. William Dodd, Master, Francis Kempe and Robert Griffeth, Wardens*

Giles [*Hugh*] Parsons, s. of Hugh Parsons of Cam, co. Glos., clerk, app. to Geoffrey [*Jeffery*] Bower [*1601*], 3 Nov. 1615

Robert Williamson, s. of Thomas Williamson of Tusmore, co. Oxon., esq., app. to Timothy Whithorne [*Whitehorne . . . 1606*], 8 Dec. 1615[1]

Thomas Dutton, s. of Ralph Dutton of Warrington, co. Lancs., cordwainer, app. to James Colbron [*1595*], 18 July 1616

[p. 202] James Wilkinson, s. of James Wilkinson of St. Bees, co. Cumb., yeoman, dec'd, adm. by redemp., 18 July 1616

Stephen Kinge [*King*], s. of John Kinge of Kings Pyon, co. Heref., yeoman, app. to Richard Nedd [*1596*], 27 Sept. 1616

[1] In Rawl. D51 this entry is followed by the date 1616 and this note:
Memorandum That the Charter or Letters Patents granted by King James dated the 28th day of January in the 14th Year of his Reigne over England France & Ireland & of Scotland the 50th Whereby the Company is incorporated by the name or title of Master Wardens and Assistants of the Society of Writers of the City of London doth here take place, being named therein for Master & Wardens The Master & those Wardens last before named and for Assistants these following. (Vizt):

John Mayle, esq., Thomas Chapman, George Samwell, Thomas Fitch, Andrew Turnor, Edward Ledsham, John Partridge, Robert Banckworth, Jeffery Place, Henry Best, Robert Hill, Robert Morgan, Peter Blower, Edward White, William Hicks, Godfrey Reynor, George Hill, James Colebrond, Charles Bostock, Francis Strange, John Hallywell, Richard Wotton, William Childe, John Woodward.

William Richbell, s. of William Richbell, citizen and merchant taylor of London, app. to John Mayle [*1589*], 3 Mar. 1616/7

Richard Bedolphe [*Bedolph*], s. of Arthur Bedolphe of Westminster, co. Middx., gent, dec'd, app. to William Swarland [*1601*], adm. *sed in arte Scriptoris inexpertus*, 3 Mar. 1616/7

Edward Pierson [*Peirson*], s. of Edward Pierson of the City of London, citizen and writer of London, dec'd [*1581*], adm. by pat., 20 May 1617

Thomas Pepper, s. of George Pepper of Warton, co. Lancs., husbandman, dec'd, app. to William Bonn[er] [*1572*], adm. *sed in arte Scriptor' inexpertus*, 20 May 1617

[p. 203] William Manley, s. of John Manley of Halberton, co. Devon, woollen draper, app. to Nicholas Reeve [*1607*], 20 May 1617

Abraham Churche [*Church*], s. of William Churche of the city of Hereford, gent., dec'd, app. to Geoffrey Bower [*1601*], 23 July 1617

John Partridge, Master,[1] *Peter Blore* [*Blower*] *and Edward White, Wardens*

Richard Ridley, s. of Richard Ridley of Doynton, co. Glos., yeoman, app. to Edward Cowper [*Cooper . . . 1606*], 9 Sept. 1617

William Holloway, s. of William Holloway, citizen and merchant of London, dec'd, app. to Francis Mosse, 2 Oct. 1617[2]

[p. 204] William Halliley, s. of William Halliley of South Milford, co. Yorks., yeoman, app. to Godfrey Reyner [*Reynor . . . 1595*], 9 Oct. 1617

John Pridgeon, s. of Richard Pridgeon of Bassingham, co. Lincs., yeoman, dec'd, app. to Robert Andrewes [*Andrews . . . 1588*], adm. *sed in arte Scriptorum inexpertus*, 9 Oct. 1617

Lawrence Newman, s. of Thomas Newman of London, writer, dec'd, app. to Thomas Preene [*1602*], 15 May 1618

John Chenery, s. of John Chenery of Isleham, co. Cambs., gent., app. to John Maye [*1597, or Bartholomew Gilman*], 15 May 1618

William Wilkinson, s. of Thomas Wilkinson of Colchester, co. Essex, yeoman, app. to Thomas Chapman [*1571*], 6 July 1618

[p. 205] *Geoffrey Place, Master, Edward White and James Colbron, Wardens*[3]

John Sharpe [*app. of Rowland Squire . . . 1598*], adm. 10 Oct. 1618

Arthur [*Alexander*] Rawthwell, adm. by redemp. 25 May 1619

Francis Pensax, s. of Edward Pensax of London, gent., app. to Thomas Hill [*1630*] 7 Oct. 1618

Anthony Anketill [*Ankehill*] s. of John Anketill of Shaftesbury, co. Dorset, gent., dec'd, app. to Robert Bankworth [*Bankeworth . . . 1583*], 17 Oct. 1618

Caleb Whitfeld [*Whitfeild*], s. of William Whitfeld of Mayfield, co. Sussex, clerk, dec'd, app. to George Smyth [*Smith . . . 1601*], 9 Jan. 1618/9

[1] In Rawl. D51 it is recorded that Partridge was 'Master for 1 Yeare from July till Tuesday after the Feast of St James the Apostle 1618'.

[2] Not in Rawl. D51.

[3] Rawl. D51 gives this heading as John Mayle and Robert Bankworth 'Fined Masters', Jeffery Place, Master, Edward White, Upper Warden, William Hicks, Godfrey Reyner and George Hill, 'fined', but the last two bracketed with James Colbron as Renter Wardens. Then occur the names of John Warren and Leonard Walworth as assistants taken in.

Thomas Sydey [*Sidey*], s. of Edward Sydey of 'dedam', co. Suff.,[1] gent., app. to William Onslow [*Onslowe . . . 1561*], dec'd, adm. 'into the company of scrivoneirs but inexpert in the same misterie', 20 Jan. 1618/9 [in English]

Michael Holman, s. of Lawrence Holman of St. Mabyn, co. Cornwall, yeoman, app. to William Childe [*Child . . .1597*], 6 July 1619

[p. 206] Thomas Wannerton, s. of John Wannerton, citizen and salter of London, app. to Edward Charnock [*1588*], 4 May 1619[2]

John Davies, s. of Thomas Davies of Leominster, co. Heref., gent., dec'd, app. to John Plukenett [*Plucknett . . . 1597*] now clerk to the Company, 6 July 1619[3] [See Frontispiece]

Francis White, M.A., s. of Edward White [*1588*], adm. by pat., *artis vero scriptoriæ non ita gnarus*, 7 July 1619

Ralph Hayward, s. of Ralph Hayward, late of Hadleigh, co. Suff., clothier, app. to Hugh Burrowes [*1607*], 7 July 1619

George Allestree [*Alestree*], s. of William Allestree of Alvaston, co. Derby, yeoman, dec'd, app. to Godfrey Johnson [*1610*], 25 May 1619

[p. 207] *Henry Best, Master, James Colbron and Charles Bostock, Wardens*[4]

George Waters, s. of Richard Waters, citizen and draper of London, dec'd, app. to John Waren [*Warren . . . 1598*], 20 Sept 1619

John Lea, s. of Roger Lea of the city of Hereford, pewterer, dec'd, app. to William Hickes [*Hicks . . . 1591*], 4 Oct. 1619

Charles Bragge [*Bragg*], s. of Charles Bragge of Stalbridge, co. Dorset, clerk, app. to William Ledsham [*1590 or Charles Bostock*], 8 Oct. 1619

George Martyn, s. of Hugh Martyn of London, gent., dec'd, app. to Hugh Osborne [*1603*], 8 Oct. 1619

Samuel Tuiford, s. of Robert Tuiford [*1600*], adm. by pat., *arte vera scriptoræ in expertus*, 12 Oct. 1619

Daniel Cooper, s. of William Cooper of Stoney Stanton, co. Leics., yeoman, app. to Henry Burnley [*1598*], 12 Oct. 1619

[p. 208] Edward Tetlowe [*Tetlow*], s. of Richard Tetlowe late of Preston [Bisset], co. Bucks., clerk, app. to [?] Owine[5] [*Edmund*] Martin [*1600*], 11 Jan. 1619/20

Philip Bisse, s. of James Bisse, S.T.P., app. to Simon Broome, dec'd, adm. *in arte vero scriptoriæ ignarus*, 21 Jan. 1619/20

Edward Awdley [*Audley*], app. to William Audley [*1612*], adm. *Arte vero Scriptor inexpertus*, 27 Mar. 1620

[1] This entry is badly written and faded. The parish, which appears to be 'dedam,' is probably Dedham in Essex. There was, however, a family of Sydey at Bures St. Mary, nine miles west of Dedham, on the Suffolk side of the River Stour. Thomas Sydey describes William Onslow as 'lat settason of london desesed.'

[2] In the left-hand margin, opposite this entry, is written: And I Job Willoughbie unexpert in the Science, have signed this wth my owne p'p' hand the xxvjth Daie of Maye 1619. He signs as Willoughby which is the form in Rawl. D51.

[3] In the left-hand margin, between this and the next entry, is written: Johannes Rye was here made free, but forgotten to bee entred. He is also entered in Rawl. D51.

[4] In Rawl. D51 this heading is followed by the names of Humfrey Pye, John Maye and Rowland Squire, who were taken in as assistants, and of Charles Bostock and Francis Strange as stewards.

[5] This name is very indistinct.

William Goodwin, s. of Nicholas Goodwin late of Knossington, co. Leics., blacksmith, app. to Thomas Fitch [*1577*], 28 Mar. 1620

Josias [*John*] White, s. of William White of Milborne Port, co. Som., dec'd, app. to Geoffrey Place [*1583*], 12 Apr. 1620[1]

[p. 209] Robert Walker, s. of Lawrence Walker, citizen and vintner of London, app. to Henry Best [*1583*], 30 June 1620

William Dexter, s. of William Dexter of Crondall, co. Hants., yeoman, app. to Charles Yeoman [*Yeomans . . . 1599*], 29 Aug. 1620

Henry Best [*deleted*] *Robert Morgan, Master*[2]

William Hunter, s. of William Hunter, citizen and clothworker of London, app. to Michael Dover [*1606*], 12 Oct. 1620

Robert Richardson, s. of Edward Richardson of Dalton in Furness, co. Lancs., yeoman, app. to John Partridge [*1583*], 12 Oct. 1620

[p. 210] *Robert Morgan, Master, Charles Bostock and Richard Wotton, Wardens, 1620*[3]

William Bower, s. of Joseph Bower of Donhead, co. Wilts., gent., app. to John Milton [*1599*], 6 Apr. 1621

Nicholas Bacon, app. to John Langham [*1606*], adm. *Artis vero Scriptori non gnarus*, 3 July 1621

Christopher Favell, s. of Roger Favell of Barford, co. Beds., yeoman, app. to James Goodyer [*1609*], 3 July 1621

Godfrey Austinson, s. of Thomas Austinson of South Milford, co. Yorks., yeoman, dec'd, app. to Henry Farley [*1606*], 3 July 1621

Roger Kingesley, app. to William Swarland [*1601*], adm. *Artis vero Scriptorie non gnarus*, 9 Aug. 1621

[p. 211] *Francis Kempe, Master, Richard Wootton and William Childe, Wardens, 1621*[4]

Richard Milton, s. of Thomas Milton of Cheltenham, co. Glos., yeoman, app. to John Milton [*1599*], 20 Sept. 1621

Henry Shelbery [*Shelbury*], s. of Isaac Shelbury of Colchester, co. Essex, dec'd, app. to Andrew Turno'r [*Turner . . . 1575*], 20 Sept. 1621

John Peirse, s. of Henry Peirse of Bedale, co. Yorks., yeoman, app. to Robert Griffith [*1590, or William Hicks*], 20 Sept. 1621

James Noell, s. of Edward Noell of Stafford, co. Staffs., mercer, app. to Edward White [*1588*], 24 Oct. 1621

Matthew Billinge [*Billings*], s. of Edmund Billinge of Weedon Beck, co. Northants., yeoman, app. to John Chester [*1609*], 19 Feb. 1621/2

[1] In Rawl. D51 this name is followed by the admission of Jonas Ramsden [app.] of Zachary Humfrey . . . 1595.

[2] Rawl. D51 gives this heading as Robert Morgan, Master, Charles Bostock, Upper Warden, Francis Strange and John Halliwell, 'fined', but the last name is bracketed with that of Richard Wotton as Renter Warden (in the singular). Then follow the names of John Halliwell and Richard Wotton as stewards.

[3] See note 2 above.

[4] In Rawl. D51 these names are followed by those of Thomas Hill and George Smith as taken in as assistants, and of William Child and John Woodwood as stewards.

Leb[b]eus Peache [*Peche*], app. to Edward Awdley [*or William Audley . . . 1620*] adm. *Artis vero scriptur non gnarus*, 4 Mar. 1621/2

[p. 212] Thomas Colbron, s. of James Colbron [*1595*], citizen and writer of London, adm. by pat., 28 Mar. 1622

John Bentley, s. of John Bentley [*1591*], citizen and writer of London, adm. by pat., 2 July 1622

Nicholas Ballard, s. of John Ballard of Boston, co. Lincs., clothier, dec'd, app. to Thomas Smith [*1614*], 30 July 1622

Edward [*deleted*] *Peter Blore, Master*[1]

Peaceable Sherwood, app. to Edward Chapman [*1614*], adm. *Artis vero Scriptorie non gnarus*, 10 Oct. 1622

Ralph Hartley, s. of Alexander Hartley of Chollerton [Chorlton] in Manchester, co. Lancs., husbandman, dec'd, app. to John Woodward [*1597*], 12 Dec. 1622

[p. 213] *Peter Blore, Master, William Child and John Woodward, Wardens, 1622*[2]

Humfrey Shalcrosse [*Shallcrosse*], s. of Humfrey Shalcrosse, citizen and painter-stainer of London, app. to Henry Best [*1583*], 12 Dec. 1622

Alexander Bowlinge [*Bowling*], s. of Thomas Bowlinge of London, gent., app. to Charles Bostocke [*Bostock . . . 1595*], 15 Feb. 1622/3

William Meeke, s. of John Meeke of Marcle, co. Heref., husbandman, app. to William Childe [*1597*], 28 Feb. 1622/3

Edward Pierce [*Peirce*], s. of Thomas Pierce of Wepre, co. Flint, gent., app. to Nicholas Reeve [*1607*], 3 Apr. 1623

William Stonehouse, s. of Richard Stonehouse of Lenham, co. Kent, yeoman, dec'd, app. to John Merick [*Merrick . . . 1614*], 7 July 1623

[p. 214] Walter Smithe [Smith], adm. by redemp., 7 July 1623

Edward White, Master, John Woodward and John Waren, Wardens[3]

Thomas Colbron (no declaration)[4]

Edward Joicelyn [. . . *of Francis Strange . . . 1596*] [no declaration]

Henry Colbron, app. to James Colbron [*1595*], adm. *artis vero scriptorio non gnarus*, 29 June 1624

Richard Morgan [. . . *of Thomas Powell*] [no declaration]

William Style [*Stile*], app. to Henry Manly [*Manley . . . 1612*], adm. *artis vero scriptorio non gnarus*, 29 June 1624

[p. 215] James Hodgkinson, app. to John Milton [*1599*], adm. *artis vero Scriptorio non gnarus*, 29 June 1624

Thomas Bower, app. to John Milton [*1599*], adm. *artis vero scriptoris non ignarus*, 29 June 1624

[1] In Rawl. D51 this heading reads: Peter Blower, Master, William Child and John Woodward, Wardens, John Milton and Geffery Bower, assistants taken in, John Warren and Leonard Walworth, stewards.

[2] See note 1 above.

[3] In Rawl. D51 these names are followed by those of John Woodford, John Hibberd, Charles Yeomans and John Macro as assistants taken in, and of Humfrey Pye and John May as stewards.

[4] Not in Rawl. D51.

James Robinson app. to Andrew Lake [*1609*], adm. *artis vero scriptorio non ignarus*, 29 June 1624
Ralph Ripley [. . . *of Thomas Mathew*] [no declaration]

Godfrey Rayner, Master, John Waren and Humfrey Pye, Wardens[1]

Thomas Wolley [no declaration]
Nicholas Wolley [no declaration]
Henry Wigmore, adm. by redemp., 4 Jan. 1624/5[2]
[p. 216] John Brooke, app. to John Woodward [*1597*], amd. *non penitus ignarus*, 4 Jan. 1624/5[3]
John Rea, app. to William Childe [*Child . . . 1597*], adm. *non penitus ignarus*, 22 Feb. 1625/6
Henry Iles, app. to Roland Squier [*1598*], adm. *non penitus ignarus*, 4 Feb. 1624/5[4]
Robert Wright, app. to Robert Holiland [*Halliland*], adm. *non penitus ignarus*, 30 Mar. 1626
Francis Webb, app. to Nicholas Reeve [*1607*], adm. *non penitus ignarus*, 30 Mar. 1626
James Reade [*Read*], app. to William Wilkinson [*1618*], adm. *non penitus ignarus*, 6 July 1626

[p. 217] *Richard Wotton, Master, Roland Squier and Francis Mosse, Wardens, 1626*

John Gibson, app. to John Ken [*Kenn . . . 1609*], 13 Oct. 1626
Richard Andrewe [*Andrews*], s. of Robert Andrewe, citizen and writer of London, dec'd [*Andrews . . . 1588*], 7 Apr. 1627[5]
Richard Mulcaster, app. to Francis Mosse [*1599, or John May*], 7 Apr. 1627
Robert Bird, app. to William Awdeley [*Audley . . . 1612*], 7 Apr. 1627[5]
Edward Turpin, app. to John Macro [*John Partridge . . . 1583*], 26 June 1627[5]
George Lawrence, app. to John Langham [*1563*], 26 June 1627[5]
Valentine Pritchard [*Prichard*], s. of Charles Pritchard of Llanfoist, co. Mon., gent., app. to John Plukenett [*Plucknett . . . 1597*], 18 Sept. 1627

[1] In Rawl. D51 these names are followed by those of William Swarland and John Ashenden as Wardens (probably an error for assistants), and of Rowland Squire and Francis Mosse as stewards.
[2] In Rawl. D51 this name is followed by the admission of George Wigmore [app.] of John Gregorie.
[3] In Rawl. D51 this entry is followed by the admissions of Peter Shofeild, Richard Griffith and Giles Parson with no other details.
[4] In Rawl. D51 this entry is followed by the admission of George Gregorie [app.] of Anthony Hudson . . . 1610. Then comes a heading: 1625 Charles Bostock, Master, Humfrey Pye, 'Uper' Warden died, John May, Renter Warden chosen Upper Warden, Rowland Squier, Renter Warden, John Langham, Bartholomew Gilman, Nicholas Reeve and Richard Alley, taken in assistants, and Thomas Hill and John Milton, stewards. As there are no entries under 1625, there is another heading: 1626 Richard Wootton, Master, Rowland Squire and Francis Mosse, Wardens, John Kenn and John Smythyer, taken in assistants, and Geffery Bower and Robert Woodford, stewards.
[5] Describes himself as *non peritus*—'being no expert' in the craft of a scrivener.

[p. 218] *William Childe, Master, Francis Mosse and Geoffrey Bower, Wardens*[1]

Mark Bradley [. . . *of Lawrence Lownes*], adm. by redemp., 25 Oct. 1627

Tristram Hill, app. to Richard Alie [*Alley . . . 1609*], 1 Nov. 1627

Morgan Mathewe [*Mathew*], app. to Thomas Powell [*1615*], 1 Nov. 1627

Anthony Best, app. to Robert Morgan [*1589*], 9 Jan. 1627/8

Richard Hawes, s. of Thomas Hawes of Westhorpe, co. Suff., yeoman, app. to John May [*Maile or May . . . 1589*], adm. *non penitus Ignarus*, 31 Mar. 1628

William Wight [*Wright*], s. of William Wight, citizen and draper of London, app. to Charles Bostocke [*1595*], adm. *non penitus Ignarus*, 29 May 1628

John Johnsons [*Johnson*], s. of William Johnsons, app. to John Waterhouse [*1606*], adm. *non penitus Ignarus*, 8 July 1628[2]

[p. 219 This page, scored with two diagonal lines, bears the words] *Inde incepit Liber novus admission'*.

[p. 220 *transcript*] M^{d} that the xxix day of Aprill in the xxiiij yer' of kynge Henry the Sixte in tyme of John Scadley & Thomas Froddesham than standyng Wardeyns of the crafte of Scryveners I John Valentyn' Screvenyr for dyv's offences as wele in langage as in other thynges be me gevyn to the sayd Wardeynes be menes th'of on my party made I have submytted and submytte my selfe in lowly Wyse Un to the sayd Wardeynes on' my knees knowlegyng myn' obstynacy and th'of have asked forgevenes and [have][3] is forgevyn' And further-more of myn' owne Fre p'fer & godewyll I have payd & geven to thencrece of the boxse for my sayd Offences vs' viijd' Furthermore where'as be an obligncon' of myn' owne hande wryten I stonde bounde to the sayd Wardeyns in xx li' st'ling upon dyv's condiciones as be the sayd oblígncion' it may apper' I of myn' owne knowlege afferme the sayd obligacion' to be gode under the condicone th'on exp'ssed and th^{t} be me to have be Wryten made seled & delyv'ed as for myn' dede & Wyll w^{t}out cohercion' in any Wyse.

Whereas the sayd Wardeyns of their' gode Wyll have geve & allowed me ageyn' xx d'. [p. 221 blank]

[p. 222 translation] *The justifications for scriveners to ignore the article that they should put their names on each deed*

First of all, we say that at the time when the said article was drawn up, the custom or the usage then was to write on each kind of deed and writing 'Dat' London' ' or 'Don' a Lonndres', except only charters of lands and tenements granted outside London which, however, were to have the date when the lands and tenements were granted; and a [?] plan was then worked out by the wise men of the kingdom, and it has always since been used to

[1] In Rawl. D51 the names of Thomas Hill and John Milton (each marked with an asterisk for which no explanation is given) are between those of Mosse (Upper Warden) and Bower (Renter Warden). John Smith and William Audley noted as assistants taken in.

[2] In Rawl. D51 this entry is followed by those given on pp. 114–27 below.

[3] Deleted.

remove the date of the grants[1] in the majority of all kinds of deeds and writings with the intention of alleging the date of the grant when it will be more suitable for the party [?] bringing an action. And, in that the writing of our names must be contrary to this kind of alleging—in a case where the alleging will take place outside the region[2] where one of us lives—the aforesaid article, that we should put our names on each deed, was never used or carried out to our knowledge and, for that reason it seems, in our humble estimation, that the said article is neither effectual nor necessary to be used.

Item, many deeds are delivered by us to various people, unsealed in our presence and [we need not sign our names] because it is possible that in our absence someone might wish, for a fraudulent reason, to seal the deed in the name of another party to the deed, without the actual party knowing and, because of the writing of our names, we would be called to vouch for the party who made the deceit, to testify to such wickedness done of which we could have no knowledge.

Item [we need not sign our names because] it could happen that someone, for a deceitful and fraudulent purpose, might wish to have a certain deed written in the name of another person, asserting that he is that person when in fact he is not and, in order to accomplish such fraud, he might wish to have the deed sealed in our presence, we knowing nothing of the deceit or the person; and afterwards it could happen that this kind of deed could be brought into court and [?] become the subject of litigation and, on the strength of the writing of our names, we could be called to vouch for the party who made the deceit before a judge, or other person, to testify to such fraud, in which case we could not know the truth concerning the identity of the person, or about the deceit.

Item [we need not sign our names because] it could happen, through deceit or through malice, that someone could forge our signatures on scurrilous and biased deeds [?] drawn up and written by other people, to our slander and disadvantage.

Item [we need not sign our names because] it could happen, through deceit or through malice, that someone might wish, in order to slander us, to erase a certain word in some deed written by one of us, and forge another word according to the sense of the same deed, in abuse of the deed and of he who wrote it, on account of the writing of his name there when he was not at all to blame.

Item [we need not sign our names because] it could happen that someone might wish to deny that a deed is his, when in fact it is his deed and was sealed in the presence of one of us; and in this matter we could be called, and required in court, to testify as to the truth before a judge, or other person, because of the writing of our name, and we would know very well about the truth and the testimonies; and notwithstanding this testimony as to the truth, it could be decided by contrived inquiry, or malicious

[1] The word is *lieux*, which means 'places', but as 'the date of the places' is meaningless it may be assumed there is an extension of the idea. However, the sense of a number of words in this passage is elusive. See footnote 1 to p. 3 of the manuscript (printed p. 3).

[2] Literally 'the watch' (*hors del garde*).

informing, that it is not his deed when in fact it is, which verdict would be very slanderous and degrading to us and therefore to our detriment.

Item [we need not sign our names because] it could happen that our names are written on a certain deed, as in ordained by the above-mentioned article, and someone through malice and enmity might wish to erase and carefully remove the name to damage us or, alternatively, someone might wish, through his position of superior power, not to allow us to write our names on deeds written by us and so, by default of writing our names, we could incur the penalty ordained for this to our great damage and detriment.

Item [we need not sign our names because] it seems to us that our entire handwriting, and that of our servants, in each deed which is not to be counterfeited, is quite sufficient [to identify us] in that the handwriting of us and our servants is and will be well known among us at all times afterwards. [pp. 223–78 blank]

[p. 279 transcript] *vicesimo Quarto die Aprilis 1615*

Forasmuch as divers Brethren of this Company being Assistantes of the same are dwelling in the cuntrie, and some others, either for want of abilitie or for some other their private endes give not such their attendance in furthering the affaires of the said Company, as is fitting, It is therefore [*word deleted*] ordered at a Court held the daie and yeare abovewritten in the p[rese]nce of such of the saide Company, as were then present, and have hereunto subscribed their names That the persons undernamed, being Brethren of this Societie, in regarde of their reputed abilitie, and expected deligence, and care for the generall good and creditt of the said Societie, shalbee, and were admitted to bee of the bodie of Assistan[tes] of the same Company. That is to saie

1. Leonard Walwoorth p[d]
2. Humfrey Pye p[d]
3. John May p[d]
4. Rowland Squier p[d]
5. Franncis Mosse p[d]
6. Thomas Hill p[d]
7. George Smith p[d]
8. Thomas Preene p[d]

theis thre undernamed were at the same time chosen to bee Assistantes

9. Robert Woodforde 9 p[d] [*deleted and*] John Milton [*written above*]
10. Jeoffrie Bower 10 p[d]
11. Robert Woodford

And for avoiding of question w[ch] hereafter maie arise, and for y[e] continuance of brotherlie love and kindnes, it was then further ordered. That none of the Assistantes of this company shall receave place of office within the same, but onlie and according to such time and times as they have been admitted or shalbee admitted to bee of the Assistantes of the same: [*Signed*] Henry Best; Ro: Hill; George Samwell; Tho. Fitche; John Partridge; Peter Blower; Francis Kemp; Rob: Griffith; Edward White; William Hickes; Godfrey Reyner; William Childe; John Waren.

decimo quarto Die Augusti 1615

M[d]. That question growing for precedencie betweene Jeoffrie Bower, and Robert Woodford It is for Divers just reasons nowe therefore ordered

by a Court of Assistantes That the said Bower shall hencefourth take place in precedencie, notwithstanding the said Woodfordes subscripcon before him in the Booke: [*Signed*] W: Dod; Fr. Kemp; Rob: Griffith; George Samwell; John Partridge; Henry Best; Ro: Hill; Jo: Hallywell; Jo: Woodward; Ro: Squyer; Fra. Mosse; Jo: Milton; Leonard Wallworth.
[p. 280 blank]

[p. 281 translation] *Remember that in the nineteenth year of the reign of King Richard the Second, in the time of John Cossier and Martin Seman, joint Wardens, the following incidents happened:*[1]

The assembly, sitting at London, [before] Martin Seman and John Cossier, men of judgment and scriveners of London, and authors [of this statement], send greeting. Wherefore, as we understand, certain public scriveners of the court letter of the City of London, of which scriveners we are appointed guardians (as is sworn), are keeping shop or their stalls [open] on holy days, Sundays and other feasts instituted to the glory of God, against the form and tenor of certain letters made and drawn up to revere, in Christ, the fathers, and [by] Lord Robert, by the grace of God, Bishop of London, and containing specific instructions[2]—and [these scriveners], with everyone arriving to avail themselves of their craft, deserve open rebuke by being liable to the penalties in the said letters, we therefore entrust to you and command you that diligent inquiry should be made concerning the names and surnames of all and singular these scriveners who contravene or do not observe the said instructions, so that we, about next Eastertide, having arranged a suitable place and time, may be able to apply the remedy due in this matter to correct such irreverence of their souls. Given at London on the last day of February under the foot of our official seal at London which presents, from the present, we have at hand, A.D. 1395.

According to which command, the aforesaid Wardens presented to the said assembly the names [*les nons*][3] in the following manner.

Scriveners

In that he keeps shop, or holds his stall open, on holy days and double feasts, and writes and pursues his craft openly on the said days in sight of the people, and hangs outside many documents and various writings to the great disgrace of all upright men of his craft, and as a wicked example to other crafts, and in clear contempt of the life-giving Mother Church and against the instruction of the Lord Bishop.

In that he keeps his shop open on holy days and double feasts and writes and pursues his craft openly in sight of the people on the said days and hangs outside many of his documents and various writings to the great disgrace of all upright men of his said craft, and as a wicked example to

[1] Then follows, in another hand, this statement (in translation): Regarding shops open on festival days, the Wardens made warning that they should be shut, and if anyone should disobey this warning, it happened as is written below.
[2] See pp. 5 and 6 of the Common Paper (printed pp. 4, 5).
[3] The sense is that what follows are the forms of allegation employed against those five unnamed scriveners who contravened the instruction about closing their premises on festivals.

other crafts, and in clear contempt of the life-giving Mother Church and against the prohibition of the guardians of his craft and against the instruction of the Lord Bishop.

In that he keeps his shop open on holy days and double feasts so that all his documents and various writings are seen, and he writes and pursues his craft openly on the said days, in sight of the people to the great disgrace of all upright men of his craft, and as a wicked example to other crafts, and in clear contempt of the life-giving Mother Church, and against the prohibition of the guardians of his craft and against the instruction of the Lord Bishop and against an earlier rebuke in the assembly in the same circumstance.

In that he keeps part of his shop open on holy days and double feasts and hangs outside his documents and various writings, and writes and pursues his craft in sight of the people to the great disgrace of upright men of his craft, and as a wicked example to other crafts, and in clear contempt of the life-giving Mother Church and against the instruction of the Lord Bishop.

In that he keeps part of his shop open on holy days and double feasts and hangs outside his documents and various writings, and writes and pursues his craft openly in sight of the people to the great disgrace of all upright men of his craft, and as a wicked example to other crafts, and in clear contempt of the life-giving Mother Church and against the instruction of the Lord Bishop and prohibition of the guardians of his craft.

They were acquitted, etc.

[p. 282] Item, soon after the said five people were thus on their own,[1] other persons of the said craft met up with them and suggested forming a party in opposition to their Wardens and their said craft, and they did not wish to come to their assembly, for which reasons the same Wardens put forward the following bill—

Most honourable sire, the Mayor of the City of London, making complaint [are] the Wardens of the craft of scriveners of the court letter of the said City against one Robert Huntyngdon', scrivener, in that the said Robert for a long time has been rebelling against the said Wardens and, through which rebellion, certain other persons of the said craft, influenced by his bad example, have become rebellious in the same way towards the said Wardens to the great trouble and disruption of the said craft, for which reason the said Wardens are deposed from carrying out their duty and are no longer able to control the said craft. For which they make plea for redress, according to the usage of the said City, in the work of charity.

By virtue of which bill, the said Robert was judged by the Mayor and Aldermen and committed to prison until he had conformed with his craft, and after an end was made to the rebellion.

[*transcript*] An oath conceaved in the time of John Partridge M^{r} &c.

I, A.B. of my owne free will do sweare upon the holie Evangelistes to bee true and faithfull unto our Sovereigne lord the kinge his heires and Successors

[1] This passage is difficult to translate; the names of the scriveners are not given.

kinges and Queenes of England, and to bee true in myne office and science and to Do my deligence that all the Deedes w[ch] I shall make to bee sealed shalbee well and trulie done after my learning and science and shalbee Dulie and advisedlie read over and examined before thensealing of the same, And especiallie I shall not write nor suffer to bee written by any of myne to my power or knowledg any Deed or writing to bee sealed where in any deceipt or falshood maie bee perceaved or in my conscience suspected to lye, nor any deed bearing date of long time past before thensealing thereof nor bearing any date of a time to come, neither shall I testefie nor suffer any of myne to testefie to my power or knowledg any blanck ch[a]rt[er] or deed sealed before the full writing thereof and neither for hast nor for covetousnes I shall take upon mee to make any deed touching inheritance of landes or estates for life or yeares nor any deed of greate charge whereof I have not cunning without good advice and informacon of councell, and all the good rules and ordinances of the Societie of Scriveners of the citie of London I shall well and trulie keepe and observe to my power, soe farr as god shall give mee grace. So helpe mee god, and the holie contentes of this Booke:

[p. 283 transcript][1] *Tempore Joh'is Hulson et Thome Wytton'*

The ceassement of the fyrste payement for wheate by a warrante dated from S[r] Thomas Lodge then Lorde Mayo[r] the thyrde daye of Octobre 1562
Thomas Wytton guard, 40*s.*; Mr Blackwell, 20*s.*; Mr Lee thelder, 20*s.*; Mr Melsham, 20*s.*; Mr Wente, 20*s.*; Mr Norden, 20*s.*; Mr Godfrey, 20*s.*; Mr Thomas Pierson, 20*s.*; Mr Wylli'm Pierson, 20*s.*; Mr Brokesbye, 20*s.*; Mr Atkynson', 20*s.*; Mr Owtred, 20*s.*; Mr Bonde, 20*s.*; Peter Baker, 20*s.*; Wylfryde Lutye, 20*s.*; John Scampion', 20*s.*; Humfrey Brooke, 20*s.*; Alexander Rotherforth, 10*s.*; Thomas Hulson', 10*s.*; John Dalton', 10*s.*; Anthony Hyggyns, 10*s.*

Tempore Thome Wytton' sole

The ceasment of the seconde payement for wheat by the sayde Lorde Mayo[rs] warrant dated the xxiij[th] daye of January, 1562
Thomas Wytton' guard, 10*s.*; Mr Blackwell, 10*s.*; Mr Lee thelder, 10*s.*; Mr Melsham, 10*s.*; Mr Went, 10*s.*; Mr Norden, 10*s.*; Mr Godfrey, 10*s.*; Mr Thomas Pierson, 10*s.*; Mr Wylli'm Pierson, 10*s.*; Mr Brokesby, 10*s.*; Mr Atkynson, 10*s.*; Mr Owtred, 10*s.*; Mr Bonde, 10*s.*; Mr Baker, 10*s.*; Anthony Hyggyns, 13*s.* 4*d.*; Paule Pope, 10*s.*; Wylfryde Lutye, 10*s.*; Humfrey Brooke, 10*s.*; Thomas Browne & Rob'te Wylson, 20*s.*; Rauf Hall, 13*s.* 4*d.*; John Lee the yonger, 13*s.* 4*d.*; Thomas Bradfo'rth, 13*s.* 4*d.*; Wylli'm Braynewood, 13*s.* 4*d.*; William Ownslowe, 10*s.*; Wylli'm Tysdale, 10*s.*; Nycholas Kyngestone, 13*s.* 4*d.*; Thomas Stafferton, 10*s.*; Frannces Bryght, 13*s.* 4*d.*; Edwarde Holme, 13*s.* 4*d.*; George Kevall', 13*s.* 4*d.*; Frannces Kydde, 10*s.*; Mychaell Howman, 10*s.*; Thomas Hulson, 10*s.*; John Dalton', 10*s.*; Wylli'm Charnocke, 10*s.*; Robert Davyson, 5*s.*; Wyllim Laying, 5*s.*

[1] In the manuscript the names are arranged in columns and the money is given in Roman figures; the latter have been converted to Arabic figures for convenience. The superscript letter r of 'M[r]' has been brought down to the line.

All whiche severall som'es Cessed and Collected in the tyme of John Hulson and Thomas Wytton amountynge in all to the some of Fouertie poundes were receyved by Thomas Atkynson one of the wardens of this Companie in Anno 1564 of Mr John Whyte Alderman And paide over by hym anno predict' as foloweth viz' To the saide Thomas Wytton' for the foote of his accompte Tenne poundes and the Residue thereoff unto the severall lenders of the same as by theire Acquitannces and Bylls delyvered in of the Receipte of the same yt dothe and maye more playnelie appere —— } x.li

[p. 284 transcript] *Tempore Georgii Kevall Mag'ri, Simonis Wrenche, et Will'mi Serche, Gardianor'*:

Jovis duodecimo die Marcii, Anno xxxij° d'ne n're Elizabeth Regine &c 1589:

Harte maior, Haywarde, Ramsey, Dixie, Barne, Bonde, Martyn, Allott, Webbe, Roe, Billingesley, Elkyn, Howse, Catcher, Offeley, Saltonstall, Mowseley, &c

This daye the Maister and Wardens of the Company of the writers of the Courte l're of this Cittie, present in this Co'te, made reporte unto the same, That where heretofore, they have att sondrie tymes, receaved precept, and Comanndemtes, from this Courte, for provision to be made by their company, for Armor, Weapon, gunepowder, wheate, and other thinges, aswell for her Mates s'vice, as of this Cittie, And that towardes the p'formaunce' thereof, they have att sondrie tymes, called before them, divers of their bretheren, free of their company, and required them to contribute, rateablie towardes the saide p'vision, Whereof some have moste wilfully and contemptuously, refused to p'forme, And that some others refuse upon Lawfull som'ons, to appeare before them, And others also, denys[1] to paie their quarteridge, and other chardges and dueties, as of right they ought to paie/ yt is therfore, ordered, and decreed, this daye, by this Courte, that if at any tyme hereafter, any member of the same company, shall refuse to yelde, to reasonable contribuc'on for the causes aforsaide, or any other the like, or to appeare upon lawfull warninge, having no reasonable excuses, to the Contrary, or to paie their quarteridge, or other dueties, That then it shalbe lawfull to and for the Mr and Wardens of the saide Company for the tyme being, to comytt ev'y suche p'son to warde, into one of the Compters of this Citie, there to remayne, untill he shall p'forme the same accordingly

Sebright

[p. 285][2] Mr Norden [and] Mr Brende, Wardens. 19 June 1575 whiche Daie Kydd, Kevall & Langham were called to be assastannts.

Thomas Godfrey, Thomas Went, Bartholomew Brokesby,[3] Peter Baker, John Dalton', Anthony Higgons, Paul Pope [*deleted*], Humfrey Broke,

[1] This word could be 'devys', i.e. devise, but it is probably a scribal error for 'denye'.

[2] This is a very confused page; it has been treated partly as a transcript.

[3] This and the two previous names are marked 'mort'.

Paul Pope, Thomas Browne,[1] Thomas Stafferton', William Squire, Ralph Carkeke, William Onslowe, Thomas Hulson, Francis Kydd, George Kevall, John Langham.

Thomas Brend, sen. [and] Francis Kydd, Wardens, 1 March 1580
Assistanntes newly taken in and elected the daye and yere aforesaid, viz'—
Bernard Garter, Thomas Shorte, John Turnor, John Walker, William Dermer, Simon Wrench, Thomas Redforth, Robert Preston, Henry Burre, William Search, Robert Mannsell', Emanuel Mannsell', John Taylor, Thomas Brende, jun.

Put at the elecc'on of theis assistentes—
The Two Wardeyns aforsaid, John Dalton', Anthony Higgens, Paul Pope, William Squyre, Ralph Karkeke, George Kevall'.
All theis were put at the elecc'on of all the said assistentes, Except the said John Turno', Robert Mannsell', John Taylo', At the elecc'on of which thre this xvij^th^ day of Julie 1581 were p'sent the said Wardeyns, the said John Dalton', Humfrey Brooke, Paul Pope, Thomas Browne,[1] George Kevall', John Walker, Emanuel Mannsell'.

In the Tyme of Mr Dalton' & Mr Squier [and] Mr Kevall, Wardeyns, was admytted Into the assistance Richard Blake.

In the tyme of Mr Poope, M[aste]r, Mr Onslowe [and] Mr Langham, Wardeyns, was taken into the Assistance the xxvj of July 1587 Richard Bouth.

[p. 286 transcript] *Temp'e Joh'is Norden & Th' Brend gardian' &c A° 1573, Annoqz Elizabeth Regine xvj° & xvij°*

A sessement off xx^{li} levyd of the Company of Scryveners of the Court l're of the Cytte of London' by v'tue of a p'cept to the same Wardens directed From s^{r} lyonell Duckket the lord Mayre of the sayd Citte the (*blank*) day of (*blank*) A° 1573 as Followeth viz'—

Imp'mis lent by John Norden & Thomas Brend, Wardens, 40*s.*; Thomas Goodfrey, 10*s.*;[2] Thomas Went, 10*s.*; Bartholomew Brokesby, 10*s.*; Anthony Bond, 10*s.*; Peter Baker, 10*s.*; John Dalton', 10*s.*; Anthony Hyggyns, 10*s.*; Nicholas Kyngstone, 10*s.*; Paul Poppe, 10*s.*; Thomas Browne, 10*s.*; Thomas Stav[er]ton, 10*s.*; William Squyer, 10*s.*; Ralph Carkeket, 10*s.*; William Ownslow, 10*s.*; Thomas Hulson, 10*s.*; Humfrey Broke, 10*s.*; George Kevall, 10*s.*; John Langham, 10*s.*; John Turner, 10*s.*; Robert Mannsell, 10*s.*; William Charnok, 6*s.* 8*d.*; Richard Reason', 6*s.* 8*d.*; Lambert Thomas, 6*s.* 8*d.*; John Walker, 6*s.* 8*d.*; William Dermer, 6*s.* 8*d.*; William Sofftley, 6*s.* 8*d.*; Thomas Redford, 6*s.* 8*d.*; Henry Bur, 6*s.* 8*d.*; Emanuel Mannsell', 6*s.* 8*d.*; Thomas Brend, jun., 6*s.* 8*d.*; Jasper Stacy, 6*s.* 8*d.*; Peter Dewes, 6*s.* 8*d.*; John Tayllo', 6*s.* 8*d.*; Francis Kyd, 5*s.*; Richard Forster, 5*s.*; Simon Wrench, 5*s.*; William Serche, 5*s.*; Thomas Lane, 5*s.*; George Cracall', 5*s.*; William Broke, 5*s.*; Christopher Cory, 5*s.*; William Bon[ner], 5*s.*; Thomas Farrand, 3*s.* 4*d.*; Richard Ruke, 3*s.* 4*d.*;

[1] The word 'mort' written against this name.
[2] Thc words, 'It' by', prefixed to the names have been omitted, the sums are given in Arabic instead of Roman figures and the spelling of Christian names has been standardized.

Thomas Shorte, 3*s.* 4*d.*; Henry Evas, 3*s.* 4*d.* S'm Recevyd of thes scriveners 19*li.* 5*s.*

J. Dewes lent at this tyme for Wheate money xxvj*s.* viij*d.* as appereth by the p[re]ceptes.

[p. 287 *transcript*][1] John Norden, 17*s.*; Thomas Brend, 20*s.* [*altered from* 30*s.*]; Thomas Godfrey, 30*s.*; Thomas Went, 30*s.*; Barth'ue Brokesby, 30*s.*; Peter Baker, 30*s.*; John Dalton, 30*s.*; Anthony Higgons, 30*s.*; Nich'as Kyngston, 13*s.* 4*d.*; Paule Pope, 30*s.*; Thomas Browne, 30*s.*; Will'm Squyre, 30*s.*; Rafe Carkeke, 30*s.*; Will'm Aunslow, 30*s.*; Thomas [*altered from* John] Hulson, 30*s.*; Humfrey Broke, 30*s.* 22^{li}–0–4^{d}[2]

Reason, 20*s.*; Lambert Thom's, 20*s.*; Walker, 20*s.*; Softley, 20*s.*; Redford, 20*s.*; Burre, 20*s.*; Brend junior, 20*s.*; Deuyce, 20*s.*; John Taylo', 20*s.*; George Kevall, 20*s.*; Robert Mansell, 20*s.*; Serche, 20*s.*; Broke, 20*s.* 13–0–0[2]

Dermer, 13*s.* 4*d.*; E. Mansell, 13*s.* 4*d.*; Stacy, 13*s.* 4*d.*; John Turno', 13*s.* 4*d.*; Wrenche, 13*s.* 4*d.* 3–6–8[2]

Corey, 13*s.* 4*d.*; Farrand, 13*s.* 4*d.*; Kydd, 10*s.*; Lane, 10*s.*; Craycall, 10*s.*; Bonner, 6*s.* 8*d.*; Sparke, 6*s.* 8*d.*; Gunby, 6*s.* 8*d.*; Cowper, 6*s.* 8*d.*; Crafford, 5*s.* 4^{li}–8–4^{d}[2]

Sm^{a} totalis 63^{li} 5^{s} 0^{d}[2] [*recte* 63^{li} 7^{s} 0^{d}].

[p. 288 transcript] *Tempore Joh'is Norden & Thome Brend gardianor' A^{o} 1573 & A^{o} Elizabeth Reg'e A^{o} xv^{o} & xvj^{o}*

Asessement of xx poundes Levyd of the Company of the Scryveners of the Court letter of the Citie of London' by v'tue of a warrant to the same warde's directed From s^{r} Lyonell Ducket knyght then lorde mayor of the sayd Cyte Dated the [*blank*] Day [*blank*] A^{o} D'ni 1573 as folowythe viz. In p'mis lent out by Joh' Norden & Thomas Brend wardens of the sayd Company viz. by ether of the' xx^{s} xl^{s}
It' lent by Thomas Goodfrey x^{s}

Thomas Went, 10*s.*;[3] Bart. Brockesby, 10*s.*; Antony Bond, 10*s.*; Peter Baker, 10*s.*; Jhon Dalton, 10*s.*; Anthony Hyggyns, 10*s.*; Nicholas Kyngston, 10*s*; Paule Poppe, 10*s.*; Thomas Browne, 10*s.*; Thomas Stav'ton, 10*s.*; Willi'm Squier, 10*s.*; Raff' Carkeke, 10*s.*; Thomas Hulsonn', 10*s.*; Humfrey Broke, 10*s.*; Willi'm Ownslow, 10*s.*; George Kevall', 10*s.*; Jhon Langh'm, 10*s.*; Jhon Turner, 10*s.*; Robert Mannsell, 10*s.*; Willia' Charnok, 6*s.* 8*d.*; Richard Reason', 6*s.* 8*d.*; Lambert Thomas, 6*s.* 8*d.*; John Walker, 6*s.* 8*d.*; Willi'm Dermer, 6*s.* 8*d.*; Willi'm Softley, 6*s.* 8*d.*; Thomas Redford, 6*s.* 8*d.*; Henr' Bur, 6*s.* 8*d.*; Emanuell Mannsell, 6*s.* 8*d.*; Thomas Brend, Juni', 6*s.* 8*d.*; Jasp' Stacy, 6*s.* 8*d.*; Peter Dewce, 6*s.* 8*d.*; John Tayler, 6*s.* 8*d.*; Frances Kyd, 5*s.*; Rich. Forster, 5*s.*; Simon Wrenche, 5*s.*;

1 In the manuscript the names are arranged in columns and the individual sums in Roman figures.

2 This total in a different hand.

3 The names are in a column and each is prefixed by 'It' by', which is omitted here. The use of capital letters for names has been regularized. The individual sums have been converted from Roman to Arabic figures. The entries on this page of the manuscript have been scored through. The names of Stephanus Alexannder and Wilfryde [*blank*] are crossed through and no money is against them.

Willi'm Serche, 5*s.*; Thomas Lane, 5*s.*; George Crakall, 5*s.*; Willi'm Broke, 5*s.*; Chr'ofer Cory, 5*s.*; Willi'm Bon', 5*s.*; Thomas Farrand, 3*s.* 4*d.*; Richard Ruke, 3*s.* 4*d.*; Thomas Shorte, 3*s.* 4*d.*; Henry Evans, 3*s.* 4*d.* [Total: £19 5*s.* 0*d.*]

[p. 289][1] John Norden [no money stated]; Thomas Brend', 30*s.*; Thomas Goodfrey, 30*s.*; Thomas Went, 30*s.*; Bartholmewe Brokesby, 30*s.*; Peter Baker, 30*s.*; John Dalton, 30*s.*; Anthony Hyggons, 30*s.*; Nicholas Kingston, 13*s.* 4*d.* [*altered from* 30*s.*]; Paule Poppe, 30*s.*; Thomas Browne, 30*s.*; William Squier, 30*s.*; Rafe Carkett, 30*s.*; John Hulson, 30*s.*; Humfre Broke, 30*s.*; Reson, 20*s.*; Lambert Thomas, 20*s.*; Walker, 20*s.*; Softlie, 20*s.*; Redforde, 20*s.*; Bur, 20*s.*; Brend, 20*s.*; Dewce, 20*s.*; John Tayler, 20*s.*; George Kevall, 20*s.*; Robert Mannsell, 20*s.*; Serche, 20*s.*; Broke, 20*s.*; Dormer, 13*s.* 4*d.*; Emanuell Mannsell, 13*s.* 4*d.*; Staci, 13*s.* 4*d.*;[2] Wrenche, 13*s.* 4*d.*; Cori, 13*s.* 4*d.*; Farrand, 13*s.* 4*d.*; Kyd, 10*s.*; Lane, 10*s.*; Crakall, 10*s.*; Bon', 6*s.* 8*d.*;[3] Sparke, 6*s.* 8*d.*;[3] Gunby, 6*s.* 8*d.*; Cowper, 6*s.* 8*d.*; Crafforde, 5*s.*

[p. 290 transcript] *Tempor' Will'm Pyersone et Steph' Alexsanndre Gardianor'*

A sessement of Ten' poundes levyd of the Company of the Scryveners of the Courte l're of the Citie of london' by vertue of a Warrannte to the same Wardeyns derected Frome s^r^ Richard Champyon knight then Lorde Mayre of the said Citie Dated the xiiij^th^ day of February 1565 as followith/ Viz'

In primis lent by William Pyersone and Stephen Alexsanndre Wardeyns of the said Company viz by either of them x^s^ xx^s^*
It'm lent by William Blackewell x^s^*
John Lee thelder, 10*s.**;[4] John Mellsam, 6*s.* 8*d.*; Thomas Pyersone, 10*s.**; Thomas Goddfray, 10*s.**; Thomas Went, 10*s.**; John Norden, 10*s.**; Bartillmew Brokesby, 10*s.**; Thomas Wyttun, 10*s.**; Thomas Atkynson, 10*s.**; Anthony Bonde, 10*s.**; Peter Baker, 6*s.* 8*d.**; Thomas Brende, 6*s.* 8*d.*; William Charnocke, 5*s.*; Nicholas Kyngeston, 5*s.*; Anthony Hyggons, 6*s.* 8*d.*; Thomas Braddforde, 5*s.**; John Dalltun, 5*s.*; Humfry Brooke, 6*s.* 8*d.*; John Lee the Jun', 5*s.**; Frannces Bright, 5*s.*; Thomas Staffortun, 5*s.*; Wylfryde Lewty, 6*s.* 8*d.*; George Kevalle, 5*s.*

Thassistence agreed upon at o^r^ Dynner kepte at the waxchanndelers hall the xij^th^ Daie of Julie A^o^ D'ni 1569 whose names are hereunder wrytten that is to saie
Thom's Wytton & Anthony Bonde then Wardens
The assistance: Will'm Blackwell, Thom's Godfrey, Thom's Went, John

[1] This page is headed *Vacat'* and the entries, probably a draft of p. 287, have been scored through with two diagonal lines. The names are in a column. The use of capital letters for names has been regularized and the figures converted from Roman to Arabic.
[2] After this name, in the centre of the column, is the signature of Thomas Mason.
[3] Altered from [?] 10*s.*
[4] For editorial method, see footnote 3 to Common Paper p. 288 (printed p. 70). The sums followed by an asterisk are marked as paid by a different hand in the manuscript.

Norden, Barthilmew Brokesby, Thom's Atkinson, Stephen Alexander, John Dalton, Jeffry Caldwell.
Admitted into the assistance the Daie and yere above saide: Peter Baker, Thom's Brende, Anthony Higgens, Rauff Haull.[1]

[p. 291 transcript] *Tempore Thome Pierson et Thome Atkynson' Gardian'*

A sessemente of Tenne poundes levied of the Company of Scryveners of the Co'te l're of the Citie of london by vertue of warrant to the same wardens directed from Sr Rychard Malery knight then lorde Maior of the saide Citie Dated the vth of Marche A^o^. 1564 as foloweth viz.

In primis[2] lente by Thomas Pierson and Thomas Atkynson Wardens of the saide Company viz' by either of them x^s^ xx^s^
Item lente by William Blakwell x^s^

John Lee thelder, 10*s.*;[3] John Melsham, 10*s.*; Barthelmewe Brokesby, 10*s.*; Thomas Wytton, 10*s.*; Thomas Wente, 10*s.*; William Pierson, 10*s.*; John Norden, 10*s.*; Anthony Bonde, 10*s.*; Peter Baker, 5*s.*; Thomas Brende, 5*s.*; Anthony Hyggons, 5*s.*; John Dalton, 5*s.*; Humfrey Brooke, 5*s.*; Rauffe Hall', 5*s.*; Nicholas Kyngston, 5*s.*; John Lee, Jun', 5*s.*; Frannces Bryght, 5*s.*; Frannces Kydd, 2*s.* 6*d.*; Paule Pope, 5*s.*; Thomas Browne and Roberte Wylson, 10*s.*; George Kevall', 5*s.*; Wylfryde Lewtie, 5*s.*; William Onslowe, 5*s.*; Rychard Reason, 2*s.* 6*d.*; Thomas Hulson, 5*s.*; John Langham, 5*s.*

[p. 292 transcript] *Primo die mens's Aprilis A^o^ D'ni 1555: tempore Richardi Mannsell et Thome Pierson' Gard'*

A benevolence grannted by the company for the buyng of Lynnen and pewter and other thing for the forniture of o^r^ house/As hereunder doth folowe their sev'all names w^t^ their p'ticler som'es That is to say.
First Richard Mannsell and Thomas Pierson then' Wardeins either of them xx^s^. S'm xl^s^
Item Mr Will'm Blakwell then Towne clerk xx^s^

John Lee thelder, 20*s.*;[4] John Melsh'm, 13*s.* 4*d.*; John Hulson, 20*s.*; Anthony Wayte, 13*s.* 4*d.*; Thomas Godfray, 20*s.*; John Stubberd, 13*s.* 4*d.*; Thomas Atkinson, 13*s.* 4*d.*; Thomas Wente, 13*s.* 4*d.*; John Norden, 13*s.* 4*d.*; William Pierson, 13*s.* 4*d.*; Thomas Wytton, 20*s.*; Barthilmew Brokesby, 10*s.*; Thomas Brend, 10*s.*; Edward Braynewood, 13*s.* 4*d.*; John Russheborowe, 6*s.* 8*d.*; John Skampyon, 10*s.*; Ellys and Rigeley p[ar]tyners togeder, 10*s.*; Edmond Bright, 6*s.* 8*d.*; Anthony Bonde, 6*s.* 8*d.*; Humfry Broke, 5*s.*; William Sympson, 5*s.* Mighell Howman, 5*s.* Will'm Dowley, 5*s.*; Rauffe Hall, 3*s.* 4*d.*; Alexander Whitehed, 3*s.* 4*d.*; Martyn Goose,

1 The meaning of this record is doubtful; the arrangement of the names in the manuscript could mean that all the thirteen men were taken in as assistants on this day.
2 In the left-hand margin at the beginning of this line: this is paide and answered in whete the viij^th^ day of June 1566 by ordre of s^r^ Richard Champyon' knight.
3 The names are in a column and each is prefixed by 'Item by', which is omitted here; all the entries are marked as paid. The individual sums have been converted from Roman to Arabic figures.
4 The names are in a column and each is prefixed by 'It'm', which is omitted here. The individual sums have been converted from Roman to Arabic figures.

3*s.* 4*d.*; William Harlowe, 3*s.* 4*d.*; John Dalton, 3*s.* 4*d.*; Edward Petinger, 3*s.* 4*d.*; Peter Baker, 3*s.* 4*d.*; Valery Lucas, 3*s.* 4*d.*; John Wayland, 2*s.* 6*d.* [p. 293 transcript] William Bowland, 2*s.* 6*d.*; Augustyne Darrys, 2*s.*; Anthony Higons, 2*s.*; Stephan Alexander, 2*s.*; Thomas Bradforth, 2*s.*; John Lee the yonger, 2*s.*; Will'm Dawson, 1*s.* 8*d.*; Will'm Browne, 1*s.* 8*d.*; Alexander Rotherforth, 1*s.*; Nich'as Kingeston, 1*s.* 1*d.*; Will'm Charnok [*nil*].

S'm tot^{t}' xviij^{li} xiij^{s} ix^{d}

Thassistence agreed upon at o^{r} supper kepte at the waxchanndelers hall the xx^{o} Day of January A^{o} D'ni 1554. whose names be'n hereunder declared. Viz'

Richard Mannsell and Thomas Pierson then Wardeyns

Assistence: Will'm Blakwell, John Lee thelder, John Melsh'm, John Hulson, Anthony Wayte, John Stubberd, Thomas Godfray, Bartilmew Brokesby, Thomas Atkinson, Thomas Wente, Will'm Pierson, Thom's Wytton', John Norden, John Rusborough,[2] Anthony Bonde.[1]

Admytted into the Assistence at the Supper holden at Wexchandelers hall the xxiij of January 1562: Antony Bonde,[2] Wylliam Owtered,[2] Geffrey Caldwell, John Dalton.

[p. 294 transcript] *Tempore* [Joh'es, deleted] *Thom's Went* & *Willi'm Pierson'*

Money Lente unto owne Late Soveraigne Ladie Marie Late Quiene of Englande the xxjth Daye of Marche in Anno d'ni Milli'mo qui'gentesimo lviij^{o} by the Company of the Scriveners as foloweth'

Firste Lente by Thomas Godfray v^{li}.

Thomas Pierson, 5*li.*;[2] Humfrey Broke, 5*li.*; Thomas Brende, 10*li.*; Thomas Atkynson, 5*li.*; Bartylmewe Brokesby, 5*li.*; Thomas Wytton, 5*li.*; Richarde Mannsell, 3*li.* 6*s.* 8*d.*; John Norden, 5*li.*; Peter Baker, 5*li.*; John Hulson, 3*li.* 6*s.* 8*d.*; John Lee thelder, 5*li.*; John Russheboroughe, 5*li.*

66*li.* 13*s.* 4*d.*

All whyche severall som'es were Repaid unto the lenders therof the viijth daye of M'che 1559 by John Norden and Bartylmewe Brokesbye Scryveners then Wardens of the said Companye.

Money lent the xxviij day of August in Anno d'ni 1560 by the Companye of Scryveners At the camanndement of Sir Willyam Hewet knight then Lorde Maire of the Citie of London towarde A p'vision for Wheate Imprimis lent by John Norden and Bartylmewe Brokesbye Wardens of the said companye videl't by everye of them xxvj^{s} viij^{d} liij^{s} iiij^{d}. Willyam Blackwell, 26*s.* 8*d.*;[3] John Lee thelder, 26*s.* 8*d.*; John Hulson, 26*s.* 8*d.*; Thomas Pierson, 26*s.* 8*d.*; Thomas Godfrey, 26*s.* 8*d.*; Thomas Wente, 26*s.* 8*d.*; Willyam Pierson, 26*s.* 8*d.*; Thomas Wytton, 26*s.* 8*d.*;

[1] Name struck through. All the names except Bonde in the first group and Caldwell and Dalton in the second have 'mort' written against them in a different hand.

[2] The names are in a column bracketed together and the word *Vacat'* is written against the bracket. Each name is prefixed by 'It'm by', which is omitted here. The individual sums have been converted from Roman to Arabic figures.

[3] Editorial method as in preceding footnote. All the entries are marked as paid.

Thomas Atkynson, 26*s*. 8*d*.; John Russheboroughe, 26*s*. 8*d*.; Peter Baker, 20*s*.; Thomas Brende, 20*s*.; Anthony Bonde, 6*s*. 8*d*.; Nicholas Kyngeston, 6*s*. 8*d*.; Humfrey Broke, 6*s*. 8*d*.; John Lee theyonger, 6*s*. 8*d*.; John Scampyon, 6*s*. 8*d*.; Anthonye Higyng, 6*s*. 8*d*. xx^{li}.
Of whyche severall som'es Last wrytten the said wardens the xxvj day of September 1560 afforesaid repaid unto everye man the fourthe parte.

[p. 295 *transcript*] Money Lent the thirde daye of Apryll Anno d'ni 1561 by the Companye of Scryveners At the Comanndme't of Sir Willyam Chester knight Lorde Mayre of the Citie of London towarde A p'vision for Corne
Imprimis Lent by John Norden & Bartylmewe Brokesbye Wardens of the said Companye Videl't by everye of them xiij^{s}. iiij^{d}. xxvj^{s}. viij^{d}.
Item Lent by William Blackwell xiij^{s}. iiij^{d}.

John Lee thelder, 13*s*. 4*d*.;[1] John Melsham, 13*s*. 4*d*.; John Hulson, 13*s*. 4*d*.; Thomas Pyerson, 13*s*. 4*d*.; Thomas Godfrey, 13*s*. 4*d*.; Thomas Wente, 13*s*. 4*d*.; Willyam Pyerson, 13*s*. 4*d*.; Thomas Wytton, 13*s*. 4*d*.; Thomas Atkynson, 13*s*. 4*d*.; John Russhboroughe, 13*s*. 4*d*.; Peter Baker, 20*s*.; Thomas Brende, 20*s*.; John Scampyon, 13*s*. 4*d*.; Anthony Hyggyns, 13*s*. 4*d*.; Humfrey Brooke, 13*s*. 4*d*.; John Lee the yonger[2]; Anthonye Bonde;[2] Nicholas Kyngeston;[2] John Owtredde;[2] Mighell Howman, 6*s*. 8*d*.; Thomas Bradforth', 6*s*. 8*d*.; John Dalton, 6*s*. 8*d*.; Alexander Rotherforthe, 10*s*.; Paull Pope, 6*s*. 8*d*.; Wylfryde Lutye, 6*s*. 8*d*.; Rauffe Hall, 6*s*. 8*d*.; George Kevall', 6*s*. 8*d*.; Willyam Charnocke, 6*s*. 8*d*.; Frannces Kydde, 5*s*.; Willyam Layng, 5*s*.; Edward Holme, 5*s*.; Frannces Bright, 5*s*.; Frannces Seager, 3*s*. 4*d*.; Thomas Turner, 5*s*.[3]

[p. 296 transcript] *Sacru' Gardianor' in Guyhald'*

Yee shall swere that ye shall wele and truly ov'see the Craft of Scryvaners Wherof yee bee chosen wardeyns for the yere and alle the good rules and ordenannces of the same Craft that been' approved here by this Court yee shall kepe and doo to be kept And all the defautes that yee fynde in the same Craft doon' to the Chamberleyn of this Citee for the tyme beyng yee shall Wele and truly present Sparyng no man for favour ne grevyng no personne for hate Extorcion' ne wrong under colour of your office shall yee noon' Doo neither Do no thing that shal be agenst the peas or profite of oure sov'ain lorde the king or the Citee ye shall consent but for alle tymes that yee been' in office wele and laufully aftir the lawes and custumes of this Citee yee shall Doo so god you help and alle seyntes and by the book'.

Sacru' cujusl't p'sone p'stit' coram Gardianis mistere p'd'ce in sua admissione in Societatem eiusd'm mistere

I. N. of myn' owne Voluntarie Will' swere upon these holy Ev'ngelies by me bodily touched for to be true and lawefull in myn' Office and occupacion' of scryvanership of court l're and to do my diligence that alle the

[1] Editorial method as in note 2 on p. 73. All the entries are marked as paid.
[2] The sums of money against these four names have been torn away.
[3] In the left-hand margin: not Laid owte by Mr Norden.

feates the Whiche I shall make unto the seale shull be wele and lawefully made after my reason' and cunnyng And in especiall' that I shall not Write nor suffre to be Writen' by eny of myn' to my power or knowleche eny man'e feat or Writyng to be ensealed beryng date longe tyme before the makyng therof ner longe tyme after ner no blank Chartre ner other feate ensealed before the Writyng therof ner cloos l're beryng Date in ferre place ner of longe tyme Whereth[?rough][1] eny untrouthe might be felt in my consoience ner no copie of eny dede ensealed but yf it be worde by worde by good examinacion' And for noon' haast or covetise that I shall not take upon me to make any feate touchyng enheritannce ner other feate of grete charge Wherof I am not of [*word deleted*] cunnyng w^{t}out good advys and informacion' of counseill and alle the good rules and ordin'nces of the seid occupacion' or Craft I shall Wele and truly kepe and obs've unto my power as nygh' as god Woll' geve me grace So help me god [and alle Seintes and by this Book' *deleted*] and the hollye contentes of this booke [*added in a different hand*].

[1] Doubtful word. This page of the manuscript is very faint and partly worn.

BODLEIAN LIBRARY, MS. RAWLINSON D51

[Rawl. D51, p. 7 edited transcript][1] *To the Right Honourable Sir John Holles,*[2] *knight, Lord Maior of the Citty of London and the Right Worshipfull the Aldermen of the same Citty*

The humble petition of William Dodd, Master, and Francis Kemp & Robert Griffith, Wardens of the Company of Writers of the Court Letter of the City of London

Shewing That where the petitioners this yeare and the late Wardens the last yeare by severall precepts by[3] your Lordship and the Court of Aldermen for the levying of £150, £75 and £50 imposed upon their Company by act of Common Councill for the generall Plantation in Ireland, and of £73 required of them by the Iremongers (with whom they are joyned in divident)[4] for their private Plantation there, have made severall cessments upon their Company for raiseing thereof (haveing noe lands nor stocke wherewith to beare out any charge)

And the petitioners in performance of their obedience to this Court have in their owne persons upon every cessment travelled three or foure times from house to house through the City to collect the said summes to their great paines and neglect of their private affaires which they have been enforced to doe for that most of the Company (except some of the Assistants and ancients[)] have not onely refused to send in their moneys charged upon them but have also omitted to appeare at the Quarter dayes being summoned

That notwithstanding the petitioners' care and travell therein there is yet uncollected of the severall cessments £87 8*s*. 8*d*. due by the severall persons named in the noate within this petition which they refuse to pay, a great part of which money uncollected is already disbursed by the petitioners and the late Wardens in payment of the £150 and £75: and if this Court shall enjoyne us to make payment of the £50 and £73 to the Iremongers the rest of this £87 8*s*. 8*d*. must be by the petitioners also disbursed, and they remedilesse for recovery of what they have and shall disburse (except by the favour and assistance of this honourable Court releived) And if any other payments hereafter should be required either for the Irish businesse or any other occasions, the petitioners are out of hope ever to collect any more cessments, such is the disorder of the Company by reason they are not incorporate and thereby want both orders and power to governe

[1] Pp. 7–55 of this manuscript are printed in the style of an edited transcript (except pp. 32, 33 and 55 which are transcribed in full) while pp. 67–75 are in calendar form.

[2] *Recte* Sir John Jolles, Lord Mayor, 1615–16.

[3] Interpolated above the word 'for'.

[4] See John Nicholl, *Some Account of the Worshipful Company of Ironmongers* (1851), pp. 413–38, and *Londonderry and the London Companies, 1609–29* (H.M. Stationery Office, Belfast, 1928), esp. pp. 135–7.

For redresse whereof and of divers other abuses and enormities the petitioners with full consent of the ancients and Assistants of their Company have resolved to become suitors to the King's Majesty for the obteyning of a Corporation if the same may stand with the likeing of this honourable Court not doubting but thereby to reduce their Company to a more civill government amongst themselves and to a more conformable obedience to this honourable Court

And therefore humbly pray that they may have the assistance of this honourable Court for the collecting of the moneyes unpaid, And likewise that with the favour and good likeing of your Lordshipp and the Court they may proceed in their intended purpose for procureing a Corporation

And according to their duty they shall ever pray for your Lordship and Worships

[Rawl. D51, p. 8] *Jolles Maior* *Jovis xj° die Julii 1616 Annoq' xiiij° Jacobi Regis*

This day upon the humble petition of the Master and Wardens of the Company of Writers of the Court Letter of London and for the especiall causes and motives therein conteyned, And forasmuch as the petitioners have this day paid into the Chamber of London all arrearages that were unpaid by the said Company for severall taxations for the Plantation in Ireland, this Court is well pleased that the petitioners shall become suitors to the King's Majesty for the o[b]teyning of a Corporation And a draught of their intended pattent and other proceedings to be first perused and considered of by Mr Common Serjeant and Mr Stone and then the same being by them perused to be presented to this Court that the same may receive the approbation and allowance of this Court And John Savage to warne and attend them

Welde

The report of the committees

We have perused and considered the draught of the intended pattent according to the order of this honourable Court, whereunto our names are subscribed, and are of opinion that the passing of it will not be prejudiciall to the Citty or the liberties thereof, But it is very requisite to be passed for the good government of the scriveners in and about this Citty.

Tho:Jones Jo:Stone

Jolles Maior *Martis x° Septembris 1616 Annoq' Jacobi Regis xiiij°*

For asmuch as upon the reading of the Company of Scriveners for a Corporation which hath been perused and considered of by Mr Common Serjeant and Mr Stone this Court doth thinke fitt that the same be corrected and amended in some points And therefore doe order that Mr Coventry shall joyne with the said Mr Common Serjeant and Mr Stone and they to amend and carefully pen the same as they shall thinke fitt to passe, and the same pattent being by them so perused and amended and subscribed under their hands as fitting and allowable to be passed, It is thought fitt and soe ordered that the same shall remaine in the office of Mr Towne Clarke of this Citty, and that a copy thereof shall be by him delivered unto the said Company of Scriveners who thereupon may proceed with their suite to his Majestie to graunt the same unto them under seale. For effecting whereof this Court will give their best furtherance approveing of what the said Committees shall do therein

Welde

The report of all the committees

We have perused this patent and corrected the same in those points which this honourable Court did thinke fitt to be reformed And [are] of opinion that this intended patent subscribed by us may passe without prejudice to the Citty

Tho:Jones Tho:Coventrye Jo:Stone

[Rawl. D51, p. 9] *To the King's most Excellent Majesty*

The humble petition of William Dod, Master, Francis Kemp and Robert Griffith, Wardens of the Company of Scriveners of the Citty of London

Shewing That whereas the Scriveners of London tyme out of minde have been an ancient Company by reputation and in that respect are charged with all manner of taxes and payments as other Companies of the Citty which are incorporated, And of late have disbursed by order and comaundement for their parts towards the generall Plantation of Coleran & London Derry in Ireland £445 and in the private plantation of that part which is allotted unto them and others £73 in toto £523:

For raiseing whereof (haveing noe land nor stocke to beare out any charge [)] they have been forced to make severall cessments throughout the Company and many perticular persons have refused to pay the cessments alleadging that for want of a Corporation the Company is not capable to receive or hold such part in the Plantation as is or shall be allotted unto them So that there is yet uncollected of those severall cessments about £100 which the Master and Wardens that now are and their p[r]edecessors the late Wardens have disbursed out of their private estates and are likely to loose being out of hope to collect the same or any other cessment hereafter to be made for that or any other service to be comaunded them either by your Majesty or the Citty unlesse they were incorporate.

Such and so great is the disorders of the Company by reason they are not incorporated and thereby want both orders and power to governe, that the greatest part of them doe refuse to[ge]ther to appeare at their Quarter dayes or to pay quarterage or any other duties whatsoever as formerly they have done, and as all other Companyes use to do so that the Company is likely to be dissolved for want of meanes to the ancients and better sort to governe the ruder and irregular part of the same.

For redresse of which disorders and of divers other abuses and enormities And that the Company may be reduced to a settled and civill government amongst themselves and to a conformable obedience to authority over them and may be made capable to hold and enjoy such part in the Plantation in Ireland as is or shall be allotted unto them

The petitioners most humbly beseech your Royall Majesty of your accustomed clemency to vouchsafe to graunt unto them a Corporation, And that your Highnesse will be pleased to give warrant to your learned councell to draw up your Majesty's letters pattents in that behalfe, the rather for that the Lord Maior and Aldermen of your City of London have given their good likeing and consent to the petitioners to become suitors to your Majesty herein; So shall the petitioners and the whole Company [(] as in duty they are already bounden) daily pray unto the Almighty God for the long life and prosperous reigne of your Majesty over these your kingdomes

[Rawl. D51, p. 10a] *At the Court at Theobalds the Second of October 1616*

His Majesty referreth the consideration of this petition to the Lords of this most honourable Privy Councill

Daniell Dun[n]e

The reference of the Lords to the Lord Maior & Recorder of London

My Lords of the Councell thinke fitt the Lord Maior and Recorder of London consider of this petition and certifie their opinions of the conveniency of the suite.

Tho: Lake

The certificate of the Lord Maior & Recorder to the Lords

To the Right Honourable the Lords and others of his Majesty's most honourable Privy Counsell

It may please your goods [*sic*] Lordships we have considered of this petition and finde the informations therein to be true, and in respect the petitioners are and have been an ancient brotherhood of this City, and of later time growne to a greater number and many of them able men that use the said art and much employed in the services of the Citty, that they may the better governe and rule the persons useing their arte and observe orders amongst themselves We hold their suite very convenient and desire to have them incorporated if it may stand with his Majesty's good pleasure

Your Lordships most humble

Jn[o]: Jolles. Maior. H: Mountague. Recorder.

The King's warrant to . . . draw up a bill

The King's Majesty is pleased upon sight of this certificate that the said Scrivenors may be incorporated as other Companyes of London are And upon such orders and paines for their government as his Majesty's attorney or sollicitor shall thinke reasonable, And thereupon either of them to make a booke for his Majesty's signature

Tho: Lake

The docquett to the bill signed under the King's sollicitor's hand

It may please your excellent Majesty—

Whereas the Scriveners of London being by reputation onely an ancient fraternity did humb[l]y petition your Majesty to be graciously pleased to incorporate them whereby they might be invested as well with power to redresse the abuses now practiced in that Company, As with capacity to take such lands as should be allotted them in the late Plantation in Ireland wherein they had bin equally charged with other Companies of the said Citty.

The consideration of which petition was by your Majesty referred to the Lords of your most honourable Privy Councell and by them to the Lord Maior and the now Lord Cheife Justice then being Recorder of London to certefie their opinions of the [Rawl. D51, p. 11] conveniency of that suite who accordingly did certefie they held the same convenient and desired also they might be incorporated.

Your Majestie thereupon is graciously pleased hereby to incorporate the said Scrivenors and to enable them with government over all persons useing that art within London and the liberties and three miles thereof, and with power to take lands to them and their successors not holden in capite or knight service to the value of two hundred markes per annum, And with such other clauses as are used in graunts of this nature

Signified to be your Majesty's pleasure by the Right Honourable
Sir Thomas Lake, knight, one of your Majesty's principall secretaries
Henry Yelverton

[Rawl. D51, p. 10c][1] *James* by the grace of God King of England Scotland France and Ireland defender of the faith &c *To all* to whome these present letters shall come, greeting *Whereas* the freemen of our Cittie of London and the suburbs of the same commonly called Writers of the Court Letter of the Cittie of London in times past and from the time whereof the memory of man is not to the contrary were and as yett are an ancient Society and fraternity of the Cittie aforesaid, and the men useing the art within the same Cittie are increased into a greater number then heretofore and very many of them are very often used and exercised in very hard matters and businesses of great moment and much trust within the same Cittie

Know yee that we for the embettering [In the margin: *The constitution of the Corporation*] and amendment of the estate of our people of the Society or fraternity aforesaid, and for the good rule and better government of all men useing the science, art or mistery of scrivenors within our Cittie of London and the libertyes and suburbs of the same and also within the circuit of three miles of the same Cittie of our especiall grace, and of our certaine knowledg and meer motion *Have* granted and given full power and authority and by these presents doe grant and give full power and authority for us our heires and successors to our beloved and faithfull liege people and subjects all the freemen of the science art or mistery of scrivenors of our Cittie of London and the suburbs of the same and by these presents will

[1] P. 10b is blank. This is the first page of the translation of the charter of incorporation of the Company of Scriveners of the City of London, 28 January 1616/17, as given in Rawl. D51. The Latin version commences on p. 11 of Rawl. D51 and is continued on pp. 12, 15, 16, 19, 20, 23, 24, 27, 28 and 31. A translation of the charter as the same was read in the Court of Common Council, 6 May 1752, upon passing the Act for regulating the Company of Scriveners, has been printed by the Company, and a copy is given to each member on his admission; an epitome of the charter is in City of London Livery Companies' Commission, *Report and Appendix*, vol. 3 (1884), pp. 756, 757.

and ordaine, and for us our heires and successors grant appoynt and declare that they from henceforth for ever may and shalbe [Rawl. D51, p. 13] one body corporate and politique of themselves in matter deed and name and one perpetuall Society and commonalty incorporate by the name of The Master Wardens and Assistants of the Company of Scrivenors of the Cittie of London. And them by the name of the Master Wardens and Assistants of the Company of Scriveners of the Cittie of London a body corporate and politique forever really and to the full in and by all things for us our heires and successors doe erect ordaine make create appoynt and establish by these presents. And that they by the same name of [In the margin: *Perpetual Succession*] Master Wardens and Assistants of the Company of Scrivenors of the Cittie of London may have perpetuall succession. And that they and their successors (from henceforth forever) [In the margin: *The name of the Corporation*] shalbe named and called by the name of Master Wardens and Assistants of the Company of Scrivenors of the Cittie of London. And that they by the name of Master Wardens and Assistants of the Company of Scrivenors of the Cittie of London may and shalbe in times perpetuall and to come persons able and capable in law to have purchase receive possesse and enjoy to them and their successors in fee as well mannors messuages lands tenements libertyes, priviledges [In the margin: *Power to purchase*] jurisdictions franchizes rents rectorys tythes revenues and other hereditaments whatsoever and also to give grant sell demise assigne and dispose the said mannors messuages lands tenements hereditaments goods and chattells or any parcell or parcells thereof from time to time. And all and singular deeds writings and things necessary about the same to performe doe seale and execute at their will and pleasure. And that they by the name of the Master Wardens and Assistants of the Company of Scriveners of the Cittie of London [In the margin: *Power to plead and be impleaded*] may plead and be impleaded and may be able and have power to answer and be answered defend and be defended before whatsoever judges and justices and other officers and ministers of us our heires and successors and other persons whatsoever in whatsoever courts and places in all and singular matters suites pleas complaints actions demaunds and causes whatsoever of whatsoever kinde nature condition or sort they be and in as ample manner and forme as any other or subjects of this our realme of England being persons able or capable in law may and can plead and be impleaded answer and be answered, defend and be defended and have receive possesse give grant and demise. [In the margin: *That they may have a common seal*] And that they the said Master Wardens and Assistants of the Company of Scriveners of the Cittie of London may have forever a common seal for themselves and their successors to serve for the doing and sealing their causes things and businesses whatsoever. And that it may and shalbe lawfull to the said Master Wardens and Assistants of the Company aforesaid and their successors the same seale at their will and pleasure from time to time to break spoyle change and new make as to them shall be thought fitt and expedient

And further of our more abundant grace [In the margin: *That there be a Master and two Wardens*] we will and ordaine for us our heires and successors by these presents that from henceforth forever in times to come there may and shalbe one Master and two Wardens of the aforesaid Company of Scrivenors of the Cittie of London to rule and governe that Company and the men of the same Company and all things matters causes and businesses touching or concerning that Company, to be chosen and appoynted in manner and forme in these our letters patents specified and limitted

And furthermore [In the margin: *That there be 27 assistants*] for the better assistance and councell of the Master and Wardens of the Company aforesaid for the time being in and about the execution of their severall offices aforesaid of our more abundant grace we will and ordaine for us our heires and successors [Rawl. D51, p. 14] by these presents that from henceforth forever there may and shalbe twenty seaven men discreet and very honest persons of the same Company (vizt) the Master and Wardens of the aforesaid Company for the time being and twenty four other persons of the Company aforesaid who shall be and shall be called Assistants of that Company for all matters causes and businesses touching or concerning that Company and the good rule state and government of the same Company to be chosen and appoynted in manner and forme in these our letters pattents specified and limitted. And that the said twenty and four men from time to time shallbe assisting aiding and councelling to the said Master and Wardens of the Company aforesaid for the time being in all things and businesses touching or concerning the Company aforesaid (as is aforesaid[)]

And besides for the better execution of the premisses and of our commands and grant in that behalfe, [In the margin: *The nomination of the first Master*], and for the good government and rule of the Company aforesaid of our more abundant grace aforesaid we have assigned named created ordained and appoynted, and by these presents for us our heires and successors doe assigne name create ordaine and appoynt our beloved subject William Dod gentleman one of the aforesaid Company to be the first and moderne Master of the aforesaid Company of Scrivenors of the Cittie of London, making oath before the Maior of our Cittie of London to exercise that office faithfully and honestly. Willing that the aforesaid William Dodd shalbe and remayne Master of the Company aforesaid from the day of the date of these presents untill Tuesday next after the feast of St. James the Apostle next following, and from the same Tuesday untill another fitt and discreet person of the same Company shalbe chosen into the office of Master of that Company, and shall make his oath to exercise that office according to the ordinances and provisions in these our letters patents specified and limitted, if the aforesaid William shall soe long live

And for the considerations aforesaid [In the margin: *The nomination of the first Wardens*] we have assigned nominated created ordained and appoynted and by these presents for us our heires and successors doe assigne nominate create ordaine and appoynt our beloved and faithfull subjects Francis Kempe gent: and Robert Griffith gent: being of the Company aforesaid to be the first and moderne Wardens of the aforesaid Company of Scrivenors of the Cittie of London, either of them likewise making oath before the Maior of the Cittie of London respectively to exercise their office faithfully and honestly, willing also that they the said Francis Kempe and Robert Griffith shalbe and remayne Wardens of the Company aforesaid from the day of the date of these presents untill the aforesaid Tuesday next after the aforesaid feast of St. James the Apostle next following, and from the same Tuesday untill two other fitt and discreet persons of the same Company shalbe chosen into the offices of Wardens of that Company, and shall make their oathes to exercise those offices according to the ordinances and provisions in these our letters patents expressed and limitted, if they the said Francis and Robert soe long shall live

And also we have assigned nominated created ordained and appoynted [In the margin: *The nomination of the first Assistants*] and by these presents for us our heires and successors doe assigne nominate create ordaine and appoynt the aforesaid William Dodd, Francis Kempe and Robert Griffith, and our well beloved subjects John Mayle, esq., Thomas Chapman, George Samdwell, Thomas Fitch, Andrew Turner, Edward Ledsham, John Partridg, Robert Banckeworth, Jeoffry Place, Henry Best, Robert Hill, Robert Morgan, Peter Bower, Edward White, William Hickes, Godfrey Reyner, George Hill, James Colebrand, Charles Bostock, Francis Strange, John Halliwell, Richard Wotton, William Child and John Woodward [Rawl. D51, p. 17] being of the Company aforesaid to be the first and moderne Assistants of the Company aforesaid, every one of the aforesaid William Dodd, Francis Kempe and Robert Griffith making oath before the Maior of our Cittie of London aforesaid and every one of the aforesaid other Assistants making oath before the aforesaid Master and Wardens of that Company or any two of them to exercise their severall offices and places aforesaid faithfully and honestly. Willing that the aforesaid William Dodd, Francis Kempe, Robert Griffith, John Mayle, Thomas Chapman, George Samwell, Thomas Fitch, Andrew Turner, Edward Ledsham, John Partridg, Robert Banckworth, Jeoffrey Place, Henry Best, Robert Hill, Robert Morgan, Peter Blower, Edward White, William Hickes, Godfrey Reyner, George Hill, James Colebrond, Charles Bostock, Francis Strange, John Holliwell, Richard Wotton, William Childe and John Woodward shalbe & remayne Assistants of the Company aforesaid for and dureing their naturall lives respectively unless any one or any more of them for any reasonable causes by the Master and Wardens and the greater part of the Assistants of the Company aforesaid for the time being, shalbe amoved and dismissed from his or their office or offices aforesaid

And further we have given and granted [In the margin: *Power to choose a Clerk and Beadle and to amove them*] and by these presents for us our heires and successors doe give and grant to the aforesaid Master, Wardens and Assistants of the Company of Scrivenors of the Cittie of London and their successors full power and authority that the Master and Wardens of the Company aforesaid and the rest of the Assistants of the same Company for the time being or the greatest part of them shall and may choose and nominate one Clerk and one Beadle or Bayliff from time to time as often and whensoever it shall please them, to serve the Master, Wardens and Assistants of the Company aforesaid for the time being in their commands and lawfull businesses whatsoever and that they shall and may from time to time for reasonable cause moveing the Master and Wardens of the Company aforesaid or the greater part of them amove and deprive them the said Clerk and Beadle or Bayliff or either of them from their offices or places.

We will also and for us our heires and successors [In the margin: *That all useing the art of scrivenors who are not freemen of some other mistery shalbe contributory with the freemen of the mistery of scrivenors in all payments*] doe grant by these presents to the aforesaid Master, Wardens and Assistants of the Company of Scrivenors of the Cittie of London and their successors that all strangers and forreigners as well outlandish as home borne and all other persons inhabiting within our Cittie of London, libertyes and suburbs of the same and within the circuit or precinct of three miles of the same Cittie, and occupying useing or exercising the mistery or art aforesaid which are not freemen of some other mistery or Company of the Cittie of London aforesaid, shall and may be from henceforth contributory with the freemen of the Company aforesaid in all payments as well to us our heires and successors, as also in the maintenance and sustentation of the art or mistery aforesaid, and shall pay and beare all such and the like charges and payments as our subjects the free men of the Company aforesaid doe pay or have accustomed or ought to pay.

We also ordaine and of our [In the margin: *That all useing the art of scrivenors shall pay* 2*s.* 8*d. by the yeare for quarterage*] like grace for the amendment and better support of the state of our people of the Company aforesaid for us our heires and successors by these presents doe give [Rawl. D51, p. 18] and grant to the aforesaid Master, Wardens and Assistants of the Company of Scrivenors of the Cittie of London and their successors that all men of the Company aforesaid and all other persons inhabiting or abodeing within our Cittie of London the libertyes and suburbs of the same, and within the aforesaid circuit or precinct of three miles of the same Cittie and occupying useing or exercising the mistery or art aforesaid shall from henceforth forever yearly pay to the Master, Wardens and Assistants of the Company of Scrivenors of the Cittie of London and their successors a yearly payment of two shillings and eight pence by the yeare at the four most usuall feasts in the Cittie of London (vizt) at the feast of the Annuntiac'on of the Blessed Virgine Mary, the Nativity of St. John Baptist, St. Michaell the Archangell, and the Birth of our Lord by equall portions to be paid (to witt) at every feast of the feasts aforesaid eight pence being an ancient payment and duty called quarterage of the freemen of the Company of the fraternity of Writers of the Court Letter of the Cittie of London to the Master or Wardens from the same fraternity from times past due and paid

And that the aforesaid Master, Wardens and Assistants of the Company of Scrivenors of the Cittie of London and their successors [In the margin: *That the Master, Wardens and Assistants may levy the same by distress*] may and shall have full power and authority from time to time forever to have receive require demand collect and by distresse and distresses to levy to their proper uses of and from all persons of the Company aforesaid and of and from all other persons whatsoever inhabiting or abideing within our Cittie of London the libertyes and suburbs of the same and within the aforesaid circuit or precinct of three miles of the same Cittie and occupying useing or exerciseing the mistery or art aforesaid, the aforesaid yearly payment of two shillings and eight pence by the yeare.

And further [In the margin: *That they may have a Common Hall*] of our more ample grace we will and by these presents for us our heires and successors doe give and grant to the aforesaid Master, Wardens and Assistants of the Company of Scrivenors of the Cittie of London and their successors that they the said Master, Wardens and Assistants of the Company of Scrivenors of the Cittie of London and their successors from henceforth forever may have a Common Hall or Councell House in some convenient place within our said Cittie of London and the libertyes of the same Cittie, and that it shall and may be lawfull to them the said Master, Wardens and Assistants of the Company of Scrivenors of the Cittie of London and to all the freemen of the Company and to all other persons inhabiting or abiding within our Cittie of London the libertyes and suburbs of the same and within the aforesaid circuit or precinct of three miles of the same Cittie and occupying useing or exerciseing the mistery or art aforesaid from time to time to meet appeare & gather themselves together in the Hall or Councell House aforesaid, or within any other convenient house in the said Cittie the libertyes of the same soe often & when as & whensoever & wheresoever it shall seeme to be expedient & necessary to the Master, Wardens & Assistants of the Company aforesaid & their successors

And that [In the margin: *And have power to keep their antient customes and lawfull ordinances*] the aforesaid Master, Wardens & Assistants of the Company of Scrivenors of the Cittie of London & their successors from henceforth forever shall & may not only have hold & enjoy to them & their successors all their ancient customes and lawfull ordinances heretofore in any wise granted to them or their successors or by them or their predecessors or by the Writers of the Court Letter of our Cittie of London or by whatsoever other name they are called or named, heretofore used or enjoyed for the good rule and government of the freemen of the mistery art or science of Scrivenors of the Cittie of London but also that the Master and [Rawl. D51, p. 21. In the margin: *And may make other constitutions &c.*] Wardens of the Company aforesaid, and the rest of the Assistants of the same Company for the time being or the greater part of them from time to time from henceforth forever for the wholsome rule and better government of the Company aforesaid as often as shall please them, shall and may lawfully and unpunishably ordaine establish and make other lawes rules orders constitutions and reasonable ordinances and agreeable to the lawes and statutes of our realme of England according to their sound discretions for the profitt of the Company aforesaid and for other lawfull causes. And [In the margin: *And put the same in execution*] the same statutes constitution and ordinances from time to time may put or cause to be put in execution without molestation disturbance impeachment or impediment of us our heires or successors or of any our justices maiors sherriffs or other offices or ministers whatsoever (any statute act ordinance custome or use to the contrary thereof in any wise notwithstanding[)] And the same statutes constitutions and [In the margin: *And revoak the same*] ordinances soe had and made or any of them from time to time change revoak and adnihilate as to them or the greater part of them shall seem to be convenient and expedient

And also we will and for us our heires and successors doe grant by [In the margin: *Power to tax all useing the art aforesaid who are not freemen*

of some other mistery for the support & maintenance of the Company aforesaid] these presents to the aforesaid Master, Wardens and Assistants of the Company of Scrivenors of the Cittie of London and their successors that the Master and Wardens of the Company aforesaid and the rest of the Assistants of the same Company for the time being or the greater part of them from time to time may and shall have full power and authority to impose and tax such reasonable payments taxations impositions and summes of money whatsoever upon the severall persons of the Company aforesaid, all other persons useing the science art or mistery aforesaid within our Cittie of London the suburbs and libertyes of the same Cittie & within three miles of the same Cittie who are not freemen of some other Company or Mistery of the Cittie aforesaid, as to them the said Master and Wardens and the rest of the Assistants of the Company aforesaid for the time being or the greater part of them shall seeme to be necessary and convenient for the supportation maintenance good rule and sound government of that Company

And further of [In the margin: *Power to tax fines upon all useing the art aforesaid for not appearing or for not fulfilling the orders & to levy them by distresse*] our more abundant grace certaine knowledg and meer motion we have ordained and for us our heires and successors doe by these presents grant to the aforesaid Master, Wardens and Assistants of the Company of Scriveners of the Cittie of London and their successors That if any person of the same Company or any other person useing or occupying the art science or mistery aforesaid within the said Cittie of London or the libertyes of the same or within three miles of the same Cittie shalbe summoned by the officer or minister of that Company to appeare at any court or assembly by the Master or Wardens of the Company aforesaid for the time being in any certaine place within the same Cittie of London or the libertyes of the same hereafter (as is aforesaid) to be holden or appoynted, and such person soe summoned shall not appeare at the day hour and place soe appoynted not having lawfull or reasonable cause or excuse by the Master and Wardens of the Company aforesaid and the rest of the Assistants of that Company for the time being or the greater part of them to be allowed Or if any person of the same Company or any other person useing the art science or mistery aforesaid within the said Cittie of London the suburbs and libertyes of the same Cittie or within three miles of the same Cittie shall refuse to pay or shall not pay [Rawl. D51, p. 22] all impositions payments taxations or summes of money upon him or them (as is aforesaid) reasonably taxed and imposed or hereafter to be taxed or imposed or shall not fulfill all just and lawfull statutes acts ordinances and constitutions by the Master and Wardens of the Company aforesaid and the rest of the Assistants of that Company for the time being or the greater part of them made or hereafter to be made, but shall infringe the same just and lawfull statutes acts ordinances or constitutions or any of them that then and soe often it shall and may be lawfull to the Master and Wardens of the Company aforesaid and the rest of the Assistants of that Company for the time being or the greater part of them from time to time to impose assesse and tax upon every such person and persons so delinquent, all such fines amerciaments and summes of money whatsoever for his or their offence or contempt in that behalfe, as to the Master and Wardens of the Company aforesaid and the rest of the Assistants of that Company for the time being or the greater part of them shall seeme to be necessary and convenient. And that it shall and may be lawfull to the Master and Wardens of the Company aforesaid and the rest of the Assistants of that Company for the time being or the greater part of them from time to time soe often and when as it shall please them to assess & distreyne as well all the freemen of that Company as all strangers and forreigners and other persons whatsoever dwelling within the said Cittie of London and the libertyes of the same or within the aforesaid circuit or precinct of three miles of the same Cittie and occupying useing or exerciseing the mistery or art aforesaid and not being free men of some other Company or mistery of the Cittie aforesaid, and the fines & amerciaments aforesaid and also all other payments taxations impositions and summes of money whatsoever upon them or any of them from time to time imposed and taxed, or to be imposed or taxed may and shall levy and collect the same by distresse and convert unto the proper use of the Company aforesaid lawfully and unpunishably without the molestation disturbance or burthen of us our heires or successors or of whatsoever justices escheators sherriffs bailiffs or other our officers ministers or subjects whatsoever

And further [In the margin: *Power to choose Master & Wardens yearly*] of our more ample grace and of our certaine knowledg and meer motion we will and ordaine and for us our heires & successors doe grant by these presents to the Master, Wardens and Assistants of the Company of Scriveners of the Cittie of London and their successors full power and authority that the Master and Wardens of the Company aforesaid and the rest of the Assistants of the same Company for the time being or the greater part of them yearly from time to time hereafter upon Tuesday next after the feast of St. James the Apostle in every yeare or at any other time when it shall seeme to them more necessary and fitt shall and may come and choose one fitt & discreet person of the Assistants of the Company aforesaid to be Master of the Company And also two other fitt and discreet persons of the Assistants of the Company aforesaid to be Wardens of that Company to rule governe and oversee the Company aforesaid and all the aforesaid men of the art or mistery aforesaid their servants and apprentices. Every one of them makeing oath before the Master and Wardens next precedent or any two of them or before the greater number of the Assistants of the same Company to exercise and execute their severall offices respectively well and faithfully in all things, and that they the said Master and Wardens soe newly nominated elected and sworne shall and may exercise their severall offices aforesaid for one whole yeare then next following and from thenceforth untill some others in the severall offices aforesaid respectively [Rawl. D51, p. 25] shall be of new nominated elected and sworne according to the tenor and effect of these presents

We will also and by these presents for us our heires and successors [In the margin: *Power to choose Master or Wardens after the amovall or death of any one within the yeare*] doe ordaine and grant that soe and as often whensoever it shall happen the Master or Wardens of the Company aforesaid for the time being or any of them to dye and depart out of this life or otherwise to be amoved from their offices for some reasonable cause before the end of the same yeare in which (as is aforesaid) he or they shalbe nominated and elected (whome we will shall be amoveable by the Master and Wardens of the Company aforesaid) who be in their offices aforesaid and by the rest of the Assistants of the Company aforesaid for the time being or the greater part of them for reasonable cause That then and soe often it shall and may be lawfull to the Master, Warden or Wardens of the Company aforesaid and the Assistants of the same Company then for the time being in full life, and in his or their office or offices or the greater part of them, within fourteene dayes next after the death or amoveall of such Master, Warden or Wardens to nominate and new elect some other fitt and discreet person or persons of the aforesaid number of Assistants in the place and stead of the same person or persons soe dead or amoved, and that he or they soe newly nominated and elected makeing oath in forme aforesaid shall and may exercise and execute that or those office or offices respectively for the residue of the same yeare and from thenceforth untill some other or others shalbe nominated and elected to the same offices according to the tenor and effect of these presents

We will also and of our like grace doe ordaine [In the margin: *To choose Assistants within three months after the death or amoveall of another*] that soe and as often and whensoever it shall happen one or more of the Assistants of the Company aforesaid for the time being to dye or be amoved from his office or place for some reasonable cause (as is aforesaid) whome we will shalbe amoveable by the Master and Wardens of the Company aforesaid and the rest of the Assistants of that Company for the time being or the greater part of them for reasonable cause, That then and soe often it shall and may be lawfull to the Master and Wardens of the Company aforesaid and the rest of the Assistants of the same Company then being in full life and in his or their office or offices, or the greater part of them within three monthes after the death or amoveall of such person from time to time to nominate and choose a new one or more other fitt person or persons of the freemen of the commonalty or Company aforesaid in the place or stead of the same person or persons soe dead or amoved, And that every such person soe nominated and elected makeing his oath before the Master and Wardens of the Company aforesaid for the time being or any two of them to exercise that office or place honestly and faithfully, shalbe one of the Assistants of the Company aforesaid for terme of the life of every such person untill he be amoved from that office for reasonable cause by the Master and Wardens and the rest of the Assistants of the Company aforesaid for the time being or the greater part of them (as is aforesaid)

And further we will and for us our heires and successors doe grant [In the margin: *A grant to hold lands and tenements, goods and chattells formerly purchased*] to the aforesaid Master, Wardens and Assistants of the Company of Scrivenors of the Cittie of London and their successors that they the said Master, Wardens and Assistants of the Company aforesaid and their successors from henceforth forever shall and may have and enjoy to them and [Rawl. D51, p. 26] their successors all goods and chattells, lands, tenements, possessions and hereditaments whatsoever which they now have hold enjoy and possesse, and which their predecessors the Master, Keepers or Wardens and Comminalty of freemen of the science art or mistery of Writers of the Court Letter of the Cittie of London and the suburbs of the same or by whatsoever other name they are called or named heretofore have had held enjoyed or possessed or ought to have hold enjoy or possesse or of which any person or persons is or was, are or were seized to the use of the Master, Keepers or Wardens or Commonalty of freemen of the science art or mistery of Writers of the Court Letter of the Cittie of London and suburbs of the same

And further know ye that we [In the margin: *Licence to purchase lands, tenements, goods & chattells*] in consideration that the said Master, Wardens and Assistants of the Company of Scrivenors of the Cittie of London and their successors shall and may the better beare and support the charges of that Company from time to time of our more ample especiall grace certaine knowledg and meer motion have granted and given licence, and for us our heires and successors doe by these presents grant and give licence and lawfull faculty power and authority to the Master, Wardens and Assistants of the Company of Scrivenors of the Cittie of London and their successors that they and their successors from time to time lawfully and unpunishably shall and may purchase receive and obtaine to them and their successors forever, as well of us our heires and successors, as of whatsoever person or persons, any messuages burgages lands tenements libertyes priviledges jurisdictions franchizes rents rectoryes tythes revenues and other possessions and hereditaments whatsoever which are not imediately holden of us our heires or successors in cheife by knights service nor are holden of us our heires or successors or any other or others by knights service without our lycence or of our heires or successors soe as such lands tenements and hereditaments soe (as is aforesaid) hereafter to be purchased and obteyned doe not exceed the cleer yearly value of two hundred marks by the yeare besides all charges and reprizes. And [In the margin: *The value of land in mortmaine*] that they the said Master, Wardens and Assistants of the Company aforesaid and their successors all and singular the same lands tenements & hereditaments heretofore (as is aforesaid) obtained or hereafter (as is aforesaid) to be purchased and obtained shall and may from time to time demise lett grant sell charge and at their pleasure dispose [In the margin: *Licence to demise & dispose of lands and tenements*] as to them shall seeme to be most expedient (The statute of lands and tenements not to be put to mortmaine or any other statute act ordinance provision or restraint to the contrary thereof made published ordained and provided or any other thing cause or matter whatsoever in any wise notwithstanding)

And further wee will and for us our heires and successors doe by these presents grant [In the margin: *A grant to enjoy all grants, priviledges, customes antiently used & granted*] to the aforesaid Master, Wardens and Assistants of the Company of Scrivenors of the Cittie of London and their successors that they the said Master, Wardens and Assistants of the Company of Scrivenors of the Cittie of London and their successors from time to time hereafter shall and may from henceforth forever use have hold and enjoy to them and their successors all and singular the same and such like lands tenements possessions hereditaments franchizes priviledges exemptions admittance jurisdictions ordinances and reasonable customes which the Master and Wardens or Keepers and Commonalty of freemen of the science art or mistery [Rawl. D51, p. 29] of Writers of the Court Letter of the Cittie of London and the subjects of the same within the Cittie aforesaid or within the suburbs of the same Cittie at the time of the makeing of these presents had, or they or their predecessors or the freemen of the aforesaid science art or mistery or the Master, Wardens & Assistants of the science art or mistery of Writers of the Court Letter of the Cittie of London aforesaid and the suburbs of the same within the same Cittie of London by whatsoever names or whatsoever name, by whatsoever corporation, or by colour of whatsoever corporation, before these times have or hath had possessed held or enjoyed or ought to have enjoy use or hold by reason or colour of any charters or letters patents in any wise heretofore made granted or confirmed by us or any of our progenitors kings or queenes of this our realme of England or by whatsoever other lawfull meanes right custome use prescription or title heretofore used had or accustomed (Any thing cause or matter whatsoever to the contrary thereof in any wise notwithstanding[)]

And further of our more ample grace [In the margin: *Power to search & oversee within three miles aswell freemen as forreignors useing the art aforesaid*] and of our certaine knowledg and meer motion we will and doe grant by these presents for us our heires and successors to the aforesaid Master, Wardens and Assistants of the Company of Scrivenors of the Cittie of London and their successors full and whole power and authority that the said Master, Wardens & Assistants of the Company aforesaid and their successors or six of them at the most whereof we will the Master or Wardens of the Company aforesaid for the time being or some of them to be alwayes one, shall and may forever enjoy and exercise within our aforesaid Cittie of London the libertyes and suburbs of the same, and within our Cittie of Westminster and the libertyes of the same, the burrough of Southwark, the precinct of St. Katherines near the Tower of London, and in all other places within three miles every way about the said Cittie of London the full and whole survey search examination correction punishment and government as well of all and singular the freemen of the said Cittie of London, as also of all and singular other men forreigners within the said Cities of London and Westminster and the libertyes and suburbs of the same, the burrough of Southwarke and precinct of St. Katherines aswell within libertyes as without in any wise useing and frequenting the said science art or mistery of Scrivenors or publiquely or openly makeing and writing any evidences charters deeds or writeings to be sealed within the same Citties the libertyes and suburbs of the same and places aforesaid or any of them, or elsewhere in any other place not distant above three miles from the said Cittie of London.

And that the Master and Wardens of the Company aforesaid and the rest of the Assistants of the same Company [In the margin: *Power to punish all offending in the art & to levy fines and amerciaments on such persons by distress*] for the time being or the greater part of them from time to time forever shall and may have full power and authority to punish and correct all men, as well freemen of the said Cittie of London as also strangers and forreigners (as is premised) frequenting or useing the science art or mistery of Scrivenors as well within the said Cittie of London and suburbs of the same and places aforesaid as within the aforesaid limitts or distance of three miles every way about the said Cittie of London for their defaults in insufficiently doeing executing and useing the science art or mistery aforesaid and to correct and amend the defaults in the same science art or mistery (if any shalbe found) [Rawl. D51, p. 30] according to their sound discretions, and to tax reasonable fines and amerciaments upon whatsoever delinquents according to the exigency of the same faults, and the same to levy collect and take to the proper uses of them and their successors by distresses And further to doe as they shall think fitt for the most proffitt of the Company aforesaid and of our people Although expresse mention is not made in these presents of the true yearly value or of the certainty of the premisses or any of them, or of other gifts or grants before these times made by us or any of our progenitors or predicessors to the aforesaid Master, Wardens and Assistants of the Company of Scrivenors of the Cittie of London or any statute act ordinance provision proclamation or restraint to the contrary thereof heretofore had made published ordained or provided or any other thing cause or matter whatsoever in any wise notwithstanding

In witnes whereof we have caused these our letters to be made patents Witnes our selfe at Westminster the eight and twentyth day of January in the fourteenth yeare of our raigne of England France and Ireland, and of Scotland the fiftyth.

By writt of privy seale &c.

[Rawl. D51, p. 32 transcript] *Leman Maior.*

Vicesimo Septimo die Februarii 1616

The Oath of William Dodd and Francis Kemp and Robert Griffith as Master and Wardens & as Assistants of ye Society

This day appeared before the Right hono^ble^ the Lord Maior of the City of London William Dod Francis Kemp and Robert Griffith Gent, all three of them free of the Society of ye Writers of the City of London and presented unto his Lordship his Ma^ts^: Letters Patents bearing date at Westminster the Eight and Twentieth day of January now last past By which it appeareth the said William Dod to be assigned and constituted the first and Moderne Master of the same Society to remaine therein from the day of the date of the same Letters Patents untill ye Tuesday next after the Feast of St James Thapostle now next ensuing, And from that Tuesday untill another fit and discreet person of the same Society shall be chosen to be Master thereof And it also appeareth by the same Letters Pattents that the said Francis Kemp and Robert Griffith are named and appointed to be the first and Moderne Wardens of the said Society to continue for the tyme aforesaid. And moreover the said William Dod Francis Kempe and Robert Griffith are therein named and assigned three of the first and Moderne Assistants of the said Society respectively dureing their naturall Lives unles for cause reasonable they shall be amoved And thereupon every of them severally and respectively accordingly as they are limitted in and by the said Letters Patents did take their corporall Oathes before his Lordshipp as

Master and Wardens and as assistants of the said Society faithfully and honestly to execute their severall places dureing so long time as every of them shall severally continue in them.

Examinatur p'me Hambletum Clarke

To the Right hono^ble^ Francis Lord Verulam Lord Chancellor of England

The humble Petic'on of the Master Wardens and Assistants of the Society of Scrivenors of the Citty of London

Shewing That the Petic'oners being an Auncient Brotherhood of the said Citty and lately by his Majesties Letters Patents dated xxviij^{o} Januarii xiij^{o} Jacobi[1] incorporated they have reduced into a Booke divers auncient Ordinances and Orders by their Predecessors heretofore made, and some others by the Petic'oners lately framed, all for the well ordering and good Government of the said Society which they humbly present unto your good Lordshipp, referring the reformac'on and alterac'on of them to your hono^{ble} Wisdome, And humbly craveing your Lordships allowance and approbac'on of them with the two Cheife Justices according to the Statute [Rawl. D51, p. 33] of xix^{o} Henrici Septimi.

And your Petic'on^{rs}: as in duty they are bound shall daily pray for the happy State of Your Lords^{p}: with increase of honor long to continue

The Lord Chancello^{rs} Reference to the Cheife Justices

I desire my Lords the two Cheife Justices first to peruse and consider of them and to deliver me their opinions xij^{o}. Octob: 1618

Fra: Verulam. Can.

The Cheife Justices Opinions of ye Ordinances

Perused by me Henry Mountague And these Ordinances as now they are I hold fitt to passe H Mountagu

I have perused them and thinke they may well passe H: Hobart.

The Lord Chancello^{rs} Warrant for ingrossing them

xxj^{o} Januarii 1618. Upon the two Lord Cheife Justices opinions let these constituc'ons be ingrossed. Fr. Verulam Canc.

[Rawl. D51, p. 34 edited transcript][2] *To all to whome* these presents shall come Francis Lord Verulam, Lord Chancellor of England, Sir Henry Mountagu, Knight, cheife justice assigned to hold pleas before our Soveraigne Lord the King, and Sir Henry Hobart, Knight and Baronett, cheife justice of the court of com[m]on pleas send greeting.

Whereas in and by a certaine Act of Parliament holden at Westminster the sixteenth day of January in the nineteenth yeare of the reigne of the late most noble prince King Henry the Seaventh, it was amongst other things ordeyned established and enacted, That no Master Wardens and

[1] Scribal error for 14 James I.

[2] Extracts from the ordinances are printed in City of London Livery Companies' Commission, *Report and Appendix*, vol. 3 (1884), pp. 757–8. A translation of the charter and a transcript of the ordinances by Jeremiah Bentham, Clerk of the Company, has also been printed; a copy is handed to each liveryman on taking his oath.

Fellowships of crafts or misteries nor any of them nor any rulers of guilds or fraternities after the feast of Pentecoste in the same Act mentioned should take upon them to make any acts or ordinances nor to execute any acts or ordinances by them before the said Act made in disinheritance or diminution of the prerogative of the King nor of other nor against the common proffitt of the people, but if the same acts or ordinances be examined and approved by the Chancellor, Treasurer of England or cheife justices of either benches or three of them or before both the justices of assize in their circuit or progresse in the sheire where such acts or ordinances be made upon paine of forfeiture of forty pounds for every tyme that they should doe contrary, as by the said Act amongst other things more plainely may appeare.

And whereas the freemen of the City of London useing the art or mistery of Scrivenors within the said Citty and suburbs of the same commonly heretofore called writers of the court letter of the City of London tyme out of mind have been an ancient society and brotherhood of the said Citty and are now lately upon due considerations incorporated by the name of Master, Wardens and Assistants of the Society of Writers of the City of London by letters patents of our now Soveraigne Lord King James under the great seale of England bearing date at Westminster the eight and twentieth day of January in the fourteenth yeare of his Majesties reigne of England France and Ireland and of Scotland the fiftieth and have divers auncient rules orders priviledges ordinances constitutions and oaths heretofore tyme out of minde by their predecessors the Master or Wardens and Governors of the said fraternity made and established and likewise have some other by the Master, Wardens and Assistants of the said Society now incorporated lately devised and made, all for the conservation rule and good order and better government and maintenance of the people useing the said art or mistery within the City of London, and the suburbs of the same, and [Rawl. D51, p. 35] within the circuite and precinct of three miles of the same Citty according to his Majesties graunt to them in that behalfe made which said rules orders acts ordinances constitutions and oaths they pray to be by us examined and approved according to the said Act of Parliament, And which said rules orders ordinances constitutions and oathes doe hereafter followe.

1. *Election of Master & Wardens yearly*

Imprimis It is ordered constituted and ordeined by the Master, Wardens and Assistants of the Society of Scrivenors of the Citty of London as followeth (That is to say) That the Master, Wardens and Assistants of the said Society for the tyme being or the major part of them yearely from tyme to tyme for ever hereafter on Tuesday next after the feast of St. James the Apostle in every yeare or some other tyme when to them it shall seem most necessary and fitt shall and may nominate and elect one fitt and discreet person of the Assistants of the Society aforesaid to be the Master of the said Society, and two other fitt and discreet persons of the Assistants of the same Society to be the Wardens of the same Society to rule governe and oversee the said Society and all the men of the art of mistery aforesaid their servants and apprentices every of them takeing his oath before the

Master and Wardens next precedent or any two of them or before the greater number of the Assistants of the same Society their severall offices respectively well and faithfully in all things to exercise and execute, And that the same Master and Wardens so newly nominated elected and sworne their severall offices aforesaid shall and may exercise for one whole year then next ensuing, and from thence untill some others into the severall offices aforesaid respectively shall be newly nominated elected and sworne.

2. *Election of the Assistants within three moneths after the death or amoveing of any*

Item That whereas the Kings Majestie by his said letters patents hath appointed and nominated twenty and foure persons of the said Society to be the present Assistants to joyne with the Master and Wardens in the good government of the same Society which in the whole number is seaven and twenty of the Assistants, It is ordered that as often and whensoever it shall happen one or more of the Assistants of the said Society for the tyme being to dye or from his or their office or place to be amoved that then and so often it shall and may be lawfull to the Master and Wardens of the said Society and the rest of the Assistants of the same Society then in full life and in their offices being, or the major part of them within three moneths next after the death of amoveing of such person from tyme to tyme to nominate and elect de novo one or more other fitt person or persons of the freemen of the commonalty or Society aforesaid in the place and stead of the same person or persons so dead or amoved And that every person so nominated and elected takeing his oath before the Master and Wardens of the Society aforesaid for the tyme being or any two of them honestly and faithfully to exercise that place or office shall be one of the Assistants of the said Society for the terme of the life of every such person untill from that office for cause reasonable by the Master, Wardens and Assistants of the Society aforesaid for the tyme being or the major part of them he shall be amoved.

[Rawl. D51, p. 36] 3. *That there shall be a convenient number of the livery who shall pay upon their admittance to the Clarke 2s. 6d. & to the Bedell 12d. & £5 to the good of the Company*

Item It is ordeyned and constituted that the Master, Wardens and Assistants of the said Society or the major part of them for the tyme being as they shall thinke fitt and see cause shall and may from tyme to tyme call nominate choose and admitt into the livery or clothing of the said Society such and so many of the freemen of the said Society being willing to accept the same as they shall thinke good honest meet skillfull and able thereunto, and that every such person so called and chosen as aforesaid other than such as heretofore were of the Assistants of the said auncient brotherhood before the said corporation graunted shall pay unto the Master and Wardens of the said Society five pounds to be employed to the generall use of the said Society, and that every person whatsoever called chosen and admitted to be of the livery shall pay unto the Clerke of the said Society for entring his name into the roll or booke of the names of the livery two shillings and six pence, And shall likewise pay unto the Bailiffe or Beadle of the same Society twelve pence, And when such person shall be chosen into the Assistants of the said Society he shall pay to the said Clarke for entring his admittance two shillings and six pence, and to the Baileife or Bedell of the same Society twelve pence.

4. *Election of the Master & Wardens within 14 days after the death or amoveing of any within the yeare*

Item That so often and whensoever it shall happen the Master or Wardens of the said Society for the tyme being or any of them to dye or depart this life or otherwise from their offices for any cause reasonable to be amoved before the end of the same yeare in which as aforesaid they shall be nominated and elected, That then and so often it shall and may be lawfull to the Master, Warden or Wardens or other the Assistants of the same Society then for the tyme in full life and in their office or offices being or the major part of them within fourteene dayes next after the death or amoveing of such Master, Warden or Wardens to name and of new elect any other fitt and discreet person or persons of the number of the Assistants in the place and stead of the same person or persons so dead or amoved, And that he or they so newly nominated and elected and takeing his oath in forme aforesaid shall and may exercise and execute that office or those offices respectively for the residue of the same yeare and from thence untill some others to the same offices shall be nominated and elected.

5. *That there shall be a dinner on the election day and another on the Lord Maiors day and two Stewards to be chosen for each dinner & every steward that refuseth to hold shall forfeit £10*

Item It is ordeined and constituted that there shall be yearly kept at the Common Hall of the said Society or the place of meeting for the tyme being two dinners (that is to say) one dinner for the Master, Wardens and Assistants of the said Society and other the freemen of the same Company to be kept yearly upon the day of the election of the new Master and Wardens, And thother for the Master, Wardens, Assistants and livery of the said Company yearly to be kept on the day when the Lord Maior taketh his oath at Westminster, And that the Master, Wardens and Assistants of the said Society or the more part of them in convenient tyme before the said election day shall choose every year from tyme to tyme out of the livery or out of the Assistants of the said Company two of the elder and better sort of the said Company which have not been Master or Wardens to be Stewards for the provision of both the dinners aforesaid, And the said Stewards so to be chosen to have towards the said [Rawl. D51, p. 37] dinner to be yearly kept on the said election day of the Master and Wardens for the tyme being three pounds six shillings and eight pence a peece and of every other person of the said Company three shillings and four pence, and whatsoever shall be more disbursed or laid out about the said dinner shall be borne and discharged at the charge of the Stewards for the tyme being respectively, And for the said other dinner the Master and Wardens to pay forty shillings a peece, and every one of the livery onely to pay three shillings and four pence a peece and the residue of the said charge to be borne by the Stewards, And if any person so chosen to be Steward as aforesaid doe or shall refuse or [*recte* to] accept the same or deny to performe the same then every person so chosen and refuseing shall forfeit and pay to the Master and Wardens for the tyme being to be by them employed in necessary expences of the said Society as occasion shall serve tenn pounds for every such offence.

6. *That there shall be a chest with four locks and four keys*

Item It is ordeined and constituted that the said Society or Company shall have one substantiall chest with four locks and four severall keyes to the same which shall stand and be placed conveniently in or neer the Common Hall which shall be used by the said Company wherein shall be put and kept all the money plate jewells and other treasure belonging to the said Society, three of which keys shall be and remaine in the keeping and custody of the Master and Wardens for the tyme being, and the fourth key shall be alwaies remaining in the custody of some one of the auncients of the said Assistants which hath bin Master or Warden of the said Society (That is to say) every of the said four persons to have a key that all four may goe and repaire together to the said chest when and as often as need shall be to put any thing into the said chest or to take any thing out of the same. And if it happen the Master and Wardens for the tyme being or the said other person to whome the keeping of one of the said keyes shall be assigned to be sicke or out of the Citty or to have any other lawfull businesse that they or any of them cannot be present at the opening the chest, That then every such of the said four person[s] haveing the charge or custody of any of the keys aforesaid shall nominate and appoint one other of the Assistants of the said Society which hath been Warden of the same Society to take his key in his absence for that tyme to goe repaire help and condiscend to the opening takeing out and putting in of any thing out of or into the same chest as aforesaid so alwaies as the said chest be not opened but in the presence of all four persons which for the tyme being shall have the custody of the said four severall keys.

7. *That every person refuseing to be Master or Warden shall pay £20 & refuseing to be an Assistant shall pay £5*

Item It is ordeyned and constituted that if any person or persons being a freeman of the said Society shall at any tyme hereafter be elected and nominated to be Master or Warden of the said Society according to the forme of his Majesties letters pattents aforesaid, and to the order and constitution herein before in that behalfe appointed, and after such election and nomination shall denye and refuse to take upon him or them any such place or office or shall denye and refuse to take his or their oath before the last precedent Master and Wardens of the said Society or any two of them for the due execution of such office, whereunto he or they shall be so elected as aforesaid (so alwaies that noe one person of the said Society dureing his life tyme shall be inforced to serve more than two yeares as Warden and two yeares as Master accompting the tymes and [Rawl. D51, p. 38] turnes which any of the said Society have already served in either of the said places before the said corporation graunted[)]. That then all and every such person and persons so denying and refuseing haveing noe just and reasonable cause and impediment to be allowed of by the Master, Wardens and Assistants of the said Society for the tyme being or the major part of them shall forfeit and pay to the Master and Wardens of the same Society for the tyme being at every tyme he or they doe or shall soe refuse the summe of twenty pounds to the generall use and supportation of the said Society, And if any person or persons being a freeman as aforesaid shall at any tyme hereafter be chosen to be of the number of Assistants of the said Society according to the said letters pattents and the constitution herein in that behalfe also made and after such election and nomination shall refuse and denye to take upon him or them the office & place of an Assistant of the said Society or shall refuse to take the oath hereafter appointed for the due execution of the said place in such sort as is prescribed haveing noe lawfull or reasonable cause for such his refuseall and denyall to be allowed of by the Master, Wardens and Assistants of the said Society or the major part of them That then every such person so offending shall forfeit and pay to the Master and Wardens of the said Society for the tyme being five pounds to be employed to the generall use and supportation of the same Society.

8. *The Accomptant Warden to make his account before Michaelmas next after his departure out of office upon pain of 40s. & so 40s. every moneth untill the account be made*

Item That if the Accomptant Warden going out of his said office shall not from tyme to tyme every year after the election and admission of the new Master and Wardens and before the feast of St. Michaell tharchangell following upon such day and before such auditors as by the new succeeding Master and Wardens and Assistants or the greater part of them shall be appointed make and give up a true and perfect accompt in writeing of all such money, plate & other goods & chattells whatsoever as dureing the tyme of his continuance in the said office have come unto his hands, or shall not then and there likewise satisfie pay and deliver over unto the Master and Wardens of the said Society next after him elected and sworne to the use of the said Society all such money, plate, goods and chattells whatsoever as upon the foot of every such accompt shall appeare to be remaining in his hands, That then every such Accomptant Warden by whom such default shall be made shall forfeit and pay unto the Master and Wardens for the tyme being forty shillings for such default and so forty shillings every moneth untill the accompt be taken and payment and delivery made as aforesaid to the use and generall supportation of the said Society.

9. *To nominate a Clarke and a Bedell & to amove them*

Item That the Master and Wardens of the said Society and other the Assistants of the same Society for the tyme being or the greater part of them shall and may elect and name one Clerke and one Bedell or Baileiffe from tyme to tyme as often and whensoever it shall pleas them to serve the Master, Wardens and Assistants of the Society aforesaid for the tyme being in all their commandements and lawfull businesse whatsoever, And that they may from tyme to tyme amove and deprive the said Clerke and Bedell or Baileiffe or either of them from their offices or places for reasonable cause, the Master, Wardens and Assistants of the said Society or the greater part of them moveing.

10. [Rawl. D51, p. 39] *That if the Master or Wardens or any of the Assistants or livery shall be knowne to be a vitious liver or convict of a notorious crime he shall be displaced*

Item It is ordeined and constituted that if the Master or Wardens or any of the Assistants for the tyme being or any of the livery of the same Company at any tyme hereafter shall be apparently and sufficiently knowne and proved to be a dishonest and vitious liver or shall be detected or convicted of or for any speciall odious and notorious crime or offence and being called before their assemblies shall not purge or cleare himselfe of the same That then and so often it shall and may be lawfull to and for the residue of the Master, Wardens and Assistants of the said Society or the more part of them to expell and put out of the Assistants and livery of the said Company, and out of and from any office and offices in the said Company every such person and persons and him and them utterly to exclude from the same be he Master or Warden or of the Assistants or of the livery or other person whatsoever.

11. *That there shall be four meetings called Quarter dayes to which all that use the art shall be summoned and whosoever doth not appear or after appeareance doth depart without leave shall forfeit 3s. 4d.*

Item It is ordeyned and constituted that there shall be kept and holden at the Common Hall or comon place of meeting of the said Society four tymes in every year hereafter four severall assemblies or meetings commonly called four Quarter dayes by the Master, Wardens and Assistants for the tyme being or the more part of them (that is to say) At the feasts of the nativity of St. John Baptist, St. Michaell tharchangell, the birth of our Lord God and thannunciation of St. Mary the Virgin or within fourteen dayes next after every of the said feasts, unto every of which said assemblies and meetings shall be summoned and warned by the Baileiffe or Bedell of the said Company or by some other thereunto to be appointed by the Master and Wardens the whole number of the freemen of the said Society and all and every other person & persons useing or exerciseing the same art, mistery or science aswell Englishmen as strangers dwelling or resideing in the City of London the liberties and suburbs thereof or within the compasse of three miles of the said Citty to appear and attend at the Comon Hall aforesaid there to pay his and their quartridge hereafter mentioned & all other duties, fines and forfeitures to be required or levied. And to the intent these present ordinances may be then and there once or twice at the summoning of them in every year read and published by the Clarke or Bedell in the said Common Hall for the better knowledge and government of themselves to avoid and eschew the danger and penalties of and for the not performing the same ordinances, And that every person so assembled shall there continue and not depart any such Court or meeting untill the end thereof without licence of the said Master and Wardens upon peine that every person so offending either for not appearing (haveing noe reasonable excuse) or after appearance for departing without licence as aforesaid shall forfeit and pay to the Master and Wardens of the said Society three shillings and four pence to the use aforesaid.

12. *That there shall be monethly Courts upon occasion for hearing & decideing of all controversies & punishing of all offences against the ordinances*

And It is also ordeyned and constituted that there shall and may be holden monethly every year and oftener if need be one Court at the Comon Hall or place of meeting aforesaid by the Master, Wardens and Assistants of the said Society or the greater part of them for the hearing, debateing, examineing and determineing of all and all manner of controversies, debates, fines, forfeitures, demaunds and questions that shall happen [Rawl. D51, p. 40] to arise or growe by any of the said Society or by any other useing the said science, denizen or not denizen, free or forreigne, English or stranger, as also for the correction, punishment, reformation or restraint of any willfull, disordered or stubborne apprentices or other persons touching or concerning any thing done or to be done contrary to these present ordinances or any part of them at the discretion of the Master, Wardens and Assistants and their successors for the tyme being.

13. *That all persons useing the art of a scrivener not being free of any other Company shall be contributory in all payments with the scrivenors to the King and otherwise*

Item It is ordered, constituted and ordeined that all straungers and forreigners and all other persons inhabiting or residing within the Citty of London the liberties and suburbs of the same and within the circuite and precinct of three miles of the same Citty, and which doe occupy use or exercise the mistery or art aforesaid which are not freemen of any other mistery or Society of the City of London forever hereafter shall be contributory with the freemen of the Society aforesaid in all payments aswell to the Kings Majestie his heirs and successors as in maintenance and sustentation of the Company and Society of Writers aforesaid and shall pay and bear all such and the like charges and payments as the Freemen of the Society aforesaid doe pay or have used or ought to pay, And that every person that shall refuse to pay and bear all such summes of money, charges and duties aforementioned as the same shall happen to be assessed and demaunded shall forfeit and pay for every tyme so offending and denying the summe of forty shillings to the Master and Wardens for the tyme being to be employed to the use of the said Society.

14. *That all useing the art shall pay 2s. 8d. per annum for quartridg*

Item That all men of the Society aforesaid and all other persons inhabiting and dweling within the City of London the liberties and suburbs of the same within the aforesaid circuit or precinct of three miles of the same Citty, and occupying useing or exerciseing the mistery or art aforesaid for ever hereafter shall yearly pay to the Master and Wardens and Assistants of the Society aforesaid and their successors at their Common Hall an annuall payment of two shillings and eight pence per annum at four feasts of the yeare in the City of London most usuall (videlicet) at the feasts of the annunciation of the Blessed Virgin Mary, the nativity of St. John Baptist, St. Michaell tharchangell and the birth of our Lord God by even portions to be paid (scilicet) at every of the said feasts eight pence being an ancient payment and duty called quarteridge by the freemen of the Ancient Brotherhood of Writers of the Court Letter of the City of London to the Master or Wardens of the same brotherhood heretofore due and paid, And that the Master, Wardens & Assistants of the Society of Scrivenors of the City of London and their successors may have and shall have full power and authority from tyme to tyme forever to have, receive, require, demaund, collect, and by distresse and distresses to their own uses to levy of and from all persons of the Society aforesaid, and of and from all other persons whatsoever inhabiting or being within the City of London the liberties and suburbs of the same and within the aforesaid circuite and precinct of three myles of the same Citty, and occupying useing or exerciseing the mistery or art aforesaid the aforesaid annuall payment of two shillings and eight pence per annum.

[Rawl. D51, p. 41] 15. *Power to tax & cesse all persons using the art not being free of any other Companyes for the supportation and maintenance of the Society*

Item That the Master, Wardens and Assistants of the said Society for the tyme being or the major part of them from tyme to tyme may impose and tax such reasonable payments, taxations, impositions and summes of money whatsoever aswell to the Kings Majestie his heires and successors as upon warrants and precepts to the said Society awarded by the Lord Maior of the City of London and other necessary burdens of the said Society upon severall persons of the said Society and all other persons useing the science art or mistery aforesaid within the Citty of London the suburbs and liberties of the same and within three miles of the saide Citty which are not freemen of any other mistery of the said Citty, as to the said Master, Wardens and Assistants or the more part of them shall seeme necessary and convenient.

16. *Power to set fines upon all men useing the art for not appearing or for infringeing any orders and to levy them by distresse*

Item That if any person of the said Society or any other person useing or occupying the art science or mistery aforesaid within the Citty of London or the suburbs and liberties thereof or within three miles of the same Citty shall be summoned by the officer or minister of the said Society to appear at any Court or meeting by the Master or Wardens of the said Society for the tyme being in any certaine place within the Citty of London or the liberties thereof hereafter to be holden or appointed, and such person so summoned shall not appear at the day hour and place so appointed not haveing lawfull or reasonable cause or excuse by the Master and Wardens and other the Assistants or the major part of them to be allowed, Or if any person of the said Society or any other person useing the said art science or mistery within the Citty of London the suburbs and liberties thereof or within three myles of the same Citty shall refuse to pay or shall not pay all impositions, payments, taxations and summes of money upon him or them as aforesaid reasonably taxed and imposed or hereafter to be taxed or imposed or shall not fulfill all the statutes, acts, ordinances and constitutions herein set downe, but the same shall infringe or breake, That then and so often it shall and may be lawfull to and for the Master, Wardens and Assistants of the said Society for the tyme being or the major part of them from tyme to tyme to impose, assesse and tax upon every such person so offending all such fines amerciaments and summes of money whatsoever for his or their offence and contempt in that behalfe as to the Master, Wardens and Assistants for the tyme being or the major part of them shall seeme necessary and convenient. And that it shall and may be lawfull to and for the Master, Wardens and Assistants of the said Society for the tyme being or the major part of them from tyme to tyme as often as it shall please them aswell all the freemen of the Society aforesaid as all straungers and forreyners and other persons whatsoever inhabiting within the City of London and the liberties thereof or within the aforesaid precinct or curcuite of three miles of the same City and occupying, useing or exerciseing the mistery or art aforesaid to distreyne and the fines and amerciaments aforesaid and all other payments, taxations, impositions and summes of money whatsoever upon them or any of them from time to tyme imposed and taxed or to be imposed or taxed by those distresses to levy and collect and to the proper use of the said Society to convert.

[Rawl. D51, p. 42] 17. *Power to amove any Master, Warden or Assistant*

Item That the Master, Wardens and Assistants of the said Society for the tyme being or the major part of them whereof the Master and Wardens or some of them to be two for just and reasonable causes to them appeareing and by them to be allowed of, shall & may from tyme to tyme displace and amove or cause to be displaced and amoved any Master, Warden or Assistant of the said Society from his or their said office or place of Master, Warden or Assistant.

18. *Power to search & survey all persons useing the art in London & 3 miles compasse & to punish them by fines and to levy the fines by distresse*

Item That the Master, Wardens and Assistants of the said Society and their successors or six of them at the least whereof the Master or Wardens of the said Society for the tyme being or any of them alwaies to be one forever shall and may have use & exercise within the City of London the liberties and suburbs thereof and within the City of Westminster and the liberties thereof, the Burrough of Southwarke, the precinct of St. Katherine neer the Tower of London and within all other places within three miles every way round about the said City of London, the full and whole view and oversight, search, examination, correction, punishment and government aswell of all freemen of the said City of London as of all strangers and forreigners and other persons whatsoever within the said City of London and Westminster, the libertyes and suburbs of the same Cittyes, the Burrough of Southwarke, the precinct of St. Katherine aswell within liberties as without that doe or shall comonly and publiquely use and frequent the said art or science within the said Citties the liberties and suburbs of the same Citties and places aforesaid or any of them or elsewhere in any other place not distant from the said Citty of London above three miles, And that the Master and Wardens and Assistants of the said Society for the tyme being or the major part of them from time to time forever may have and shall have full power and authority to punish and correct all men aswell freemen of the said City of London as strangers and forreigners as aforesaid frequenting or useing the art or mistery aforesaid aswell within the said Citties of London and Westminster the liberties and suburbs of the same and the places aforesaid as within the said limitts or distance of three miles every way round about the said Citty of London for their offences for insufficiently executeing, doing or useing the science art or mistery aforesaid, and the defects and defaults in the same science or mistery (if any shall be found) to correct and amend according to their sound discretions, And fines and amerciaments reasonable upon whatsoever offendors, according to their offences to tax, and to the use of the said Society for supportation of the generall burthens thereof by distresses to levy, gather and take, and every offendor against this present ordinance at every tyme denyeing or refuseing to be searched, surveyed or examined to forfeit and pay to the Master and Wardens for the tyme being forty shillings to be employed to the use of the said Society.

19. *That noe person shall be made free of the Society till he be examined for his sufficiency & takeing the oath prescribed*

Item That noe person hereafter shall be infranchised or admitted into the freedome or liberties of the said Society to make open profession of the aforesaid science or art untill such tyme as he shall have first been duely examined touching his sufficiency and hability to use and exercise the same art or mistery before the Master, Wardens and Assistants [Rawl. D51, p.43] of the said Society or any six of them, And shall be by the said Master, Wardens and Assistants or such six of them as aforesaid upon such examination declared and aproved to be of sufficiency and hability and shall have taken an oath as is hereafter appointed.

20. *That noe person shall use the art but such as shall be free of the Society and have taken his oath*

Item That no person hereafter shall publiquely use or exercise the art mistery or scyence aforesaid and make it his profession or meanes of liveing within the Citty of London the suburbs and liberties thereof or within three miles compasse of the said Citty unlesse he shall be first admitted into the freedome of the said Society and enfranchised with the liberties of the said Citty, and shall have taken such an oath before the Master and Wardens of the said Society or any two of them as the freemen of the same Company shall usually take at the tyme of their admissions according to the auncient usage and according to the forme in these presents on that behalfe prescribed.

21. *That every person free of the Society shall take the oath prescribed*

Item That every person which hereafter shall be duely infranchised into the said Society shall upon his admission take an oath before the Master and Wardens of the said Society or any two of them according to the forme in these presents in that behalfe prescribed, And that every one which shall take the said oath shall witnes the same oath to be by him taken by writeing under his proper hand to be by him entred into the Comon Booke of the said Society.

22. *That none keepeing shopp shall keep in his service or employment in the science any but such as are free of the Society*

Item That no person of the said Society keeping shopp and useing the said art or mistery and makeing it his profession and meanes of liveing within the Citty of London the suburbs and liberties thereof and the fore-said circuite of three myles about the same Citty shall reteyne or keep in his service and employ about his affaires in the said art either as servant or partner or otherwise any other person whatsoever (except such as shall be his or their apprentice or apprentices) which shall not be free of the said Society upon paine to forfeit and pay unto the Master and Wardens of the said Society for the tyme being to the use of the said Society forty shillings for every moneth that he keepeth or employeth any such person as afore-said.

23. *That none take an apprentice for lesse than 7 years nor agree to releas any part of his tyme*

Item That none of the said Society keeping shopp and useing the said art or mistery and makeing it his profession and meanes of liveing shall take any apprentice to be bound to serve him in the art or mistery aforesaid for any lesse terme than for seaven yeares at the least, nor shall take any apprentice to the intent or upon any agreement to release him any part of the terme for which he shall be bound as aforesaid upon peine that every one so offending shall forfeit and pay to the Master and Wardens of the said Society five pounds for either of the said offences.

24. *That every apprentice shall be enrolled & presented within six moneths, upon paine of 6s. 8d. for each offence*

Item That every apprentice so taken shall be enrolled in the Chamber of London and presented to the Master and Wardens of the said science, and his indenture of apprenticehood there entred in a booke for that pur-pose to be kept and that such enrollment and presentment shall be made and done alwaies within six moneths next after the sealing of such inden-tures of apprenticehood upon paine that every one offending in either of the cases aforesaid shall pay unto the Master and Wardens of the said Society for the tyme being [Rawl. D 51, p. 44] for each of those offences so often as they happen six shillings and eight pence.

25. *That none shall set over his apprentice to any useing any other trade or occupation upon pain of five pounds*

Item It is ordeyned and constituted that noe person or persons what-soever useing the said art or mistery within the said Citty and suburbs and the compasse before declared shall from henceforth set over his or their apprentice or apprentices being once bound to him or them to any other person or persons useing any other trade, handicraft or occupation or useing the same art science or mistery which shall not be free of the said Society without the licence consent and agreement of the Master and Wardens of the Society aforesaid and the greater part of the Assistants of the same Society upon peine to forfeit and pay for every such offence five pounds to the aforesaid Master and Wardens for the tyme being to be employed to the generall use of the said Society.

26. *That none being once free of the Company shall be translated upon peine of £20*

Item It is ordeined and constituted that noe manner of person or persons whatsoever being once made free and accepted into the freedome and Society aforesaid whatsoever his or their trade or occupation is or shall be, shall at any tyme hereafter change or alter his copy or become free of any other Company or fellowshipp within the City of London without the knowledge consent and agreement of the Master, Wardens and Assistants of this Society or the major part of them upon paine that every person so offending or doing any thing contrary to this ordinance shall forfeit and pay to the Master and Wardens for the tyme being twenty pounds to be employed to the generall use of the said Society, Except such person or persons doe or shall necessarily change his said copy by reason of his or their election into and service of any capitall office or cheife place of magistracy within the said Citty of London.

27. *That noe person shall give any reproachfull speeches to another or sweare in the Hall upon paine to forfeite 3s. 4d.*

Item That noe person or persons whatsoever of the said Society or any other useing the said art openly or privily shall revile or any waies misuse with evill speeches or words of reproach or disgrace any other person of the same Society or shall swear any oath vainely or wilfully blaspheme the name of God in their said Common Hall or in any assembly or meeting upon paine to forfeit and pay to the Master and Wardens for the tyme being for every tyme soe offending three shillings and four pence.

28. *That if any useing the art shall have summons left to appeare at any Court or to attend the Lord Maior & Aldermen at any other meeting appointed & shall not appear every such person shall forfeit 3s. 4d.*

Item It is ordeined and constituted that all persons of the said Society and all other persons aforesaid useing the aforesaid art or mistery which shall have any summons or warning given to himself or left at his dwelling house or place of abode by the Bailiffe or Beadle of the said Company for his attendance or appeareance before the Master and Wardens of the said Society for the tyme being at any certaine houre tyme or place upon the said quarter dayes or any of them or at any other Court or Comon Assembly for or about any of the affaires of the Kings Majestie his heires or successors or to attend upon Lord Maior, Aldermen and Sheriffs to Westminster or at the buriall or funeralls of any brother of the said Society or about any other necessary affaires of the said Society, and such person so summoned or warned doe or shall make any default in his or their appeareance or attendance at any such tyme or place aforesaid, That then every such person so offending haveing noe reasonably excuse or just occasion to be allowed of by the said Master, Wardens and Assistants or the major part of them shall pay unto the Master and Wardens for every [Rawl. D51, p. 45] such offence three shillings and four pence. And if any person doe or shall become [In the margin: *And being obstinate or disdaining to appear to forfeit 10s.*] obstinate or wilfull or doe disdaine to appear or attend then he or they soe offending to forfeit and pay for every such offence tenn shillings in manner and forme aforesaid.

29. *That every person shewing himselfe disobedient to these ordinances shall forfeit 40s.*

Item It is ordeyned and constituted that if any person of the said Society aforesaid or any other person whatsoever useing the art mistery or science aforesaid within the Citty of London the liberties and suburbs thereof or within the circuite and precinct of three myles distant from the same Citty shall at any tyme hereafter be found obstinate, willfull, perverse or disobedient in any thing or matter conteyned in these ordinances or any part of them herein mentioned against the said Master, Wardens and Assistants and their successors or any of them for the tyme being, whereby they are, shall or may be hindred, letten, denyed or any waies interrupted from the executeing of the said ordinances or any part of the same according to their offices and charge and the tenor and true meaning of the same ordinances, Than [*sic*, *recte* that] then every such person and persons whatsoever, English or straunger, freeman or forreine, denizen or not denizen so offending (the same offence appearing to the said Master, Wardens and Assistants or to the major part of them for the tyme being) shall forfeit and pay for every such offence and tyme of offending forty shillings of lawfull money of England to the said said [*sic*] Master and Wardens to be employed to the use of the Society aforesaid.

30. *The forme of every freemans oath*

I, N: D: doe sweare upon the holy evangelist to be true and faithfull unto our soveraigne lord the King his heires and successors Kings and Queenes of England and to be true and just in mine office and science, and to doe my dilligence that all the deeds which I shall make a deed [*sic*] to be sealed shall be well and truly done after my learning skill and scyence and shall be duely and advisedly read read [*sic*] over and examined before thensealing of the same, And especially I shall not write nor suffer to be written by any of mine to my power or knowledge any deed or writeing to be sealed wherein any deceipt or falsehood shall be conceived or in my conscience suspected to lye nor any deed bearing date of long tyme past before thensealing thereof nor bearing any date of any tyme to come neither shall I testifie nor suffer any of mine to testifie to my power or knowledge any blanck charter or deed sealed before the full writeing thereof, And neither for haste nor for covetousnesse I shall take upon me to make any deed touching inheritance of lands or estate for life or yeares nor any deed of great charge whereof I have not cunning without good advice and information of councell, And all the good rules and ordinances of the Society of Scriveners of the City of London I shall well and truly keep and observe to my power so farr as God shall give me grace, so help me God and the holy contents of this booke.

31. *The Master and Wardens oath*

You shall sweare that you shall be true and faithfull to our soveraigne lord the King and to his heires and successors Kings or Queenes of this realme and that after the best manner you can you shall justly and indifferently execute or cause to be [Rawl. D51, p. 46] executed your office of Master or Warden of this Society in every respect, And all the good and lawfull ordinances in this booke of ordinances expressed without spareing any person or persons for affection, reward, meed, dread, malice or promise of reward dureing the tyme you shall execute and continue in the same office of Master or Warden. You shall to the uttermost of your power and hability truely and faithfully observe and keepe and of all and every such goods, jewells, plate, summes of money, deeds, guifts, graunts, commodities or of any other thing or things whatsoever that by reason of your said office shall come to any of your hands you and every of you shall respectively according to all the ordinances in this booke specified make a good true and plaine accompt and shall deliver all the said goods, deeds, guifts and other things whatsoever aforesaid to the safe custody of the Master, Wardens and Assistants for the tyme being at the Common Hall aforesaid at the tyme thereunto appointed or else to pay such fines as you shall be ordered to pay by them for your not soe doing. You shall not for malice, love or affection assesse any person or persons in any greater or lesser summe than after the quallity & quantity of his or their offence or offences after your discretion and according to the said ordinances therein mentioned, so help you God and the holy contents of this booke.

32. *The oath of the Assistants*

You and every of you shall be true to our soveraigne lord the King and to his heires and successors Kings or Queenes of this realm and every of you shall after the best manner you can by your selfes justly and indifferently execute or cause to be executed your office and place of an Assistant to the Master and Wardens of this Society in every respect, And all the good and lawfull ordinances in this booke of ordinances expressed without spareing any person or persons for affection, reward, meed, dread, malice or promise of reward dureing the tyme you shall execute and continue in the same office or place of an Assistant you shall to the utmost of your power and hability truly and faithfully observe and keep. You shall not for malice, love or affection assesse any person or persons in any greater or lesse summe than after the quantity and quallity of his or their offence or offences after your discretion and according to the ordinances herein mentioned, so help you God and the contents of this booke.

33. *The Clarkes oath*

You shall be true to our soveraigne lord the Kings Majestie of England now being and to his heires and successors Kings or Queenes of England, you shall be obedient to your Master, Wardens and Assistants of the said

Society for the tyme being in all lawfull and honest comaundements and attendant upon them at all their meetings, you shall from tyme to time read all the ordinances and make due and true entries of all things which the Master & Wardens aforesaid shall commaund you without spareing any person for affection, lucre or malice, you shall not deliver any copies of the bookes or orders concerning the Company nor any part of them nor of any of the articles or ordinances whereby the said Society may or shall take [Rawl. D51, p. 47] any hurt neither shall shew the same bookes or ordinances to any person or persons without the consent, comaundement or agreement of the said Master and Wardens for the tyme being. You shall from tyme [*recte*, from time to time] upon the comaundement and according to the direction of the Master and Wardens for the tyme being warne and summon all the Assistants and livery of the said Society to appeare at the Common Hall or generall meeting place of the said Society at all quarter dayes and other Court dayes, and in all other things incident or belonging to your said office or place you shall faithfully and honestly demeane and behave your selfe, so help you God and the contents of this booke.

34. *The Beadles oath*

You shall be true to our soveraigne lord the Kings Majestie of England now being and to his heires and successors Kings or Queenes of England, you shall be obedient to the Master, Wardens and Assistants of the said Society for the tyme being in all their lawfull and honest comaundements and attendant upon them at all their meetings. You shall from tyme to tyme upon the comaundement and according to the direction of the Master and Wardens or any of them warne and summon all the freemen of the said Society and all others useing the art science or mistery aforesaid within the Citty of London the suburbs and liberties thereof or within three miles of the same Citty to appear at the Common Hall or generall meeting place for the said Society at all quarter dayes and other Court dayes. You shall alsoe truly execute your office in carrying of any person or persons to ward and in releaseing him or them againe at the comaundement of the said Master and Wardens, and in all other points incident or belonging to your office you shall faithfully and honestly demeane and behave your selfe, soe help you God and by the contents of this booke.

All and singular which said ordinances and constitutions we the said Lord Chancellor, Sir Henry Mountagu and Sir Henry Hobart have perused and examined, and doe by these presents approve them and allow of them, And in testimony thereof we have signed the same with our signes manuall the nine and twentieth day of January, and in the yeares of the reigne of our soveraigne lord James by the grace of God of England, Scotland, France and Ireland King defender of the faith &c. of England, France and Ireland the sixteenth and of Scotland the two and fiftieth.

Fr. Verulam Canc. H. Mountague. H. Hobart.

[Rawl. D51, p. 48] *To all people* to whome this present writeing shall come, Thomas Lord Coventry, lord keeper of the great seale of England, Sir John Bramston, knight, cheife justice assigned to hold pleas before our soveraigne lord the King, and Sir John Finch, knight, cheife justice of his

Majesties court of common pleas at Westminster, send greeting in our Lord God everlasting.

Whereas in and by one Act of Parliament holden at Westminster the sixteenth day of January in the nineteenth yeare of the reigne of the late most noble prince of famous memory King Henry the Seaventh, it was amongst other things ordeyned, established and enacted that no Master, Wardens and Fellowships of Crafts or Misteries nor any of them nor any rulers of guilds or fraternities after the feast of Pentecost in the same Act mentioned should take upon them to make any acts or ordinances nor to execute any acts or ordinances by them before the said Act made in disinheritance or diminution of the prerogative of the King nor of other nor against the comon proffitt of the people. But if the same Acts and ordinances be examined and approved by the Chancellor, Treasurer of England or cheife Justices of either benches or three of them, or before both the justices of assizes in their circuite or progresse in the sheir where such acts or ordinances be made upon peine of forfeiture of forty pounds for every tyme that they should doe contrary, as by the same Act of Parliament amongst other things therein conteyned more at large appeareth

And whereas the freemen of the Citty of London useing the art or mistery of scrivenors within the said Citty of London and suburbs of the same comonly heretofore called Writers of the Court Letter of the Citty of London time out of minde have been an auncient society and brotherhood of the said Citty, and are lately upon due considerations incorporated by the name of the Master, Wardens and Assistants of the Society of Writers of the Citty of London by letters patents of our late soveraigne lord King James under the great seale of England bearing date at Westminster the eight and twentieth day of January in the foureteenth yeare of his said late Majesties reigne of England, France and Ireland, and of Scotland the fiftieth, by which [Rawl. D51, p. 49] said letters pattents our said late soveraigne lord King James did give and graunt for him his heires and successors unto the Master, Wardens and Assistants of the said Society and their successors, That they the said Master and Wardens of the said Society and the rest of the Assistants of the same Society for the time being or the greater part of them from tyme to tyme forever after that should and might lawfully and freely ordeine establish and make statutes, rules, orders, constitutions and ordinances reasonable and agreeable to the lawes and statutes of this realme of England according to their sound discretions for for the proffitt of the Society aforesaid as often as they should please, and the same statutes, constitutions and ordinances from time to tyme to put in execution and cause to be executed without molestation, hindrance or impediment of the said late King his heires or successors or of any his or their justices, maiors, sherriffs or other officers or ministers whatsoever, any statute, act, ordinance, custome or usage to the contrary thereof in any wise notwithstanding, And the same statutes, constitutions & ordinances so had and made or any of them from tyme to tyme to change alter or revoake and annihilate as to them or the major part of them shall seeme to be convenient and expedient as in and by the said letters pattents (amongst other things) may appeare

And whereas the Master, Wardens and Assistants of the said Society have divers ancient rules, orders, priviledges, ordinances, constitutions and oathes heretofore time out of minde by their predecessors the Master or Wardens and Governors of the said fraternity made and established, and likewise have some other by the Master, Wardens and Assistants of the said Society after the said letters patents of incorporation devised and made, all for the conservation, rule, good order and better government and maintenance of the people useing the said art or mistery within the Citty of London and the suburbs of the same and within the circuit and precinct of three miles of the same Citty according to the graunt to them in that behalfe made by the letters patents aforesaid, all and singular which said ordinances and constitutions were by the late right honourable Francis, Lord Verulam, Lord Chancellor of England, Sir Henry Mountague, knight, cheife justice assigned to hold pleas before the said late King James, now Earle of Manchester and lord privy seale, and Sir Henry Hobart, knight and baronett, cheife justice of the court of comon pleas under their hands and seales the nine and twentieth day of January in the sixteenth yeare of the reigne of our said late soveraigne lord King James approved and allowed according to the foresaid Act of Parliament as by the said ordinances & constitutions under their hands and seales more at large may appear, some of which said ordinances and constitutions by the Master, Wardens and Assistants of the said Society devised & made the now present Master, Wardens and Assistants of the said Society upon speciall reasons and considerations, and for the conservation, rule, good order and better government of the people of the same Society have in part altered and changed and in leiw and stead thereof have made certaine other ordinances and constitutions which they pray by us to be examined and approved according to the said Act of Parliament, and which said orders, ordinances and constitutions soe altered and new made doe hereafter followe.

[Rawl. D51, p. 50] *Whereas* our late soveraigne lord King Charles[1] by his letters patents of incorporation bearing date at Westminster the eight and twentieth day of January in the fourteenth yeare of his reigne amongst other things assigned, ordeined, created and constituted seaven and twenty persons of the Society of Writers of the City of London in the same letters pattents perticularly named to be the then present Assistants of the same Society for the good government of the said Society *And* that as often and whensoever it should happen one or more of the Assistants of the said Society for the tyme being to dye or for a reasonable cause to be removed from his or their office or place, That then and so often it should and might be lawfull to and for the Master and Wardens of the said Society and other the Assistants of the same Society then in full life and in their offices being or the greater part of them within three moneths after the death or removeing of such persons from time to time to nominate and elect of new one or more other fitt person or persons of the freemen of the cominalty of the Society aforesaid in the place and stead of such person or persons so dead or removed *And* that every such person so nominated and elected takeing the oath by the said letters patents in that behalfe prescribed and appointed should be one of the Assistants of the said Society for the terme of his life

[1] A scribal error for James.

untill by the Master, Wardens and Assistants of the same Society or the greater part of them for reasonable cause he should be removed as by the said letters patents (amongst other things) may appeare

And whereas sithence the said letters patents of incorporation amongst divers other ordinances, orders and constitutions by the Master, Wardens and Assistants of the said Society made by force and vertue of the said let[t]-ers patents for the good rule and government of the said Society, and by the late right honourable Francis, Lord Verulam, Lord Chancellor of England, Sir Henry Mountague, knight, cheife justice assigned to hold pleas before the said King, now Earle of Manchester and the lord privy seale, Sir Henry Hobart, knight and baronett, cheife justice of the court of common pleas under their hands and seales the nine and twentieth day of January in the sixteenth yeare of the reigne of our late late [*sic*] soveraigne lord King James approved and allowed according to an Act of Parliament holden at West-minster the sixteenth day of January in the nineteenth yeare of the reigne of the late King Henry the Seaventh in that behalfe made, it was ordeined and constituted that the Master, Wardens and Assistants of the said Society or the major part of them for the tyme being as they should thinke fitt and see cause should and might from time to time call, nominate, chose and ad-mitt into the livery or clothing of the said Society such and so many of the freemen of the said Society being willing to accept the same as they should thinke good, honest, meet, skillfull and able thereunto *And* alsoe that there should be yearly kept at the Common Hall of the said Society two dinners (that is to say) one dinner for the Master, Wardens and Assistants of the said Society and other the freemen of the same Company to be kept yearly upon the day of the election of the new Master and Wardens, and the other for the Master, Wardens, Assistants and livery of the said Company yearly to be kept on the day when the Lord Maior taketh his oath at Westminster [Rawl. D51, p. 51] and that the Master, Wardens and Assistants of the said Society or the major part of them in convenient tyme before the said elec-tion day shall choose every yeare from time to time out of the livery or out of the Assistants of the said Company two of the elder and better sort of the said Company which have not been Master or Wardens to be Stewards for the provision of both the dinners aforesaid, and the said Stewards so to be chosen to have towards the said severall dinners to be yearly kept as afore-said of the Master, Wardens and Assistants and of the livery and generally of the said Company, the severall summes of money in the same ordinances respectively specified, and the residue of the said charge to be borne by the Stewards, and that if any person so chosen to be Stewards as aforesaid doe or should refuse to accept the same or denye to performe the same, then every person so chosen and refuseing should forfeit and pay to the Master and Wardens for the tyme being to be by them employed in neces-sary expences of the said Society as occasion should serve tenn pounds for every such offence *And also* that if any person or persons being a freeman of the said Society should at any tyme be chosen to be of the number of the Assistants of the said Society according to the said letters patents and the constitutions aforesaid in that behalfe also made, and after such election and nomination should refuse and denye to take upon him or them the office and place of an Assistant of the said Society, or should refuse to take the oath by the said constitutions appointed for the due execution of the said place in such sort as is prescribed haveing no lawfull or reasonable cause for such his refuseall and denyall to be allowed of by the Master, Warden and Assistants of the said Society or the major part of them, That then every such person so offending should forfeit and pay to the Master and Wardens of the said Society for the tyme being five pounds to be employed to the generall use and supportation of the same Society

And whereas many and severall persons of the said Society since the said letters patents of incorporation graunted and since the makeing of the ordinances and constitutions aforesaid have been duely chosen to be of the number of the Assistants of the said Society according to the said letters patents and the constitutions aforesaid in that behalfe also made, and after such election and nomination have refused and denyed to take upon them the office and place of an Assistant of the said Society and have refused to take the oath by the said letters patents and constitutions prescribed and appointed for the due execution of the said place, albeit they had noe lawfull or reasonable cause for such their refuseall and denyall, but finding the said fine of five pounds for such their refuseall to be so easie a fine, and well knowing, that by such their refuseall to be of the Assistants they (as the ordinances of the said Company now stand in force) doe escape and free themselves from bearing the offices of Stewards, Wardens and Masters of the said Company for five pounds, whereby great inconveniencies doe arise to the said Company which places of an Assistant, Steward, twice Warden and Master of the said Society would in a few yeares come to forty pounds a man in charge at the least besides much labour, travell and expences in attending about the necessary affaires and at the Courts of [Rawl. D51, p. 52] Assistants of the Company and other matters and businesse for the good government of the said Society

And whereas by the said former ordinances two Stewards for the provision of the said dinners were appointed to be elected yearly out of the livery or out of the Assistants of the said Company *And* forasmuch as upon many speciall reasons and weighty considerations and for the good of the said Company, the Master, Wardens and Assistants of the said Society have hitherto forborne and omitted to establish and settle a livery or cloathing for the said Company or to call, nominate, choose and admitt into the livery or clothing of the said Society any of the freemen of the said Society so as by that means the two Stewards have yearly been chosen out of the Assistants of the said Society onely (there being no livery) and so is to be continued if redresse in that behalfe is not made *And* for that at this present tyme all the Assistants of the said Company which are capable by the said former ordinances to be chosen Stewards have served the said place of Steward [(]saveing onely one man which was lately taken into the Assistants) so that the two Stewards for this next yeare, upon the election of the Master and Wardens which will be about halfe a yeare hence being to be elected out of the number of Assistants onely, it will fall out that one of the same two Stewards so to be chosen for this next yeare must needs be one of the Assistants that hath already served the same place of Steward, and so likewise it is unavoidably likely (except provision be made to the contrary) that hereafter also many of the Assistants must be chosen and be enforced to hold the place of Stewards of the said Company which have already to their great charge served the same place, which will be a heavy charge and burthen to those of the Assistants for the tyme being and will deterr others to accept the place of Assistants hereafter but the rather for that cause to pay the said small fyne of five pounds, for remedie, redresse and avoiding of all which mischeifes and inconveniencies that may hereafter ensue for the time to come in like cases

That the Stewards shall be chosen yearly aswell out of the generality as out of those the Assistants & every person refuseing to pay £10 fine

It is now ordered, constituted, ordeined and appointed by the Master, Wardens and Assistants of the said Society of Writers of the Citty of London as followeth (That is to say) That the Master, Wardens and Assistants of the said Society or the major part of them in convenient tyme at or before the election day of the new Master and Wardens of the said Society shall choose every yeare yearly from tyme to tyme aswell out of the Assistants of the Company as out of the generallty and cominalty and residue of the freemen of the said Society two of the elder and better sort of freemen of the said Company which have not been Master or Wardens of the said Society to be Stewards for the provision of the dinner by the former constitutions appointed to be yearly kept for the Master, Wardens and Assistants of the said Society and other the freemen of the same Company upon the day of election of the new Master and Wardens, albeit the said Stewards or any of them for the tyme being to be chosen as aforesaid be not or shall not be of the Assistants of the said Society or of the livery or clothing of the said Company. *And* that the said Stewards so to be chosen shall have towards the [Rawl. D51, p. 53] said dinner to be yearly kept on the said election day, of the Master, Wardens and Assistants of the said Society and of every other person of the said Company such severall summe and summes of money respectively as by the said former ordinances in that behalfe are severally and respectively allowed and appointed to be paid unto the said Stewards and that whatsoever shall be more disbursed or laid out or fitt to be disbursed or laid out for or about the said election dinner shall be yearly and from tyme to tyme borne and discharged at the proper costs and charges of the Stewards for the tyme being, And that if any person so chosen to be Steward as aforesaid doe or shall refuse to accept or execute the said place or office of Steward or doe or shall deny or omitt to disburse the monyes or to performe the other services incident or belonging to the said office or place of Steward, that then every such person so chosen and refuseing, denying or omitting as aforesaid shall forfeit and pay for every such offence unto the Master, Wardens and Assistants of the said Society for the tyme being to be by them employed in the necessary expences of the said Society as occasion shall serve the foresaid summe or fine of tenn pounds by the said former constitutions and ordinances in that behalfe appointed to be paid.

That every person of the Company chosen to be an Assistant & refuseing shall pay £20 fine & yet be lyable to be chosen Steward

Item It is also ordered, constituted, ordeined and appointed by the

Master, Wardens and Assistants of the said Society that if any person or persons being a freeman of the said Society shall at any tyme hereafter be chosen to be of the number of Assistants of the said Society according to the said letters pattents, and the said former constitutions in that behaffe [*sic*] also made, and after such his election and nomination shall refuse or denye to take upon him or them the office and place of an Assistant of the said Society or shall refuse to take the oath by the said letters patents and former constitutions appointed to be taken for the due execution of the said place in such sort as by the former constitutions or ordinances is prescribed haveing no lawfull or reasonable cause for such his refuseall and denyall to be allowed of by the Master, Wardens and Assistants of the said Society or the major part of them, That then every such person so offending shall forfeit and pay for every such offence to the Master, Wardens and Assistants of the said Society for the tyme being twenty pounds to be by them employed to the generall use and supportation of the said Society. *And* that yet neverthelesse every such person so offending shall be subject to be elected Steward for the election dinner of the new Master and Wardens as if he had not [been] fined for an Assistant and shall hold and serve the office and place of a Steward when he shall be thereunto elected or shall pay such further fyne for the not holding of the Stewards place as by the last precedent ordinance is appointed in that behalfe.

Which said orders, ordinances and constitutions by the new Master, Wardens and Assistants of the said Society lately made and herein before specified, we the said Thomas, Lord Coventry, Sir John Bramston and Sir John Finch have perused and examined, and do by these presents approve them and allowe of them, and in testimony thereof we have signed the same with our signes manuell the eight and twentith [Rawl. D51, p. 54] day of May 1635 and in the eleaventh yeare of the reigne of our soveraigne lord King Charles by the grace of God King of England, Scotland, France and Ireland, defender of the faith &c.

Tho: Coventry Cs. John Bramston. Jo: Finch.

[Rawl. D51, p. 55 transcript] *An Annuall Catalogue* begun to be collected in the Year 1664 and from thence continued out of the Bookes & Papers now extant of the Company of Scrivenors of the City of London formerly a Brotherhood by the Name or Title of *The Writers of the Court Letter of the Citty of London* And by King James by his Charter or Letters Patents dated the 28th day of January in the 14th Year of his Reigne over England France & Ireland and of Scotland the 50th Incorporated by the Name or Title of *Master Wardens and Assistants of the Society of Writers of the City of London* Of all the Persons who, for so much as those Bookes & Papers shew (some others haveing miscarried) doe appear to have been or be Members of the said Company or subscribed or submitted to the Rule Government and Orders therof. With a Genealogie or Pedegree of many of them shewing of whom they proceeded And who of them by Service or Patrimoney. And also of those that have been called to bear Office, have fined for or borne the Office in the said Company, of Stewards Assistants Wardens or Masters. With an Alphabeticall Table of all the Names directing to the Year when each Person was according to those Bookes and

Papers made free, subscribed or became a Member. Or was first menc'oned to be soe.[1]

[Rawl. D51, pp. 67, 68 calendar] *1628. John Woodward, Master, Jeffery Bower and Robert Woodford, Wardens*

Henry Manley and William Alexander, Assistants taken in.
William Swarland and John Langham, Stewards.

John Hatton, app. of John Milton [1599][2]
Thomas Wilcox, app. of Edward Chapman [1614]
David Jones, app. of George Foster [1591]
Isaac Gold, app. of Charles Yeomans [1599]
John Wingrave, app. of Philip Bisse [1619]

1629

George Wilkinson, app. of Anthony Hudson [1610]
Samuel Berry, app. of Richard Bedolph [1616]
Arthur Rutter, app. of Robert Pye [1611]

John Warren, Master, Robert Woodford and John Macro, Wardens

Thomas Powell, Richard Alsop and Stephen King, Assistants taken in.
Richard Alie, Bartholomew Gilman, John Smithier, John Smith, William Awdley and Henry Manley, Stewards.

Humfrey Hayward, by redemption
Edward Coddington, app. of Richard Bedolph [1616]
Edward Parker, app. of Lawrence Newman [1618]
Thomas Boys, s. of Thomas Boys, scrivener [1581]
Matthew Baynes, app. of William Halliley [1617]
James Milton, app. of Francis Strange [1596]
Sidenham Lukins, app. of William Childe [1597]
Robert Till, app. of Bernard Garter [1600]

1630

Thomas Colwell, app. of John Macro [1603]
Robert Wallis, by redemption 'of Ric^{d} Alsop'
John Robinson, app. of Rowland Squier [1598]
John Townesend, app. of Francis Mosse [1599]
John Bower, app. of Abraham Church [1617]

John Maye, Master, John Macro and Richard Alie, Wardens

George Berisford and John Linton, Assistants taken in.
William Alexander and Thomas Powell, Stewards.

Thomas Hill, s. of Thomas Hill, scrivener [1601]
George Frithe, s. of Thomas Frithe, scrivener [1595]

[1] The entries in Rawl. D51 from 1392 (p. 55) up to and including the first three entries under 1628 (p. 67) have been incorporated in the calendar of the Common Paper on pp. 20–62 above in so far as there is any variation between the two records (see note 1 on p. 20). The calendar of entries which here follows represents the last line of p. 67 and pp. 68–75 inclusive of Rawl. D51, thus bringing the list of members of the Company up to 1678. The alphabetical table, or index of names, mentioned above is on pp. 77–87 of Rawl. D51 and has been omitted from this present book. P. 76 of Rawl. D51 is blank.

[2] The date in square brackets is the year of the admission of the master.

Richard Shelbury, app. of Henry Shelbury [1621] or John Macro
John Hitchens, app. of William Wilkinson [1618]
John Edmunds, app. of John Eaton [1615]
Edward Packer, app. of William Child [1597]

1631

Christopher Nailer, app. of Ralph Hanmer [1606]
Robert Filbrick, app. of Thomas Wanmerton [1619]
John Bell, app. of John Atkins [1612]
Andrew Dickenson, app. of Edward Chapman [1614]
Richard Holeman, app. of Michael Holeman [1619]

Rowland Squier, Master, Richard Alie, Upper Warden, Bartholomew Gillman,[1] John Smithier, Renter Warden*

Abraham Church, Assistant taken in.
Stephen King and Edward Chapman, Stewards.

James Evans, app. of Thomas Powell [1615]
Thomas Browne, app. of Michael Holman [1619]
Walter Meredith, translated from the Girdlers' Company

1632

William Stanninough, app. of Thomas Wannerton [1619] or Caleb Whitfeild
John Bastard, app. of John Linton [1615]
George Thurgarland, app. of Ralph Hartley [1622]
William Smith, app. of Peter Shofeild

Francis Mosse, Master, John Smither and John Smith, Wardens

William Wilkinson, John Atkins, John Partridge and Thomas Wannerton, Assistants taken in.
George Berisford and Abraham Church, Stewards.

Francis Sheppard, app. of John Woodward [1597]
John Burt, Martin Hardrett and James Smither [bracketed together and the word 'Gent' written alongside]
John Wescott, app. of John Rea [1624]
Edward Finch, app. of [blank]
Edward Jackson [no other details]
Bartholomew Bigmore, app. of Robert Woodford [1599]
John Baker, gent.
William Richbell [no other details]

1633

Martin Dallison, app. of John Woodward [1597]
Francis Harrison, app. of John Davies [1619]
John Underwood, app. of Richard Milton [1621]
Philip Lugger, jun. [s./app.][2] of Philip Lugger, scrivener [1598]
Ralph Hardwick [s./app.] of Ralph Hardwick, scrivener [1597]

[1] No explanation is offered in the manuscript as to the significance of the asterisk, but it probably means that the man refused to serve as Warden or even as Master.
[2] This indicates that no information is given in the manuscript as to whether the man admitted was the son or apprentice (or both) of the man named as master.

Thomas Hill, Master, John Smith, Upper Warden, William Audley,*[1] *William Alexander, Renter Warden*

Christopher Lawe and William Thomasin, Assistants taken in.

John Atkins and John Pridgeon, Stewards.

John Carter [no other details]
Henry Deane [s./app.] of Elias Deane [1604]
Thomas Ashby, app. of James Noell [1621]
John Nicholls, app. of Robert Morgan [1589]
Daniel Woodgate, app. of Edward Chapman [1614]
John Halliwell, s. of John Halliwell, scrivener [1584]

1634

Thomas Bostock [s./app.] of Charles Bostock [1595]
Henry Owen, app. of Matthew Billing [1621]
Isaac Rowlett, app. of [blank]
John Fox, app. of Stephen King [1616]

*John Milton**[1]

[Rawl. D51, p. 69] *Charles Yeomans, Master, William Alexander and Stephen King, Wardens*

William Richbell, Robert Minchard and Michael Holeman, Assistants taken in.

Thomas Wannerton and Robert Minchard, Stewards.

William Johnson, app. of George Beresford [1615]
Thomas Bradley, app. of Christopher Favell [1621]

1635

Edward Michell, app. of William Dexter [1620]
Matthew Lock, app. of Francis Mosse [1599]
Robert Abbott, app. of Francis Webb [1626][2]
William Horne, app. of William Awdley [1612]
John Massy, app. of John Langham [1606]
Edward Perry, app. of William Childe [1597]
Joseph Alport, app. of Charles Yeomans [1599]

John Macro, Master, Stephen King, Upper Warden, Edward Chapman,*[1] *Abraham Church, Renter Warden*

John Rye, Assistant taken in. Michael Holman and John Rye, Stewards.

Thomas Purnell, app. of Henry May [1610]
John Norton, app. of William Wilkinson [1618] or Edward Duck
Benjamin Ward, app. of Abraham Church [1617]
Henry Mosse, s. of Francis Mosse, scrivener [1599]
Henry Bradshawe, app. of Humfrey Shalcrosse [1622]
Christopher Townesend, app. of Richard Alsope [1614]
Francis Manestye, app. of Ralph Hartley [1622]

1636

John Prestwood, app. of Jeffery Bower [1601]

[1] See note 1 on p. 115; the same remark applies to asterisks on pp. 117–122.

[2] See Jasper A. R. Abbott, 'Robert Abbott, City Money Scrivener, and his account book, 1646–52', in *Guildhall Miscellany*, no. 7 (Aug. 1956), pp. 30–9.

John Howard, app. of John Wicks [1615]
Arthur Dove, app. of John Pridgeon [1617] or of [blank] Dove
Roger Caly, app. of Bartholomew Gilman [1607]

Bartholomew Gilman, Master, Abraham Church and John Atkins, Wardens

Henry Shelbury, James Noell and Ralph Hartley, Assistants taken in.
Henry Shelbery and James Noell, Stewards.

John Taylor, app. of Francis Pensax [1618]
Richard Ridgar, app. of John Linton [1615]
Richard Black, app. of John Atkins [1612]

1637

Thomas Radcliffe, s. of Thomas Radc[l]iffe, scrivener [1589]
Edward Arnold, app. of Peter Hughes [1600]
Thomas Farmer, app, of Stephen King [1616]
Robert Singer, app. of Edward Cottington [1629]
Thomas Francis, app. of Stephen King [1616]

John Smither, Master, John Atkins, Upper Warden, John Pridgeon, Thomas Wannerton, Renter Warden*

Humfrey Shalcrosse, Assistant taken in.
Ralph Hartley, Humfrey Shalcrosse and George Alistree, Stewards.

Martin Noell [s./app.] of James Noell [1621]
Nicholas Gruytt, by redemption 'of Thomas Wannerton' [1619]
Christopher Chishall, app. of Robert Wright [1628]
Thomas Conn, app. of John Meyrick [1614]
John Smyther, s. of John Smyther, scrivener [1611]

1638

John Taylor, app. of John Wicks [1615]
Richard Duke, app. of Francis Webb [1626]
James Frithe [no other details]

John Smith, Master, Thomas Wannerton and Robert Mincherd, Wardens

George Allistree, Assistant taken in.
Matthew Billing and Walter Smith, Stewards.

John Perrott, app. of Henry Shelbery [1621]

1639

William Audley, Master, Robert Minchard, Upper Warden, Michael Holeman. John Rye*, Henry Shelbery, Renter Warden*

Matthew Billing and William Smith, Assistants taken in.
Anthony Hudson, William Dexter and Nicholas Bacon, Stewards.

Robert Lane, app. of Stephen King [1616]
Nicholas Gouge, app. of John Macro [1603]
William Stannard, app. of John Atkins [1612]

1640

Jonathan Blackwell, app. of Ralph Hartley [1622]
John Clifton, app. of John Rea [1624]
Nicholas Hunlock, app. of John Smither [1611] or Henry Deane

William Alexander, Stephen King, Master, Abraham Church,*[1] *Henry Shelbery, Upper Warden, James Noell*, Ralph Hartley*, Humfrey Shalcrosse*, George Allistree, Renter Warden*

Henry Colbron, Nicholas Bacon, Thomas Bower, Henry Iles, John Rea and Mark Bradley, Assistants taken in.

William Richbell, Henry Coleborne, Thomas Bower, Henry Iles, John Rea, Richard Andrews and Mark Bradley, Stewards.

John Moore, app. of Robert Minchard [1615]
Nathaniel Stakes, app. of Sidenham Lukins [1629]
William Deane, app. of John Meyrick [1614]
Abdiell Silsby, app. of Thomas Wannerton [1619]
[Rawl. D51, p. 70] John Oake, app. of John Brooke [1624]
John Dermer, app. of Edward Coddington [1629]

1641

Abraham Church, Master, Henry Shelbery, Upper Warden, George Alistree and Matthew Billing, Wardens

Lawrence Newman and Thomas Bower, Assistants taken in.

Lawrence Newman, Francis Webb and Thomas Wilcocks, Stewards.

Robert Morgan, app. of John Smither [1611]
Richard Alsop, s. of Richard Alsop, scrivener [1614]

John Pridgeon, Master, George Allistree and Matthew Billing, Wardens

John Lugger, s. of John Lugger, scrivener [1588]
George Townerow, app. of Francis Mosse [1599]
William Barber, app. of John Halliwell, jun. [1593]
Thomas or George Fossick, app. of Abraham Church [1617]

1642

John Alsop, app. of William Johnson [1634] or Christopher Towneshend

Thomas Wannerton, Master, Matthew Billing, Upper Warden, Walter Smith, Nicholas Bacon, Renter Warden*

Michael Smith [s./app.] of Walter Smith [1623]
Richard Collen, app. of John Atkins [1612]

1643

Michael Holeman, Henry Iles*, Thomas Wannerton, Master, Matthew Billing and Nicholas Bacon, Wardens, Henry Colbron*, Henry Iles* and Thomas Bower**

Thomas Colwell and Richard Shelbery, Stewards.

Thomas Crosse, app. of William Audley [1612]
James Windus, app. of Charles Yeomans [1599]
Timothy Bourne, s. of Charles Bourne, scrivener [1613]

1644 [*no entries*]

1645

Thomas Wannerton, Master, Matthew Billing[2]

Solomon Seabright, app. of Francis Mosse [1599]

[1] No asterisk against his name. [2] No further details.

Joseph Rutland, app. of John Taylor [1636 bracketed with 1638]
John Bruce, app. of Walter Smith [1623]
Hugh Ford, app. of Robert Minchard [1615]
Henry Williamett, app. of David Jones [1628]
John Sprackling, s. of Jeremy Sprackling, scrivener [1588], translated to Goldsmiths' Company [Fishmongers *in another hand*]

1646

Thomas Wannerton, Master, Matthew Billing[1]

Benjamin Sheppard, app. of Thomas Wannerton [1619]

1647

Thomas Wannerton, Master for part of the year until Francis Kempe was chosen Master, Matthew Billing[1]

Humfrey Hayward, Sidenham Lukins, Thomas Colwell, Richard Shelbery and Edward Coddington, Assistants taken in.

Alexander Donne, app. of John Prestwood [1636]
Samuel Osborne, app. of Nicholas Gruytt [1637]
Arthur Miles, app. of Francis Harrison [1633]
Joseph Cooke, app. of Francis Mosse [1599]
Thomas Bland, app. of Ralph Hartley [1622]

1648

Henry Shelbery, Master, Matthew Billing, Senior Warden for part of the year until displaced and James Noell served the remainder, Mark Bradley, Junior Warden

John Robinson, Richard Holeman and Richard Andrews, Assistants taken in.

John Robinson and Richard Holeman, Stewards.

John Leader, app. of John Bell [1631]
George Perrier, app. of James Noell [1621]
Thomas Goodwin, app. of Richard Duke [1638]
William Heron, app. of Matthew Billing [1621]

1649

Hercules Comander, app. of John Smyther [1611 bracketed with 1637]

James Noell, Master, Mark Bradley, Upper Warden, Francis Webb, Humfrey Hayward, Renter Warden*

Martin Dallison and Daniel Woodgate, Assistants taken in.

Martin Dallison, Daniel Woodgate, John Halliwell, Thomas Bostock, Henry Owen, Thomas Browne and Robert Abbott, Stewards.

Thomas Massam, app. of Martin Noell [1637]
William Taylor, app. of Edward Coddington [1629]

1650

Bartholomew Stannard [s./app.] of William Stannard, scrivener [1639]
Philip Kitfeild, app. of Mark Bradley [1627]

[1] No further details.

William Bower, app. of Henry Bradshawe [1635]
Robert Mayne, app. of John Rye [1619]

[Rawl. D51, pp. 70, 71] *Ralph Hartley, Master, Humfrey Hayward, Senior Warden, John Rea*, Thomas Colwell, Junior Warden*

John Halliwell, Thomas Bostock and Henry Owen, Assistants taken in.
John Halliwell, John Westcott, (blank) Perry and Henry Mosse, Stewards.

Thomas Porter, app. of John Rea [1624]

1651

John Bird, app. of John Ashenden [1604]
William Brewer, app. of Richard Shelbery [1630]
Edmund Burton, app. of Bartholomew Bigmore [1632]

Humfrey Shalcrosse, Master, Thomas Colwall and Richard Shelbery, Wardens

Robert Abbott, Edward Perry and Joseph Alport, Assistants taken in.
James Read and Christopher Townsend, Stewards.

Leonard Bates, app. of Ralph Hartley [1622]

1652

Daniel Bowman, app. of Richard Andrews [1627]

Walter Smith, Master, Richard Shelbery and Richard Holeman, Wardens

Henry Mosse, Assistant taken in.
Thomas Browne and Christopher Townesend, Stewards.

John Byrt, app. of Christopher Townesend [1635]

1653

John Jarmyn, app. of John Bruce, [1645]
John Dorney, app. of Matthew Billing [1621]
Robert Richardson, app. of John Perrott [1638]
Thomas Hinde, app. of James Read [1626]

Nicholas Bacon, Henry Coleborne*, Mark Bradley, Master, Richard Holeman, Upper Warden, Martin Dallison*, John Halliwell, Renter Warden*

John Ridgar, Martin Noell, Thomas Conn, John Smither, Richard Duke and John Perrott, Stewards.

Daniel Bunting, app. of Thomas Conn [1637]

1654

John Spicer, app. of John Alsop [1642]
William Daynes, bound to John Macro but upon his death turned over to Robert Abbot [1635]

Nicholas Bacon, Humfrey Hayward, Master, John Halliwell and Martin Dallison, Wardens*

John Smyther, John Underwood, Richard Andrews, John Bell, William Stannard, John Merrick, Robert Mayne and Nicholas Humlocke, Stewards.

James Noell, s. of James Noell, scrivener [1621]
John Smith, app. of Edward Coddington [1629]
Nicholas Scull, app. of John Bell [1631]
Rowland Simpson, app. of John Bell [1631]

1655

William Warne,[1] app. of John Hatton [1628] and turned over to Robert Yarway, Merchant Taylor
Peter Bell, app. of John Brooke [1624]
John Radford, app. of William Smith [1632]

Thomas Collwell, Master, Martin Dallison and Daniel Woodgate, Wardens

Martin Noell, Assistant taken in.

Godfrey Austinson, John Fox, John Robinson, James Read, Jonathan Blackwell and Benjamin Ward, Stewards.

1656

John Billing [s./app.] of Matthew Billing [1621]

Richard Shelbery, Master, Daniel Woodgate, John Rea, John Robinson, Wardens*

(blank) Fox, (blank) Ward, John Bentley, John Alsop and James Windus, Stewards.

James Needler, app. of Christopher Townesend [1635]

1657

Timothy West, app. of John Perrott [1638], assigned to Robert Richardson, scrivener
John Kendall, app. of John Bruce [1645]

Richard Holeman, Master, John Robinson and Thomas Bostock, Wardens

Richard Andrews and Henry Owen, Assistants taken in.

Arthur Dove, Henry Deane, John Clifton, Benjamin Ward, William Barbour, Benjamin Shepard, Solomon Seabright and Arthur Miles, Stewards.

Thomas Carpender, app. of John Bruce [1645]
Robert Minchard, s. of Robert Minchard, scrivener [1615]
William Audley, s. of William Audley, scrivener [1612]

1658

William Cornhill, app. of John Bruce [1645]
Thomas Barbour, app. of Richard Shelbery [1630]
John Shenton, app. of Thomas Bostock [1634]

John Halliwell, Master, Thomas Bostock, Robert Abbott, Edward Perry, Wardens*

Thomas Browne, Richard Ridger, John Smither, Richard Duke and John Underwood, Assistants taken in.

[1] At the east end of the north aisle of the church of St Martin Ludgate, City of London, stands a bell which is inscribed: THE GVIFT OF WILLIAM WARNE SCRIVENER TO THE PARISH OF ST MARTINS LVDGATE 1683.

[Rawl. D51, p. 72] John Morris, Robert Clayton and Thomas Browne, apps. of Robert Abbott [1635]
Francis Clarke, app. of Mark Bradley [1627]

1659

Paul Donne [s./app.] of Alexander Donne [1647]
Jeremy Jeneway, app. of Francis Mosse [1599]

Martin Noell, Daniel Woodgate, Master, Edward Perry and Joseph Alport, Wardens*

George Perrier, Thomas Goodwin, Hercules Comaunder and Thomas Massam, Stewards.
Samuel Houghton, app. of Christopher Townesend [1635]
Gerrard Usher, app. of Henry Colbron [1623]

1660

Richard Marshall and John Gopp, apps. of George Perrier [1648]

John Robinson, Master, Joseph Alport and Henry Mosse, Wardens

William Stannard, Assistant taken in.
Philip Kiftell, Hercules Commander, William Bower, John Dermer and Leonard Bates, Stewards.
John Gibbs, app. of James Windus [1643]

1661

Joseph Batelhaie, merchant, 'redem. at Large'
John Mitcheson, app. of John Bell [1631]
William Stucks, app. of William Audley [1612]
Arnold Griffith and Andrew Francklin, apps. of Thomas Colwell [1630]
William Curtis, app. of Hercules Comaunder [1649]
Edward Harding, app. of Daniel Woodgate [1633]

Thomas Bostock, Master, Henry Mosse and Richard Andrews, Wardens

John Alsop, James Windus and Benjamin Shepard, Assistants taken in.
John Bird and Philip Kiftill, Stewards.
Robert Cressener, app. of James Read [1626]
James Peters, app. of Richard Shelbery [1630]

1662

James Frithe, s. of James Frithe, scrivener [1638]

Edward Perry, Master, Henry Mosse and Richard Andrews, Wardens

Nicholas Gouge, John Clifton, Philip Kiftell and William Taylor, Stewards.
Joseph Andrews, app. of John Bell [1631]
Rowland Read, app. of Robert Richardson [1653]
Foulk Jones, app. of Benjamin Ward [1635], turned over to John Parry

Edward Perry, Master, Richard Andrews and Henry Owen, Wardens

Solomon Seabright, Assistant taken in.

William Swalden, app. of Ralph Hartley [1622]

1663

Abraham Harrison, app. of Solomon Seabright [1645]
John Barne, app. of John Bell [1631]
Samuel Astley, app. of Daniel Woodgate [1633]
Michael Tyler, app. of Jonathan Blackwall [1640]
John Wing, app. of Christopher Townesend [1635]
John Knight, app. of Philip Kiftell [1650]
Zorobabell Parker, app. of John Underwood [1633]

Joseph Alport, Master, Richard Andrews and Henry Owen, Wardens

William Daynes, Rowland Simpson, Nicholas Scull and William Warne, Stewards.

Joseph Alport, Master, Henry Owen and John Smyther, Wardens

Arthur Miles and Joseph Cooke, Assistants taken in.
William Taylor, Peter Bell and John Dorney, Stewards.

1664

John Hardrett, app. of Hercules Comaunder [1649]
John Brandreth, app. of Thomas Bostock [1634]
Thomas Luckett, app. of Francis Shepard [1632]
Robert Monck, app. of Daniel Woodgate [1633]
Francis Mosse [s./app.] of Henry Mosse [1635]
William Guise, app. of Richard Andrews [1627]
Peter Tilly, app. of Henry Mosse [1635]

Henry Mosse, Master, John Smither and Richard Duke, Wardens

Thomas Bland, Assistant taken in.
John Clifton and William Barber, Stewards.
Francis Minshall, app. of Matthew Billing [1621]
Samuel Lawe, app. of Joseph Cooke [1647]
Richard Noell, s. of James Noell, scrivener [1621]

1665

William Braxton, app. of John Alsop [1642]
Matthew Browne, app. of William Audley, sen. [1612]
Josias Pike, app. of George Perrier [1648]

Richard Andrews, Master (died); Henry Owen, Master, Richard Duke and John Underwood, Wardens

George Perrier, Thomas Goodwin, Hercules Comaunder, Thomas Massam and William Bower, Assistants taken in.
Elizabeth Billingsley, app.[1] of James Windus [1643] and Anne his wife

1666

Lucy Saunderson, app.[1] of James Windus [1643] and Anne his wife

[1] In the absence of any information to the contrary, it must be assumed that this person was made free of the Company and was nominally an apprentice.

[Rawl. D51, p. 73] John Bargeman, app. of John Alsop [1642]
Giles Steele, app. of Thomas Bland [1647]
Philip Lugger, s. of Philip Lugger [1633]

Richard Duke, Master, John Underwood and John Alsop, Wardens

William Barber, James Needler, John Morris and Robert Clayton, Stewards.

Mary Watson, app.[1] of Arthur Miles [1647] and Bridget his wife
Sir Robert Hanson, kt., one of the present sheriffs of London
John Mosyer, esq., 'Councellor at Lawe'
William Fashion, app. of James Windust [1643]
Thomas Grunwin, app. of Henry Mosse [1635]
John Whitehall, app. of William Stannard [1639]

1667

James Clement, app. of Daniel Bunting [1653]
Thomas Woodward, app. of William Bower [1650]

John Underwood, Master, John Alsop and James Windus, Wardens

Leonard Bates, Assistant taken in.
Thomas Browne, Samuel Houghton, James Needler and Jeremiah Jeneway, Stewards.

Richard Walker, app. of Rowland Simpson [1654]

1668

Joseph Osburne, app. of Arthur Miles [1647]
Richard Hotchkis, app. of Daniel Woodgate [1633]
Edward Allen, app. of William Bower [1650]
Bazill Cotterill, app. of Samuel Houghton [1659]

John Alsop, Master, James Windus and Solomon Seabright, Wardens

William Daines and William Warne, Assistants taken in.
Gerard Usher and Richard Marshall, Stewards.

William Holeman, by patrimony of Michael Holeman [1619]
Joseph Ward, by patrimony of Benjamin Ward [1635]

1669

Miles Lukins, by patrimony of Sidenham Lukins [1629]
Richard Bradey, app. of John Bell [1631]

James Windus, Master, Solomon Seabright and Arthur Miles, Wardens

John Morris, esq., Assistant taken in.
Rowland Simpson, John Kendall and John Gopp, Stewards.

John Ewing, by redemption
John Wheatley, app. of Joseph Alport [1635]
Humfrey Cuthbert, app. of Leonard Bates [1651]

1670

Jonathan Andrew, app. of Gerard Usher [1659]
Thomas Wright, app. of William Taylor [1649]

[1] See note 1 on p. 123.

John Morris, esq., Master, Arthur Miles and George Perrier, Wardens

Robert Clayton, esq., Assistant taken in.

John Gibbs and Arnold Griffith, Stewards.

John Hervy, by redemption

Richard Sheppard, by patrimony of Francis Sheppard [1632]

1671

John Wickham, app. of Richard Marshall [1660]

Sir Robert Clayton, kt., Alderman and one of the sheriffs of London, Master, George Perrier and Joseph Cooke, Wardens

Memorandum. That upon the Companies respect to the said Sir Robert Clayton as being in the capacity aforesaid, the persons next following did, in persuance of an order of the 17th of September 1671, take upon them the livery or cloathing. Vizt—The aforesaid Master and Wardens

Assistants: Thomas Colwall, esq.; John Morris, esq.; Abraham Church; Walter Smith; Humfrey Hayward; Henry Mosse; John Underwood; John Alsop; James Windus; Solomon Seabright; Arthur Miles; Thomas Goodwin; Hercules Comaunder; Thomas Massam; William Bower; Leonard Bates; William Daines; William Warne; Thomas Browne; James Needler; Gerrard Usher.

Stewards: Philip Kiftell; Samuel Houghton; Richard Marshall; Rowland Simpson; John Kendall; John Gopp; Arnold Griffith; Andrew Francklyn; William Curtis.

Younger Members: James Peters; Foulk Jones; John Barne; John Wing; John Brandreth; Matthew Browne; Giles Steele; William Fashion; Thomas Grunwin; James Clement; Thomas Woodward; Richard Walker; Joseph Osborne; Richard Hotchkis; Edward Allen; Bazill Cotterill; John Ewing; John Wheatley; Humfrey Cuthbert.

[*In the margin*][1] More younger members since taken: John Starkey; Michael Bignall; Edward Cole; William Antrobus; Ebenezer Jones; Thomas Lemman.

Memorandum. Also that upon the same occasion, the said Mr. George Perrier, the Upper Warden, of his owne charge, gave to the Company a staffe for the Beadle to carry before the Company upon all fitting occasions, adorned or topped with the Companies arms in silver, and haveing engraven thereon, Ex dono Georgii Perryer Guardiani Societatis 1671.

[Rawl. D51, p. 74] Thomas Browne, James Needler and Gerrard Usher, Assistants taken in.

Andrew Francklin and William Curtis, Stewards.

Henry Deane, by patrimony of Henry Deane [1633]

John Starkey, app. of John Wing [1663]

Michael Bignall, app. of Thomas Bland [1647]

Edward Cole, app. of James Windus [1643]

1672

George Marsh, app. of Henry Mosse [1635]

John Colwall, by patrimony of Thomas Colwall, esq. [1630]

[1] In a different hand.

Solomon Sebright, Master, Joseph Cooke and Thomas Goodwin, Wardens

James Peters and Foulk Jones fined Stewards and the Company made the election dinner.

1673

Thomas Robinson, app. of George Perryer [1648]
Thomas Peirce, app. of Thomas Bostock [1634]
Thomas Smith, app. of Solomon Sebright [1645]

Thomas Colwall, esq., Master, Thomas Goodwin and Thomas Massam, Wardens

Richard Marshall, Assistant taken in.

John Wing, John Brandrith, Giles Steel and William Fashion fined S[t]ewards.

1674

Thomas Carpinter, app. of John Bruce [1645], made free of the Company in 1657 and now of the City.
Nathaniel Eenderby app. of Thomas Woodward [1666]
William Leader, s. of John Leader [1648], by patrimony

George Perryer, Master, Thomas Massam and Hercules Comander, Wardens

Rowland Simpson and John Gopp, Assistants taken in.

John Barne, fined by giving bill to pay, James Clement and Thomas Woodward, fined, Stewards.

Edward Bulwer, esq., son-in-law to the Master, adm. a 'Brother at Large'.
George Hodges, app. of James Needler [1656]
Martin Dallison, s. of Martin Dallison [1633], by patrimony
William Antrobus, app. of Thomas Goodwin [1648]

1675

George Welch, app. of Giles Steele [1666]
William Burnham, app. of William Smith [1632]

Joseph Cooke, Master, Hercules Comander, William Bower fined for Renter and Senior Warden, Leonard Bates, fined for Renter Warden, William Daines, Wardens

John Gibbs and Arnold Griffith, Assistants taken in.

Matthew Browne, gave bond to pay fine, John Whitehall gave bond to pay fine, Richard Hotchkis fined, Edward Allen fined, Stewards.

Silvester Chilcott and Adam Prince, apps. of John Alsop [1642]
Sarah Dutton, daughter of Thomas Dutton [1616], by patrimony[1]

1676

John Harwar, app. of Joseph Ward [1668]
John Lloyd, app. of William Bower [1650]

Thomas Goodwin, Master, Leonard Bates and William Warne, Wardens

Andrew Francklin, William Curtis and James Peters, Assistants taken in.

[1] In the absence of any information to the contrary, it must be assumed that the Company allowed the daughter of a member to be made free.

John Ewing fined, John Wheatly gave bond, John Wickham fined, Stewards.
Ralph Edowes, app. of William Bower [1650]
Richard Fathers, app. of William Fashion [1666]

1677

William Moyle, app. of Richard Hotchkis [1668]
Thomas Warren, app. of James Needler [1656]
Joseph Beane, app. of George Perrier [1648]
Ebenezer Jones, app. of Richard Marshall [1660]

William Bower, Master, William Daines and Thomas Browne, Wardens

Miles Lukins gave bond to pay £20 or serve next year, John Starkey fined £10, Michael Bignall and Edward Cole served without any contribution by the Master and Wardens, Stewards.
Thomas Sonds, app. of John Wickham [1671]
[Rawl. D51, p. 75] Margaret Alsop, app.[1] of James Windus [1643] and Christian his wife
Daniel Shilling, app. of Joseph Cook [1647]
Thomas Lemmon, app. of Sir Robert Clayton, kt. [1658]

1678

Edmund Mantle, app. of John Brandrith [1664]
Richard Frith, s. of James Frith [1638], by patrimony

Leonard Bates, Master, William Warne and James Needler, Wardens

Note. Pages 77–87 (p. 76 is blank) of Rawl. D51 are not reproduced. The pages are: The Alphabeticall Table of all the Names directing to the Yeare when each person was (according to the Bookes and Papers of the Company of Scriveners) made free subscribed or became a Member of the Company. Or was first menc'oned to be soe.

[1] In the absence of any information to the contrary, it must be assumed that this person was made free of the Company and was nominally an apprentice.

INDEX OF PERSONS, PLACES AND SUBJECTS

Notes

An attempt has been made in this index to indicate a man's progress in the Scriveners' Company. The page references immediately following a name denote that it is mentioned on those pages; page references preceded by one of the following abbreviations indicate references to the man as—

ap., apprentice	*s.*, steward
ser., servant	*w.*, warden
a., admitted	*m.*, master
as., assistant	*l.m.*, Mayor or Lord Mayor of London

Ald., Alderman of London

Where there are several references to two men of the same name, the descriptions, sen. and jun., have been added, but it is often impossible to distinguish them accurately. In the same way, two men of the same name, divided by a good many years, have been designated as (I) and (II), e.g.—

Chapman:
  Edward (I)
  Edward (II)

The occurrence of a man's name more than once on a page in the same capacity has not been indicated in the index, but a variation in the spelling of a surname occurring more than once on a page has been noted. Cross-references have been made where there is a wide variation in the spelling of a name and where one form would be widely separated, alphabetically, from another. It should be remembered that the letters i and y, in particular, were often interchanged, e.g. Bideford could easily be recorded as Bydeford, Clifford as Clyfford, or Picot as Pycot. There was also a good deal of phonetical spelling and frequently no simple form for an unusual surname. To save space, names will be found with variants within the main form, e.g. Grigg(e)s means that the name will be found either as Grigges or Griggs and Hunte(r) as Hunte or Hunter. Forms of name which occur in the text both with and without a terminal apostrophe have been indexed without the apostrophe.

Places are provided with the names of their counties and counties have cross-references to the names of the parishes concerned. Prefixes such as Le, Little, North, South, etc., are under the first word, e.g. West Sheen is under 'West'. Places in London are principally under the entry for London, but cross-references have been provided where thought desirable.

An index of subjects usually presents problems of selection and nomenclature, but it is hoped that an adequate number of cross-references has been provided. Some occupations which could be confused with surnames are followed by the abbreviation '(occ.)'.

Attention is also drawn to the list of contents on pp. v and vi for quick reference to important subject matter, and to the headings of the clauses in the Letters Patent, 1616/17, and in the Ordinances, 1618/19, to be found under Scriveners, charter of incorporation of, and Ordinances of Scriveners' Company on pp. 151 and 147 respectively of the index.

LONDON RECORD SOCIETY

The London Record Society was founded in December 1964 to publish transcripts, abstracts and lists of the primary sources for the history of London, and generally to stimulate public interest in archives relating to London. Membership is open to any individual or institution; the annual subscription is £3 3*s*., which entitles a member to receive one copy of each volume published during the year and to attend and vote at meetings of the Society. Prospective members should apply to the Hon. Secretary, Mr. Brian Burch, c/o Leicester University Library, University Road, Leicester.

The following volumes have already been published:

1. *London possessory assizes: a calendar*, edited by Helena M. Chew. (1965)
2. *London inhabitants within the Walls, 1695;* with an introduction by D. V. Glass. (1966)
3. *London Consistory Court wills, 1492–1547*, edited by Ida Darlington. (1967)

Price to members £3 3*s*. each, and to non-members £3 10*s*. each.

A leaflet describing some of the volumes in preparation may be obtained from the Hon. Secretary.